"Cauffman and Weggeman propose a way to extend the solution-focused approach into the field of applied psychology. They call their approach a Solution-focused Applied Psychology Protocol (SoFAP-P) by using a scientific innovation called Design Science Research as a methodology to ground their practice. Their conceptualization and presentation of SoFAP-P is true to the assumptions, spirit, and practices of the approach's founders, Steve de Shazer, Insoo Kim Berg, and their colleagues at the Brief Family Therapy Center in Milwaukee, Wisconsin, U.S.A. Practitioners, researchers, and theorists alike will find much to admire and use in this clearly written, lively, and engaging book."

Prof. Dr. Peter de Jong, *PhD, M.S.W., Calvin University, USA*

"By developing a scientific basis for a psychological treatment – the SoFAP-P design – they have played a pioneering role in the application of DSR to the field of applied psychology. As a co-developer of DSR, I hope this book stimulates further innovative developments to bring DSR methodology to the field of psychology."

Prof. Dr. Joan van Aken, *Eindhoven University of Technology, Netherlands*

SOLUTION-FOCUSED APPLIED PSYCHOLOGY

This book presents a research-based solution-focused applied psychology protocol (SoFAP-P) that is efficient and effective in helping clients address challenges and can be applied to a wide range of psychological domains.

Lessons learned from preceding psychological models, including psychoanalysis, behavioral therapy, humanistic psychology, family systems therapy and the pioneering contributions of Milton Erickson and the groundbreaking solution-focused therapy of Steve de Shazer and Insoo Kim Berg, culminate in this innovative SoFAP-P approach. Based on a thorough analysis of many solution-focused case studies, this tested and validated scientifically based protocol can be used as a learning guide to better understand the SoFAP-P, as well as the innovative qualitative methodology used to validate it. Cauffman and Weggeman show how this design science research (DSR) methodology is used to design, test and validate a generic set of actions that yield interventions to effectively apply to solution-focused client cases.

The book demonstrates the importance of SoFAP-P to both psychological science and society and offers a glimpse into its growing potential as an intervention model. Those interested in the field of DSR will benefit from the overview of one of the first applications of DSR methodology in the psychological sciences, as well as students and academics in applied psychology.

Louis Cauffman is a Clinical Psychologist and Business Economist. One of the first to introduce the solution-focused approach in Europe, Louis remains passionate in his further development of the solution-focused approach as an epistemological tool. He is owner-director of SOLT.E.A.M, an international training institute, author of *Developing and Sustaining a Successful Family Business: A Solution Focused Guide* (Routledge 2022) and *Creating Sustainable Results with*

Solution-Focused Applied Psychology: A Practical Guide for Coaches and Change Facilitators (Routledge 2023).

Mathieu Weggeman is a Full Professor of Organizational Science and Innovation Management at Eindhoven University of Technology (TU/e). At that university, he also obtained his MSc in Industrial Engineering and he holds a PhD in Strategic Management from Tilburg University, the Netherlands. In recent years, Weggeman has been particularly committed to further developing and applying the design science research methodology within the *Sciences of the Artificial* (Simon 1969).

SOLUTION-FOCUSED APPLIED PSYCHOLOGY

A Design Science Research Based Protocol

Louis Cauffman and Mathieu Weggeman

Designed cover image: Photograph taken by author. Private collection.

First published 2024
by Routledge
4 Park Square, Milton Park, Abingdon, Oxon OX14 4RN

and by Routledge
605 Third Avenue, New York, NY 10158

Routledge is an imprint of the Taylor & Francis Group, an informa business

© 2024 Louis Cauffman and Mathieu Weggeman

The right of Louis Cauffman and Mathieu Weggeman to be identified as authors of this work has been asserted in accordance with sections 77 and 78 of the Copyright, Designs and Patents Act 1988.

All rights reserved. No part of this book may be reprinted or reproduced or utilised in any form or by any electronic, mechanical, or other means, now known or hereafter invented, including photocopying and recording, or in any information storage or retrieval system, without permission in writing from the publishers.

Trademark notice: Product or corporate names may be trademarks or registered trademarks, and are used only for identification and explanation without intent to infringe.

British Library Cataloguing-in-Publication Data
A catalogue record for this book is available from the British Library

Library of Congress Cataloging-in-Publication Data
Names: Cauffman, Louis, author. | Weggeman, Mathieu, author.
Title: Solution-focused applied psychology : a design science research based protocol / Louis Cauffman and Mathieu Weggeman.
Description: Abingdon, Oxon ; New York, NY : Routledge, 2024. | Includes bibliographical references and index.
Identifiers: LCCN 2023015777 (print) | LCCN 2023015778 (ebook) | ISBN 9781032519319 (hardback) | ISBN 9781032519272 (paperback) | ISBN 9781003404477 (ebook)
Subjects: LCSH: Psychology, Applied. | Solution-focused therapy.
Classification: LCC BF636 .C383 2024 (print) | LCC BF636 (ebook) | DDC 158--dc23/eng/20230624
LC record available at https://lccn.loc.gov/2023015777
LC ebook record available at https://lccn.loc.gov/2023015778

ISBN: 978-1-032-51931-9 (hbk)
ISBN: 978-1-032-51927-2 (pbk)
ISBN: 978-1-003-40447-7 (ebk)

DOI: 10.4324/9781003404477

Typeset in Times New Roman
by KnowledgeWorks Global Ltd.

*Problems help to understand the past.
Solutions help to live the present and shape the future.*

CONTENTS

Introduction on the content   xii
Prof. Dr. Peter de Jong
Introduction on the methodology   xiv
Prof. Dr. Ir. Joan van Aken
Note from the Authors   xvii

1 Introducing a solution-focused applied psychology protocol (SoFAP-P)   1

    1.1 Introduction: The futile quest for a comprehensive theory 1
    1.2 Beyond the solution-focused method 3
        1.2.1 Developments in the solution-focused method 4
        1.2.2 The rise of psychotherapy research 4
        1.2.3 Our ambition with SoFAP-P 6
    1.3 Structure of the book and reading guide 7

2 Field problem and design objective   9

    2.1 Exploration of field problems and methodological flaws in applied psychology theories 9
        2.1.1 Psychoanalysis and psychodynamic approaches 10
        2.1.2 Behaviourism and cognitive behavioural therapy (CBT) 11
        2.1.3 Humanistic psychology 13
        2.1.4 Family systems therapy 14
        2.1.5 Ericksonian practices 16
        2.1.6 Solution-focused therapy (SFT) 20

      2.1.7   Extended solution-focused therapy
              (extended SFT) 24
      2.1.8   On the limitations of the reviewed applied
              psychology theories 28
  2.2 Points of attention and lessons learned for
       developing SoFAP-P 29
      2.2.1   Points of attention (PAs) for the design of SoFAP-P,
              derived from limitations of preceding theories 29
      2.2.2   Condensed lessons learned for the design
              of SoFAP-P 30
      2.2.3   On the lessons learned from the reviewed applied
              psychology theories 31
  2.3 Field problem, design objective and the design science
       research methodology 33
      2.3.1   From field problem to design objective 33
      2.3.2   The research approach 36
      2.3.3   Research activities 43

3 Empirical grounding of the SoFAP-P design   48
  3.1 Lessons learned from professional and scientific literature 48
  3.2 Best and bad practices applied by
       solution-focused practitioners 52
  3.3 Design propositions (CIMOs) derived from client cases 54
  3.4 Answering the three support questions 62
      3.4.1   Characteristics of the SoFAP approach (SQ1) 62
      3.4.2   Area of application (SQ2) 65
      3.4.3   Productivity characteristics (SQ3) 68
  3.5 Summary of building blocks for a solution-focused
       applied psychology protocol 71

4 SoFAP-P: A solution-focused applied psychology protocol   75
  4.1 SoFAP-P, an arrangement of interventions 75
      4.1.1   SoFAP-P flowchart guidelines 89
      4.1.2   Dynamic representation of the
              SoFAP-P flowchart 90
  4.2 Indications and contra-indications for using SoFAP-P 90
      4.2.1   Indications 91
      4.2.2   Contra-indications 93
      4.2.3   Pseudo-contra-indications 93
      4.2.4   The SoFAP-P design up to specification 94

5   Validating SoFAP-P   98
    5.1 Validating the building blocks of SoFAP-P, based on a
         survey among solution-focused practitioners (α-testing) 98
    5.2 Validating the application of SoFAP-P
         based on cases ex post (β-testing) 104
         5.2.1 Case – Keep your friends close, and
                your contractors closer 104
         5.2.2 Case – The Italian way 108
         5.2.3 Case – The devil is in the details 112
         5.2.4 Case – Miles & Son Inc. 116
    5.3 Conclusions 122

6   Evaluation of SoFAP-P and a glance into the future   123
    6.1 Suggestions for further research 123
         6.1.1 Specifying in detail the mechanisms (the M's)
                in the CIMOs 123
         6.1.2 Field testing of SoFAP-P with trained
                practitioners 123
    6.2 Contribution of SoFAP-P to practice and society 124
         6.2.1 Contributions of SoFAP-P to Practice, (CP's) 125
         6.2.2 Contributions of SoFAP-P to Society, (CS's) 127
    6.3 Desirable developments in solution-focused
         applied psychology 129
         6.3.1 Beware of trendy fog banks 130
         6.3.2 SF is no SF 131

Appendix A: *SoFAP-P cases ex ante*   *133*
Appendix B: *The four minimax decision rules in detail*   *172*
Appendix C: *Use of building blocks in the SoFAP-P design*   *178*
Appendix D: *Opinion survey among solution-focused applied*
               psychology practitioners; questions and results   *180*
Literature   *192*
Acknowledgements   *197*
Curriculum Vitae   *198*
Author Index   *199*
Subject Index   *201*

INTRODUCTION ON THE CONTENT

Prof. Dr. Peter de Jong

For over 30 years now, I have been practising, researching and writing about solution-focused brief therapy (SFBT). For me, the approach has been an exciting, effective and hope-filled way to work with clients. Over the years, I have come to marvel at its efficacy across a wide range of client systems and presenting problems. Pretty much whatever a 'client' is struggling with – and the client can range from an individual to a couple to task groups to a complete organization – skilful, face-to-face solution-focused conversing can lead to a preferred future and a more satisfying life that the client wants.

In this new book, Cauffman and Weggeman propose a way to extend the solution-focused into the field of applied psychology. They call their approach a solution-focused applied psychology protocol (SoFAP-P) by using a scientific innovation called design science research as a methodology to ground their practice.

Their conceptualization and presentation of SoFAP-P is true to the assumptions, spirit and practices of the approach's founders, Steve de Shazer, Insoo Kim Berg and their colleagues at the Brief Family Therapy Center in Milwaukee, Wisconsin, USA.

SoFAP-P is client focused – not model focused – and begins the therapeutic process by building a working relationship with the client around what the client wants different in the future. Thus, it is essentially future and solution-focused, not past and problem-focused. It respects and draws on client resources and past successes to help clients generate realistic and context-specific solutions directly tied to what they want. In brief, SoFAP-P is a straightforward, concrete and efficient set of tools for working with clients that privileges the client's voice in setting the direction of their wished-for change process, the design of eventual solutions and the continuous calibration of client progress.

Ever since the development of SFBT, some have argued that it is simply a set of techniques without a theoretical base and, therefore, has less value and credibility than other approaches. It is accurate that de Shazer and his colleagues originally developed SFBT's signature techniques inductively and pragmatically in the late 1970s and 1980s. But, between 1990 and 2005 when he passed away, de Shazer wrote three books and several articles articulating what he called 'interactional constructivism'. This set of theoretical axioms is consistent with the tenets of the social constructionism of psychologist Kenneth Gergen and others. The theory maintains that practitioners and clients jointly construct (or co-create) new and re-shaped meanings (including solutions) together through their language interactions (therapy and coaching conversations).

So there is now a theory that sheds light on how SFBT works, and there is increasing empirical support for that theory. Moreover, sufficient randomized control studies have been conducted that support the efficacy of SFBT.

I agree with Cauffman and Weggeman that now is the right time to introduce SFBT more definitively into the field of applied psychology. Their proposed SoFAP-P, complete with case data, captures the essential features and practices of SFBT, along with the developing theory and research on which it now rests. It also provides a research methodology for validating the application of SoFAP-P (design science research methodology). As a bonus, the book contains a review of other approaches prominent in applied psychology and, through comparison, highlights what is different and promising about SoFAP-P. I believe practitioners, researchers and theorists alike will find much to admire and use in this clearly written, lively and engaging book.

Prof. Dr. Peter de Jong, PhD, M.S.W.
Calvin University Grand Rapids MI USA
International Microanalysis Associates
Co-author with Insoo Kim Berg, *Interviewing for Solutions*

INTRODUCTION ON THE METHODOLOGY

Prof. Dr. Ir. Joan van Aken

In this book, Cauffman and Weggeman develop a scientific basis for the psychological facilitation of human change, namely solution-focused applied psychology protocol (SoFAP-P). In practice, SoFAP-P, developed on the basis of experiential learning, has proven to be an effective approach for a wide range of clients and application contexts.

Experiential learning is a powerful process for learning to operate effectively in complex situations. This applies to everyday life, but also to doctors, psychotherapists and coaches, for example. Experiential learning can lead to knowledge about what 'works' where and when and where and when it doesn't. However, often this process produces only limited understanding of the mechanisms by which an intervention produces in a given context the observed outcomes. Furthermore, psychological facilitation inevitably produces varying outcomes. This makes it difficult to validate the effectiveness of psychological facilitation processes when it is primarily based on experiential learning. The desire to gain knowledge about the above mechanisms and to have a scientifically justified validation method is an important reason to develop a scientific basis for psychological treatment. For this, Cauffman and Weggeman have chosen the methodology of design science research (DSR).

DSR has been developed in the past two decades for the field of management research to develop generic solutions for complex organizational problems. More specifically, this concerns the development of intervention theories, which propose what can be done to solve a certain class of organizational problems.

Developing such intervention theories must solve a methodological core problem. This problem is caused by the fact that organizational problems are always context-determined: The problems are unique, their causes and backgrounds are context-dependent and so are the outcomes of interventions, used to solve these problems. The same applies to psychological problems. This makes it extremely difficult to develop generic statements for solving classes of problems. Situations where problems are context-determined have been characterized by Donald Schön (1983) in his well-known metaphor of the 'swamp of practice' (in contrast to the high ground of theory).

The starting point of DSR for developing generic solutions for problems in the 'swamp' is learning from comparable cases. But how can one develop an intervention theory from observations in the 'swamp', what should it look like and how can one then validate it? This methodological core problem cannot be solved in a scientifically justified manner, at least if the term 'scientific' directly or indirectly refers to the generic scientific method (the GSM) from the philosophy of science. The GSM has been developed based on proven effective research methods in the natural sciences, in particular physics. The material objects and processes in physics are subjected to the laws of nature. Therefore, in physics strong universal and invariant mechanisms are dominant.

The GSM is generic in its principles concerning rigorous scientific research. But for developing and validating theories, her principles are only useful for contexts with strong mechanisms. These principles cannot be applied in the 'swamp' of psychological practice with its weak psychological mechanisms. Developing theories in the 'swamp' therefore requires a different form of science than the methodology used for the 'high grounds' of theory, like physics.

DSR is able to solve the described methodological core problem of developing theories for contexts with weak mechanisms. It is inspired by Herbert Simon's groundbreaking book *The Sciences of the Artificial* (1969). In this book, Simon puts design at the centre of the kind of research aimed at innovation and improvement. Furthermore, he describes the fundamental differences between the 'Sciences of the Artificial' (A-disciplines, such as the engineering sciences, medicine, applied psychology and management research) and the 'Sciences of the Natural' (N-disciplines, such as the natural sciences).

Design is the key process of research in the A-disciplines. Design makes A-discipline research different from the kind of research in the N-disciplines, where explaining is the key process. Applied psychology is an A-discipline, largely dealing with weak psychological mechanisms. Psychological issues are almost always context-determined. Psychological interventions can therefore be characterized as interventions in the 'swamp' of practice and therefore have the same methodological core problem as management research. Operating in the 'swamp' of practice is inevitably based on limited knowledge. Unlike in physics, psychological scientific research cannot provide certainty nor eliminate risks.

As mentioned, in the DSR methodology, intervention theories are developed by learning from comparable cases. The basic structure of a DSR project consists of executing and studying cases on a class of problems in various contexts. From this, one learns what interventions do 'work' where and when and where and when they don't. The core of each case study consists of analysing the applied interventions and their outcomes, using the CIMO logic: For this-problem-in-context (C), this intervention (I) was applied, triggering mechanisms (M), which produced the outcomes (O). The essence of the case analyses is getting insight into the working mechanisms of the applied interventions. Subsequently, based on cross-case analyses and knowledge of effective mechanisms, an intervention theory is designed: a generic version of an intervention (or an arrangement of interventions), plus knowledge to make this generic intervention case-specific.

Theories for contexts with context-determined issues cannot be validated with the congruence theory of GSM. In the GSM, validation is based on directly recognizable reproducibility of the outcomes of interventions. Instead, DSR employs in the philosophy of science the most commonly used alternative to the congruence theory, namely the coherence theory. This theory states that a theory is valid if it agrees with all other knowledge relevant to the theory to be validated. Validating a medical guideline is, for example, an example of coherent validation: A forum of experts from the relevant medical disciplines assesses the effectiveness of a proposed medical intervention as objectively as possible, based on all available evidence.

The emphasis of the development of intervention theories by DSR is on getting insight into the why of the effectiveness of interventions. Psychological treatments are often based on an overarching explanatory psychological theory. In DSR, however, the theory is based on a careful synthesis of a collection of a large number of mechanisms found in the cases. Each local mechanism can be based on one or more underlying psychological theories, but the synthesis of a generic theory on the basis of many local mechanisms makes this theory more context sensitive than an overarching explanatory theory.

There are no canonical descriptions and textbooks of DSR yet. DSR today consists of a collection of related publications, such as the articles on DSR cited in this book.

Because of this, Cauffman and Weggeman use the insights and methods of DSR given in this literature on the basis of their own interpretation. By developing a scientific basis for a psychological treatment – the SoFAP-P design – they have played a pioneering role.

As a co-developer of DSR, I hope this book stimulates further innovative developments to bring DSR methodology to the field of psychology.

Prof. Dr. Ir. Joan van Aken
Professor em. Organization Science
Faculty of Business Administration
Eindhoven University of Technology

NOTE FROM THE AUTHORS

Our goal and ambition with this book is threefold.

First, we want to extend solution-focused thinking and working to different application domains so that, *second*, the epistemological tool of co-creating alternative realities between involved parties enters the domain of applied psychology.

Our *third* goal and ambition is that we want to present design science research as a methodology for validating applied psychological approaches, and to demonstrate how it works in the concrete case of SoFAP.

This book *Solution-Focused Applied Psychology: A Design Science Research Protocol* (SoFAP-P) offers a scientific foundation for the solution-focused arrangement of interventions used to facilitate change. It is mainly written for students and academics who are interested in discovering how evidence-based interventions can be developed by using design science research methodology.

The accompanying book, *Creating Sustainable Results with Solution-focused Applied Psychology: A Practical Guide for Coaches and Change Facilitators* (Routledge 2023), provides an in-depth practical guide to facilitate adding the intricacies of solution-focused thinking and working to the existing professionalism and expertise of practitioners.

Scanning the QR code on the next page brings you to the content of this book.

xviii Note from the Authors

FIGURE 0.1

1
INTRODUCING A SOLUTION-FOCUSED APPLIED PSYCHOLOGY PROTOCOL (SoFAP-P)

This chapter tells the story of the futile quest for a comprehensive theory about the functioning of the human mind that started in the late nineteenth century. In this quest, the emphasis was on what is wrong with psychological functioning and why that is so. Consecutive theories and models took centre stage and the client had to conform to them. In contrast with the traditional problem-oriented models, the development of solution-focused thinking and working emphasizes what is going well despite the problems, focuses more on facilitating change than on understanding why the problems are there and falls back on the *Image of Humankind* that every human system always has resources available, things that do work. The chapter provides a helicopter view of developments within the solution-focused approach and sketches the emergence of research on those factors that make psychotherapy work. Finally, the ambitions of the solution-focused applied psychology protocol (SoFAP-P) are outlined, with the term 'protocol' carefully defined.

1.1 Introduction: The futile quest for a comprehensive theory

With the emergence of psychology as a science in the late nineteenth century, the quest had begun for a comprehensive theory about the functioning of the human mind and ways to influence it. A theory is defined here as a system of coherent concepts that aim to offer a universal explanation for a certain field of expertise. Theories tell us about the why and how of aspects of the natural world. Psychology is a scientific discipline that studies mental states and processes and behaviour in humans and other animals (Mischel, 2020). Modern psychology has mainly concentrated on trying to understand mind and behaviour of humans, with an emphasis on what goes mentally wrong in the existence of a human being, why that happens and how it can be remedied. These understandings were embedded in theories, models and methods which succeeded each other. Each new theory or method with corresponding intervention models, pretended to be more all-encompassing, more profound or more effective than previous ones. But they all have their flaws and deficiencies, from which lessons are drawn that lead to yet another theory.

Theories and models tend to reduce the complexity of the subject studied, to phenomena that fit the theory. But you may come across a phenomenon that does not fit the theory you believe in, nor in any other theory. Moreover, you run the risk of becoming so attached to a particular theory or method that you only discover the misfit when it is too late, because your mind is blinded to alternative possibilities.

How this blinding works is easily understood. The *Sunken Cost Fallacy* kicks in: You have invested too much time, energy and passion in studying this particular approach, and it feels like a great loss to doubt the soundness of your beloved theory. On top of that, psychological theories are studied, taught and therefore learned through schools of thought: faculties, associations, training institutes and the like. Enter: *group think*. And to complete the blinding cycle, *confirmation bias* makes its appearance: One sees what one believes.

Consequently, rather than questioning the theory in use and then revising or adjusting it, the question will be asked whether there is perhaps something wrong with the description of the phenomenon that should fit within the theory, or with the way in which it was diagnosed.[1]

This brings us to our friend Procrustes, who had the unpleasant habit of offering guests a free stay at his inn, provided each of them would fit precisely into the available bed. If not: ... *the height of the guest was adapted to the length of the beds. If the guest was too tall, his legs were chopped off. If the guest was too short, he was stretched out on the rack* (Diodorus, 60–30 BC).

Because of their theoretical background, traditional therapies tend to require clients to conform to the model and underlying theories. Diagnosis and assessment are required to determine the fit. If not, the client must look for another 'therapy hostel'.

If the client fits into the framework but does not conform to the therapy provided, practitioners often call this 'resistance'. If all goes well and the therapy has relieved the client of a large part of his complaints and symptoms, the client has been helped. However, this exclusive focus on reducing symptoms that characterizes most traditional applied (psychotherapeutic) psychology approaches comes at a price. That is, the client must then work on his own to further his growth and well-being. Traditional therapies take the client so to speak from the minus to the zero: The negative has become neutral. To get from the zero to the plus is an another – traditionally: not told – story.

Every psychological theory or approach falls back on an underlying image of the Humankind. For the solution-focused therapist, the human being is a singular individual who functions in a social network and who – no matter how big the (temporary) problems are or seem to be – always has resources to get closer to his ultimate goal: to grow as a human being and enjoy well-being.[2] The American psychiatrist and psychotherapist Dr. Milton Erickson, whose work underlies the extended-solution-focused therapy, stated in this context: *Each person is a unique individual. Hence, psychotherapy should be formulated to meet the uniqueness of the individual's needs, rather than tailoring the person to fit the Procrustean bed of a hypothetical theory of human behavior* (Zeig & Geary, 2000).

Let the journey begin!

1.2 Beyond the solution-focused method

The image of Humankind behind the solution-focused thinking and working is based on the working hypothesis that all people always have resources at their disposal, albeit that these are sometimes hidden under the rubble of human misery. Resources can be defined as whatever it is that the client can use to reach his goal. That goal is to get rid of complaints, learn how to solve them in the future and learn to do something else so that the mother of all goals, well-being, can be accomplished, even tentatively and temporarily.

Treatment, therapy or, more broadly, facilitation that focuses exclusively on solving the client's problems ignores the essence of what ultimately drives human beings: growth, well-being and contentment. In this study, our aim is to provide tools to help the client and the professional to extend the step from mere treatment and care to grounded self-healing (that in this view equals growth) and well-being.

There are only two kinds of therapy and facilitation: good and bad, and it is the client who makes the definition. This premise puts the client at the centre of the therapy process. On the other hand, thanks to research on the non-specific therapeutic variables, we know what the discriminating factors for good therapy are.

The solution-way of thinking and working approaches the concept of a problem from a solution-focused angle. Instead of looking for root causes, a problem is seen as a wish for change that can be outspoken (*Instead of my problem, I would like to ...*) or tacit, for example in the case of psychosomatic complaints. By asking the right questions, the practitioner helps the client translate his problems – in casu wishes for change – into challenges. A challenge is considered here to be a client goal that has become so desirable that the client is willing to go to great lengths to achieve it. Metaphorically speaking, the client goal has become a *strange attractor*.

This *modus operandi* helps to avoid becoming problem-phobic when working solution-focused. After all, the more problems the better because the more problems, the more wishes for change and the more exciting the overall challenge.

Steve de Shazer and Insoo Kim Berg founded the *Brief Family Therapy* in Milwaukee, USA in 1978. Steve's first books, *Putting Difference to Work* (1980) and *Patterns of Brief Family Therapy: An Ecosystemic Approach* (1982), launched a worldwide movement of solution-focused therapy. This innovative development was in sharp contrast with classical psychotherapy because it moved away from analysing the root causes of problems. In the 1980s and 1990s, the solution-focused approach spread rapidly and found its place in the psychotherapy industry. From the very beginning, the major ambition of Steve de Shazer and his team was to find methods to diminish the time patients had to suffer from their problems and to move as quickly as possible to better times. The working hypothesis was that people who become patients always have moments when their problems are different, less or even temporarily absent. The concept of exceptions to the problems was the base for the philosophical stance that problems belong to a different logical class than solutions. Berg and de Shazer were both more interested in the future than in the past and they looked more into the differences, however, small, in problem perception of clients. This insight of 'exceptions to the problem' led them to develop a series of questions that invited the client to think about, and therefore become aware of, instances when the client is not overwhelmed by his perception of the problem. The evolution of their thinking caused them to explore what became two important epistemological keystones of their approach: differentiation in problem perception and future orientation. To facilitate the client's use of these key insights, they developed specific techniques. The *scaling questions* help the client to focus on differentiation while the so-called *miracle question* helps the client focus on the future.

On top of this, Steve de Shazer declared that the solution-focused approach was an a-theoretical method that did not seek to understand the mechanism of human functioning but that only was out to find what was the most helpful to a particular client at that moment in time.

1.2.1 Developments in the solution-focused method

After the initial clinical success, the solution-focused approach needed some theoretical substance. Clinical practitioners worldwide were happy but very soon criticism reared its head. So, although it became a popular approach for social workers and psychotherapists, academia was only minimally interested. In some circles, solution-focused therapy was frowned upon as 'that superficial bag of tricks'. Steve de Shazer and Insoo Kim Berg the founders of the first solution-focused training institute were perfectly aware of these critical voices. In an attempt to find an academic grounding for their approach, de Shazer embarked on a journey of trying to integrate the work of Jacques Lacan and later, that of Ludwig Wittgenstein. But his heart and mind remained focused on clinical practice. He and his team decided to stick to their 'core business', namely finding ever better ways to help and support people – students and trainees included – to use a solution-focused perspective.

1.2.2 The rise of psychotherapy research

Research in psychotherapy was slowly developing and almost limited to academic circles. Outcome research was modelled after medical research where the randomized controlled trial paradigm was adopted in the (vain) hope of emulating research in the hard sciences like physics: to find the truth and nothing but the truth, once and for all.

Much closer to daily clinical practice was the concept of evidence-based medicine as coined by Gordon Guyatt from McMaster University (Canada) in 1991. His colleague David Sackett co-authored in 1996 the article *'Evidence-Based Medicine: What It Is and What It Isn't'*. In the article, they define EBM as: *'the conscientious, explicit, and judicious use of current best evidence in making decisions about the care of individual patients'*. Today one can broaden this definition so that EBM is health care in which treatment decisions are based on the best available knowledge from clinical research, the experience of the doctor and the individual preferences and expectations of the patient. This implies that what today is seen as the best basis for treatment decisions plays out in the nexus between research and the two main stakeholders in this dynamic, namely the professional and (the idiosyncrasies of) the client.

Following the rise of evidence-based medicine, the world of psychotherapy followed in the same path. To understand the mechanisms behind positive change and to find evidence of what appeared to be the most effective interventions, a proliferation of different therapy schools, each with their own research agenda, was the result. As might be expected, this led to a bidding war over what was the most effective model and who had the honour of being the leading expert in the field. Lewis Carroll[3] taught us the DODO-effect: 'All have won, so all must have prices'.

The developers of the solution-focused approach were not deterred by this evolution. Satisfied by enough outcome research studies that proved its effectivity, the solution-focused approach kept its focus on the further deepening of its clinical and practical relevance. After de Shazer's next books, *Keys to Solution in Brief Therapy* (1985) and *Clues: Investigating Solutions in Brief Therapy* (1988), their rapidly growing international reputation led them to worldwide training workshop and conferences.

As a result, the approach knew a rapid expansion, albeit it strictly limited to the field of psychotherapy. Many books, articles and book chapters came out, mainly dealing with further specifications in the use of the techniques of scaling questions and the miracle question that became the icons of this approach. Alas, after Steve de Shazer and Insoo Kim Berg passed away in 2005 resp. 2007, who were not only the originators but also the guardians against trivialities, an ever-bigger accent was led on techniques and an ever more secluded focus on the approach itself. After 2007, solution-focused thinking no longer tried to deepen its understanding of the mechanisms of change and with that, its incisive power to elicit positive changes for clients. Most of the attention went into applying the same solution-focused principles in all kinds of (clinical) contexts: SF-methods with autism, SF-methods and the mentally disabled child, SF-methods in group therapy, SF-methods and coaching of the high potential etc.

In 2001, Berg and Cauffman presented a workshop in Washington, under the title *From Couch to Coach* where the solution-focused approach was applied to the field of coaching. This workshop introduced solution-focused thinking and working into the realm of organizations and into the context of business ventures. In 2006, Cauffman published *The Solution Tango: Seven Simple Steps to Solutions in Management and Coaching* that offered both a practical and a theoretical deepening of the approach for the field of management. It became a bestseller that even brought the solution-focused approach to China. In 2022, the book *Developing and Sustaining a Successful Family Business: A Solution-Focused Guide* was published (Cauffman, 2022). This book specifies solution-focused approaches for use in the complex economic world where family and business meet.

Cauffman's (2023) book *Creating Sustainable Results with Solution-Focused Applied Psychology* meticulously dissects, explains and formulates the latest developments in solution-focused applied psychology as a guide for beginners and seasoned change agents alike.

1.2.3 Our ambition with SoFAP-P

We have a triple ambition for our work on solution-focused applied psychology.

First, we want to make explicit the epistemology that lies behind the solution-focused approach as it is broadly applicable for use in all kinds of fields, especially where it concerns human interaction and influence. Since it is a process-like method where the content comes from the client and his context and not from the methodology, solution-focused applied psychology must be considered a generic tool.

Second, we want to broaden the solution-focused approach into a more general applied psychology. Rather than reflecting on the workings of the human mind that centre around fallacies, what doesn't work and why, solution-focused applied psychology protocol (SoFAP-P) focuses on the things that do work well. More specifically, SoFAP-P offers insight into what works well (enough) to lead a fulfilling life, and what elements in the workings of the mind can be used as focal points for creating a constructive vision of and in relationships with other people, systems and ideas.

Third, the time has come for a scientific substantiation of the expanded solution-focused approach that goes beyond techniques, simplified descriptions and personal stories and experiences. SoFAP-P reaches beyond the classical evidence-based methodology where the outcome of research is based on the average client with average problems being helped by an average intervention. We exploit a scientific method that uses an individualized design that is based upon scientific methodologies as used in engineering, medicine, architecture etc.

The scientific tool we will describe in detail and apply to achieve this ambition is called design science research.

> **A NOTE ON THE WORD 'PROTOCOL'**
>
> Merriam-Webster (2016) defines 'protocol' as:
>
> 1. an original draft or record of a document or transaction
> 2. a preliminary memorandum of diplomatic negotiation
> 3. a code prescribing strict adherence to correct etiquette and precedence
> 4. a set of conventions for formatting data in an electronic communications system
> 5. a detailed plan of a scientific or medical experiment, treatment or procedure
>
> Coming from the Greek the prefix πρoτo (*prōto*: first) and the noun κολλα (*kolla*: glue) πρoτoκoλλov (*prōtokollon*) gave us our word *protocol*. In the late nineteenth century, it began to be used in reference to the etiquette observed by the Head of State of France in ceremonies and relations with other dignitaries. This sense has since extended in meaning to cover any code of proper conduct.
>
> The word *protocol* as used in this book denotes a set of master rules (rules that govern rules at a lower operational level) or instructions that guide the ordering of interventions that a change facilitator can use to work in an effective and efficient manner. The content of the facilitation process comes from the situation in which these master rules can be applied to elicit change and is thus specific to situation X in context Y, with respect to stakeholder(s) Z.
>
> The change process is guided by a generic protocol that provides guidelines for choosing which interventions in which order, following a consecutive, stochastic, iterative, cumulative and, if necessary, recursive path. We therefore conclude by emphasizing that the word *protocol* in this book does not mean a standardized procedure or uniform method.

1.3 Structure of the book and reading guide

The most important announcement to be made here is that those who are primarily interested in the practical application of the SoFAP-P can go straight to Chapter 4. For that reason, Chapter 4 has been set up as a self-contained section of the book, explaining the use of SoFAP-P.

Those, who would like to go deeper into the scientific foundation of the design presented in Chapter 4, will find this justification in Chapters 2 and 3. Chapter 2 explores the problems and deficiencies currently experienced in the practice of applied psychology. Based on this inventory, the design objective is drawn up. Subsequently, it is explained how the design objective can be realized by applying design science research methodology. Chapter 3 contains the empirical basis for the SoFAP-P design presented in Chapter 4: lessons learned from literature and cases as well as bad and best practices derived from interviews with practitioners.

Chapter 5 shows how the protocol presented in Chapter 4 was validated (with a survey among practitioners and based on ex post cases).

Finally, in Chapter 6, contributions of the solution-focused SoFAP-P to science and society are elaborated.

Notes

1 The term 'diagnosis' often leads to problematic interventions as if diagnosis A strictly requires treatment A+. The term 'diagnosis' is best replaced by the term 'classification' which leaves more room for a broader scope of interventions.
2 We prefer the term well-being over 'happiness' for the simple reason that a relentless pursuit of happiness often results in the opposite: frustration, dissatisfaction, discomfort and the feeling of never being able to reach the ultimate happiness. Moments of happiness are side effects of the pursuit of well-being.
3 Lewis Carroll, *Alice's Adventures in Wonderland* (1865).

2
FIELD PROBLEM AND DESIGN OBJECTIVE

This chapter starts by exploring problems and methodological imperfections encountered in current applied psychology practice (Section 2.1). The lessons learned from this for the development of the envisioned SoFAP-P design are listed in Section 2.2. This section also mentions limitations that should be taken into account when designing the SoFAP-P design.

The final section of this chapter builds on the previous ones by defining a field problem and a design objective based on it (Section 2.3).

Chapter 2 ends with an explanation of design science research (DSR) methodology that is used to design and validate the intended solution-focused applied psychology protocol.

2.1 Exploration of field problems and methodological flaws in applied psychology theories

In this section, we will provide an overview of those applied psychological theories that have given rise to the intention to develop the SoFAP-P design.

It is therefore not our intention here to provide an exhaustive overview of all possible psychological models. We limit ourselves to those theories that are relevant in the context of mental problems and challenges.

The following applied theories are discussed successively:

- Psychoanalysis and psychodynamic approaches
- Behaviourism and cognitive behavioural therapy (CBT)
- Humanistic psychology
- Family systems therapy
- Ericksonian practices

DOI: 10.4324/9781003404477-2

- Solution-focused therapy (SFT)
- Extended solution-focused therapy (extended SFT)

For each of the applied theories, we will briefly articulate the change model and mention some of the renowned experts.

The brief exposition of each theory ends with the identification of its limitations and lessons that can be learned from that theory, for the development of the envisaged SoFAP-P design.

2.1.1 Psychoanalysis and psychodynamic approaches

Sigmund Freud developed psychoanalysis as the first talking therapy in history. His seminal first books are *Studien über Hysterie* (1885) and *Die Traumdeutung* (1899). The psychoanalytic approach considers psychological problems to be based on unconscious meanings and motivations. The change model explicates these unconscious meanings and motivations by the technique of 'free association': The patient lies on the couch and tells whatever comes to his mind. The therapist, occasionally, offers an interpretation of the patient's story and uses theoretical concepts to do so. The number of sessions are between three and five per week, and the complete psychoanalysis may take up many years. The focus is on the history of the patient, including all the theoretical processes (sublimation, repression, contortions, etc.) that create the intrapsychic setup of the individual. Insight is needed to find a way to deal with these processes. The current ecosystem of the patient is not relevant but only serves as a canvas on which the neuroticism of the patient is outlined. If the patient did not make progress, this phenomenon was called 'resistance'. Resistance is seen as an unconscious defensive manoeuver by the patient.

Some of the historically important contributors to psychoanalysis are – besides Sigmund Freud – Carl Gustav Jung, Alfred Adler, Melanie Klein and Anna Freud. For the psychodynamic approach, the central figures are Peter Sifneos at Harvard Medical School, David Malan at the Tavistock Clinic in London and Habib Davanloo, a professor of psychiatry at McGill University in Montreal.

In later years, psychoanalysis evolved from a therapeutic tool into a philosophy that was used as a reflective and explanatory tool, used in an amalgam of fields of study, ranging from politics and cultural phenomena, to religion and aesthetics in art.

Limitations of the approach

- The limitations of psychoanalysis are the long, in some cases even lifelong duration of the therapy, and consequently, the costs in time and fees. This led to the development of the psychodynamic approach which operates on the same principles as the classical psychoanalysis but aims at a shorter duration: 25–30 sessions over a period of 6–8 months.

- The psychodynamic approach shares similar limitations: unclear results, the fact that many of the concepts used are obscure and require a specific language for explanation.
- In psychoanalysis and psychodynamics, the model is the centre of the approach and the patient needs to adapt to the model. These models are problem oriented and focus on the intrapsychic dynamics that are used to explain the 'why' of the problems.

Lessons learned for the development of the envisaged SoFAP-P design

Sigmund Freud lay the very foundation for the industry of psychotherapy and his ideas pervaded art, culture, anthropology and so many other domains.

The limitations of psychoanalysis and psychodynamic therapy showed what was necessary in order to make progress in the psychotherapy field, namely clear results that benefit the patient.

So if we want clear results that benefit the client, fuzzy concepts need to be avoided and replaced by more realistic ones that can be connected to what happens in the here and now. The patient then can become a client who has a say in the therapeutic process, albeit that he[1] still needs to accept that the treatment model is prominent. The problem-focused 'why' needs an explanation that goes beyond intrapsychic concepts that stem from pure imagination or, in the case of Freud himself, from personal convictions. The answers to the 'why' want to ground themselves in a sound theory with interventions that can be replicated when dealing with similar problems.

2.1.2 *Behaviourism and cognitive behavioural therapy (CBT)*

Classical conditioning started out as a research project for biologists. Experts like B.F. Skinner (1904–1990) and Ivan Pavlov (1849–1936) founded behaviourism in which the effect of learning mechanisms on animal behaviour was studied. Their projects were limited to rather mechanistic learning processes that connected a simple input to a simple output. Pavlov trained a dog to salivate when hearing a bell before food was administered. In the 1960s, behavioural models of psychotherapy were operated under the premises that cognition influences behaviour. Founders of the cognitive behaviour therapy approach are Albert Ellis (1913–2007) and Aaron T. Beck (1921–2021).

The change model argued that incorrectly learned problematic cognitions cause problematic behaviour. Therefore, change the cognitions and the accompanying behaviour will change. The cognitive behavioural approach took up a central role in the clinical field, and since the 1960s, it has become the most researched form of psychotherapy. The approach unfolds along the following lines: After analysing the set of problematic cognitions, these cognitions are substituted by more suitable cognitions so that the behaviour that stems from the problematic cognitions is replaced by more adjusted behaviour. This change process happens in real time and is – obviously – intrapsychic in nature. The ecosystem of the patient is not involved. In the earlier CBT, emotions were seen as mere physiological expressions that accompanied cognitions. In recent decades, emotional distress that elicits dysfunctional coping mechanisms (e.g. stress-related substance abuse and bulimia) is analysed in order for the patient to be able to create cognitions that run counter the distress reactions. This enhanced approach was developed by Emma Gray in 2006 and goes by the moniker of cognitive emotional behavioural therapy. Behaviourism and especially the cognitive behaviour therapy approach is both cost-effective and efficient. In a relative short timeframe, clients are able to change problematic behaviour and cognitions into more healthy ones. The CBT approach is problem focused and relies on intrapsychic mechanisms for change. The interventions are based on the diagnosis of the detrimental cognitions and accompanying behaviour. Therefore, the model prevails over the wishes and goals of the clients and uses protocol-like intervention schemes.

Limitations of the approach

- Therapeutic interventions in behaviourism and CBT are based upon a diagnosis of problematic cognitive-behavioural causal chains. Neither the person of the client nor the influence of his ecosystem is taken into account. The approach is therefore less appropriate for addressing problems where emotional imbalance is central.
- Most CBT-interventions are protocolized. This facilitates knowledge transfer but reduces the tailoring of interventions to the needs of a particular individual.
- Behaviourism and CBT underrate the need for agency in human beings and ignore the influence of relevant others in the individual's life. The approach is purely problem focused and gives no attention to resources in the client system that are still working (sufficiently) well.
- In behaviourism, change is reduced to (re)learning processes. Concepts such as meaning, spirituality and growth do not fit into the CBT-model.

Lessons learned for the development of the envisaged SoFAP-P design

The transition from pure behaviourism into CBT and, more recently, cognitive emotional behavioural therapy demonstrates the flexibility in thinking among practitioners in this field.

The C(E)BT-studies show good outcome results. Nevertheless, there is a fairly high dropout rate in most studies, which could be attributed to the protocol-based interventions derived from diagnosis-cause-action chains in which there is little or no room for tailoring the approach to a specific client.

Indications for the approach are limited to problems of behaviour and cognition within a single individual. When ideas of agency, growth, inter-relational influence and the power of emotion are considered, the scope of indications and coherent interventions is broadened. This will increase the effectiveness and efficiency of C(E)BT interventions.

2.1.3 Humanistic psychology

This approach has the characteristics of a general stance rather than of a consortium of intervention techniques. It was developed in opposition to the two mainstream trends in twentieth century psychology: behaviourism and psychoanalysis. Humanistic psychology criticizes psychoanalysis for its deterministic orientation which postulates that one's early experiences and drives as a child determine one's behaviour. The critique on behaviourism is that it is too concerned with the study and analysis of people's conduct and neglects the fundamental aspects of man as a feeling, thinking and acting individual.

The humanistic approach is concerned with the growth of each individual in terms of fulfilment, self-esteem and autonomy. It is the first psychological approach to make room for the concept of love: love for one another and love for oneself. In this way, feelings and emotions receive as much attention as cognition and behaviour.

Abraham Maslow (1908–1970) argued in his major works – *Motivation and Personality* and *Toward a Psychology of Being* – that every human being has a hierarchy of needs, ranging from basic physiological requirements (food, shelter and safety) and belonging and love, to self-worth and self-actualization. With each need satisfied, the next level in the hierarchy dominates the person's conscious functioning. This ultimately leads to self-actualization which is seen as the highest human need to be satisfied. When this need is met, people can have peak experiences. These experiences were originally described by Maslow as *moments of highest happiness and fulfillment* (1964).

Another famous humanistic psychologist, Carl Rogers (1902–1987), argued that individuals perceive their world according to their own experiences, which guide their behaviour to meet the basic human needs of self-actualization, self-maintenance and self-enhancement. His book, *Client-Centered Therapy: Its Current Practice, Implications and Theory* (1951), launched the client-centred movement. As the title of the book indicates, the individual was no longer seen as a passive participant in therapy. The patient became a 'client', which suggests some equality between the caregiver and the people to whom care is provided. Humanistic psychology places the client at the centre of the encounter and not the model or method. The humanistic approach chooses to focus on the person and not their problems. What happens in the 'now' prevails over the past and the future.

Limitations of the approach

- There is a lot of emphasis on the self: self-awareness, self-enhancement and self-actualization. In that intrapsychic space, there is little room for the client's ecosystem.

- It is not clear if the humanistic approach is problem oriented because it limits itself to the development of the person and does not focus on his problems.
- The concepts used are vague, ill-defined and perhaps even hard to define.
- The goals that the humanistic approach strives for are general and difficult to operationalize. These goals do not come from the client but from the convictions that steer the model. So, these goals are more general in nature than tailored to the needs of the individual client.
- Outcome results are difficult to assess.

Lessons learned for the development of the envisaged SoFAP-P design

Progress will be made when the concepts underlying the approach are better defined, making it possible to translate them into concrete, realistic and achievable objectives.

Instead of focusing solely on working towards increasing self-awareness, self-enhancement and self-actualization, one can also identify which aspects of these three elements are already present. This gives the client a head start.

Seeing the individual client in the context of his ecosystem can increase the usefulness of the approach. When the goals of the client (and not those of the model) determine the interventions, progress can be made more easily and results can be assessed more easily.

2.1.4 Family systems therapy

The growth of the social work movement after the World War II was instrumental in coping with the seriously disturbed social fabric in society. Combined with the frustration over the frequent relapses of psychiatric patients after their return home, the idea that the patient's ecosystem is influential started to dawn. Yet, at the same time, it could be observed how many war-traumatized soldiers (in today's parlance: post-traumatic stress disorder) readjusted and healed after returning to their families and communities. In short, the time was ripe to move from the intrapsychic to an interactionist view, even though most practitioners were trained psychoanalysts. Many pioneers of the interactionist approach came from very different backgrounds: social work (Henry Richardson), anthropology (Margaret Mead, Gregory Bateson), cybernetics (Ludwig von Bertalanffy), mathematics (Paul Watzlawick, Norbert Wiener), communication theory (Jay Haley), linguistics (Noam Chomsky) and chemistry (John Weakland).

Murray Bowen (1913–1990) is one of the early pioneers. His statement *Family systems theory is a theory of human behaviour that views the family as an emotional unit and uses systems thinking to describe the complex interactions in the unit* marks the birth of the field of family therapy. His book *Family Therapy in Clinical Practice* collects all of his major contributions to the field since 1954.

The anthropologists Margaret Mead (1901–1978) and Gregory Bateson (1904–1980) studied how people function in their contexts and how these contexts influence the way humans interact within the community. In the 1940s, Bateson played an important role in introducing ideas from cybernetics and systems theory into the realm of social and behavioural sciences. This resulted in the 'Bateson Project' (1953–1963). In collaboration with Don D. Jackson, Jay Haley and John D. Weakland, they first studied human communication in propaganda. As the threat of war subsided, funds dried up and they shifted their focus to research in psychiatry and psychotherapy. This culminated in the Mental Research Institute in Palo Alto which became a major research and teaching facility for family and systemic psychotherapy. There John Weakland became a mentor for Steve de Shazer, the founder of the solution-focused approach.

The family systems approach moves its focus of attention from the intrapsychic functioning of the individual to how a person functions in his ecosystem, of which the family usually is the most important subsystem. The field of cybernetics inspires the rules of interaction and communication that govern the actions and interactions between the members of the ecosystem. The mathematician Norbert Wiener defined cybernetics as *the scientific study of control and communication in the animal and the machine* (1948).

The early family systems therapy school looks for repetitive interactional patterns in the relationships among family members. The idea is that some of these repeating patterns can negatively affect one or more family members[2] to the extent that they get into problems, and how their reactions to these recurring interactions then perpetuate the problematic interactional cycle.

A well-known example of this thinking is a 'schizophrenogenic mother' where the theory is that it is the mother's interactional and communicative style that provokes the schizophrenia in the 'identified patient'. One recognizes the diagnosis-causation chain of the problem-oriented model. The symptoms of the identified patient have a function: They keep the system in homeostasis, albeit an unhealthy equilibrium. Improvement in mental health then comes from changing the interactions among the members of the system in such a way that another, more healthy homeostasis (inner system balance) is installed.

The family systems approach is more interested in trying to understand how human systems interact than in explaining the causes of dysfunction. The literature on family systems is gradually developing a theoretical framework based in part on insights from related sciences such as cybernetics and communication theory. The result is a slightly mechanistic interpretation of the functioning of people and their interactions.

Limitations of the approach

- This systemic and interactional approach, which is a step forward from the exclusive focus on the intrapsychic, derives its theoretical insights from related

sciences that are mechanistic in nature and therefore cannot fully consider the unpredictable serendipities of human life.
- The family systems approach places understanding (the rules of) interactions above explanation but is not clear about what to do to improve the situation.
- The approach is problem oriented as it places the origin of the problems in repetitive patterns of dysfunctional interaction. Change lies in changing interaction patterns among the members of the system, and there is no focus on what happens to the individuals of the system.
- Although a family is a biological system that operates in cognition, behaviour and emotions, the emphasis in systemic family therapy is not on those factors but rather on dysfunctional interactive patterns.
- No attention is paid to the goals of the individual members of the ecosystem nor to the ecosystem-as-a-whole. The approach starts with the implicit assumption that the individual members of the ecosystem must want to change their dysfunctional interactions.
- Change is seen as change in relational patterns and not in what happens to and within the individuals involved.

Lessons learned for the development of the envisaged SoFAP-P design

Making room for serendipity, unpredictability and uncertainty in the life of human development is frightening, relieving and revealing. This acceptance helps suppress the well-intentioned but unhelpful urge to control our lives and our clients' developments. To do this, one must have the courage to abandon methods aimed at fully explaining and understanding the mechanisms of human interactions within the ecosystem and with the world. Understanding how problems arise in interactional systems is nice to know. Offering interventions that help clients find better ways to cope with what life brings is a step forward. The family systems or the broader ecosystem obviously has an important influence on everyone, but the individual still has his own free will and the possibility of making choices of his own. The emotions of every individual can influence how he and others function and bring about changes in their ecosystem. This cannot be underestimated and must be taken into consideration. Goals of individuals and of ecosystems structure the perception of their paths forward. The way forward in the family systems approach is to give room to what each member of the ecosystem sees as its purpose and destination. Therefore, the unit of change must include the individual choices, needs and goals of each member of the ecosystem.

2.1.5 Ericksonian practices

Psychiatrist and psychologist Dr. Milton Erickson (1901–1980) was highly influential in the field of psychotherapy. Over decades, many of the important contributors to the field of family therapy, system therapy, psychiatry, anthropology and even sports coaching consulted with him. It can be that Erickson was a pivotal figure from whom many experts and new models of psychotherapy drew their inspiration. During World War II, Dr. Erickson and Margaret Mead were commissioned by the American Intelligence Service to study the psychology of the 'average German'. After many academic consultations on the topics of schizophrenia, communication and relationships, Gregory Bateson became a lifelong friend of Erickson. In 1973 Jay Haley wrote a famous book about the innovative and often counterintuitive methods Dr. Erickson used in his treatments: *Uncommon Therapy*. The Mental Research Institute in Palo Alto based its strategic approach to therapy on Erickson's work. The founders of NLP (Neuro Linguistic Programming)[3], Bandler and Grinder, claim that their methodology can codify the structure inherent in the therapeutic 'magic' as performed in therapy by Erickson.

There is a large body of literature that attempts to decipher, understand, analyse and demystify his approach. To this day, it is very difficult to explicate unequivocally what it is that is so powerful in Erickson's case studies. The following quotes from Dr. Milton Erickson (Cauffman, 2010) give an impression of his way of thinking in which most of the lessons from the models discussed earlier are integrated, and they foreshadow the emergence of the solution-focused approach:

- It is the patient who does the therapy. The therapist only furnishes the climate, the weather. That's all. The patient has to do all the hard work.
- Anything that can affect good cooperation between patient and physician in achieving an important goal is worth of consideration.
- Therapy is what the therapist does to the patient. Healing is what the patient does to himself. Treatment is helping from the outside. Healing is helping from within.
- In the relationship between patient and clinician, you have one goal in common. The patient wants some type of care and you are prepared to give the desired care. They are two people joined together, working for a common goal – the welfare of the patient.
- The therapist's task should not be a proselytizing of the patient with his own beliefs and understandings. No patient can really understand the understandings of his therapist nor does he need them. What is needed is the development of a therapeutic situation permitting the patient to use his own thinking, his own understandings, his own emotions in the way that best fits him in his scheme of life.
- The patient's behaviour is a part of the problem brought into the office. It constitutes the personal environment within which the therapy must take effect; it may constitute the dominant force in the total patient-doctor relationship.
- The clinician should avoid fixating on what the client must stop doing. Growth-oriented therapy focuses on what the patient can start doing.

- You want patients to realize that illness is the only part of their total life experience. No matter what the illness, patients can always find something to appreciate about themselves. In talking to them, make them aware of all other gifts they have.
- Future-oriented thinking requires that the future imagined reflects a nascent personal direction that already awaits fulfilment, not some unrealistic fantasy.
- The sine qua non of psychotherapy should be the present and the future adjustment of the patient, with only that amount of attention to the past necessary to prevent a continuance or a recurrence of past maladjustments.

In the Ericksonian therapy approach, the client is put at the centre of the treatment, whereas the therapist provides the tools for treatment. The working relationship, in which both parties strive to help the patient achieve his goals by using his possibilities and his resources, is more important than the therapist's model. The ecosystem of the client, his personal environment, must become an active ingredient in the intervention. The present and future are the guidelines for the client's growth-orientation, while the past deserves only that amount of attention necessary to avoid falling into old useless habits.

Limitations of the approach

- The theories and explanations that Erickson offers in many of his early writings in the late 1930s and early 1940s are more thinking exercises than attempts to construct a coherent body of knowledge. Very soon, he concentrated on his clinical practice and his writing turned to case studies. His extensive travelling and teaching in the 1950s and 1960s combined with extraordinary therapeutic results became a magnet for his ever-growing private practice. Although highly controversial in the contemporary psychiatric scene of his time, his name and fame attracted both patients and students from around the world.
- The fact that there is no solid theoretical background on which Erickson grounded his controversial, yet successful interventions, limits the possibility of knowledge transfer. The many case studies, however innovative and even disruptive they were in the years he published them, offer hardly opportunities to learn how to practice the Ericksonian therapy.
- Because of his 'single-case design', even the publication of all his cases cannot possibly provide full insight in the overall effectiveness of his approach.
- There are no full transcripts, nor audio- or videotapes available that could shed light on how the therapeutic process with his patients worked out in practice. Erickson's *thinking behind his thinking* can only be reconstructed based on his many case studies. Since the early 1980s with the establishment of the Milton H. Erickson Foundation (www.erickson-foundation.org), a study and research centre focused exclusively on Erickson's work, much effort has been done in this regard.

Lessons learned for the development of the envisaged SoFAP-P design

Because of the intrinsic idiosyncratic and client-situation specificity of Erickson's approach, it is impossible to find out what the effectiveness is of the approach. Comparative single-case studies seem the best method to unravel his practice, if one includes as comprehensive an account as possible of the 'what, how and why' of each of the constituent elements of the intervention. The beliefs, (mis)conceptions, situational context that comprises people and ideas, are all to be seen as part of the ecosystem. This explication should be done in a way that facilitates the transferability of the know-how (and the 'do-how'). In other words, a hands-on translation of quotations like the ones above and information from the case studies can help to turn Erickson's mythical (and for some neo-Ericksonian's even mystical) approach into a practical tool. To safeguard the subtlety of the Ericksonian approach, mechanistic protocols are to be avoided.

POSITIVE PSYCHOLOGY AND APPRECIATIVE INQUIRY, AN INTERMEZZO

Hermann Ebbinghaus observed: *'Psychology has a long past, but only a short history'* (Boring, 1950). In that short history, concepts emerged and evolved in succession, in parallel and in accordance with the spirit of the times. After decades of trying to understand and explain the flaws in *La Condition Humaine*, Dr. Milton Erickson was one of the first practitioners to point to resources and resilience in the clients and offer interventions to help clients actively use those factors to improve their lives, despite the difficulties. The solution-focused approach is a practical and more teachable version of his seminal work. The *zeitgeist* of the 1990s spawned two closely related areas of research: positive psychology and appreciative inquiry.

In his role of President of the American Psychology Association, Martin Seligman coined the moniker **positive psychology** (PP) in 1998. Based on the work of Nobel Laureate Daniel Kahneman and Mihaly Csikszentmihalyi (1934–2021), PP urges that human goodness and excellence are as authentic as disease, disorder and suffering. PP explores what makes life worth living, and the PP expert offers some general interventions that are helpful in doing so (Peterson, 2006). Based on similar principles, PP differs in practice from the solution-focused approach. PP is more focused on a reflective attitude of studying and knowing what generally underlies human fulfilment, whereas the solution-focused attitude is more directed towards providing practical and tailored help to the client in question.

Appreciative inquiry (AI) originates in the field of organizational development.

The first article by David Cooperrider and Suresh Srivastava (1987) was an expansion of Cooperrider's doctoral thesis of 1986 and sparked an innovative movement in the field of organizational development. AI advocates asking the collective of the client organization questions that constitute an inquiry into the best of what is, to imagine what could be, followed by collectively designing a desired future state that is compelling and thus invites all stakeholders to participate in what is necessary to make the planned change happen (Bushe, 2013). The framework that structures large-scale interventions is called the 4-D model: *Discover, Dream, Design* and *Deploy*. Simplified, this amounts to asking many questions about what is still going well, formulating a vision for future change that is translated into the architecture of the intervention that reflects what has been learned in the previous stages, and then putting these plans into action. Offering continuous appreciation is oil in the cog of change. AI provides a framework for large-scale interventions by following a fairly strict protocol of intervention steps. In AI, the model is guiding, whereas in the solution-focused approach, the goals and resources, or desires for change and associated personal possibilities, are guiding.

Starting from similar principles, but different in the way they convey their core messages, neither PP nor AI refers to the solution-focused approach that preceded them in time.

2.1.6 Solution-focused therapy (SFT)

As already mentioned in Section 1.1, Steve de Shazer (1940–2005) and Insoo Kim Berg (1934–2007) were the founders of the *Brief Family Therapy Center (BFTC)* (1978) in Milwaukee, USA. In its early days, years, the BFTC was both a therapy research centre and a provider of psychotherapeutic services. Gradually in the first decade of its existence, team members, early adopters, academically interested and visitors from all over the world came to learn from behind the one-way mirror in de Shazer and Berg's office – to name just a few from that large group: Eve Lipchik, Wallace Gingerich, Michelle Weiner-Davis, Yvonne Dolan, Peter de Jong, Brian Cade, Bill O'Hanlon, Scott Miller, Gale Miller and so on. Insoo Kim Berg acted as the master clinician while her husband, Steve de Shazer functioned as the thinker, theoretician and writer of the BFTC. Over the years and accompanying books, de Shazer's thinking and working evolved in an increasingly subtle way. In the last few decades, a plethora of developments and conversation techniques based on his work was used in attempts to structure the solution-focused approach into a more protocolized form.

In de Shazer's first book, *Putting Difference to Work* (1980), he clarifies the difference with other forms of therapy and their philosophical underpinnings. The following metaphor makes this clear: If the key fits the lock, the lock can open without disassembling the lock. In other words, it is not necessary to understand the mechanism of the lock (the problem) nor does one needs to know the intrinsic characteristics of the key (the model). If the key (model) fits the lock (the problem), combining the two will open the lock (offer a solution). His famous quote, *the class of problems belongs to another logical class than the class of solutions*, elucidates this. In other words: One does not necessarily need to understand neither the nature nor the underlying root cause of a problem to help the client find a solution.

de Shazer's second book, *Patterns of Brief Family: An Ecosystemic Approach* (1982) honoured those on whose shoulders he stood to look beyond. Here de Shazer introduced the importance of working with the client's ecosystem. In all his subsequent books, de Shazer did not just look further but he looked differently. Inspired by the work of Milton H. Erickson, his focus of interest shifted to exceptions to the problems and, especially, to the client's resources.

The solution-focused approach, which in the beginning was more of a methodology, a set of consecutive tools, evolved in incremental steps. When talking with the clients about their problems, de Shazer and his team realized that there were times when the problem was not as prominent, a little different as before or even absent. They called these moments 'exceptions to the problem' and it became a major point of interest to analyse what the client was doing differently at those moments.

Next, the de Shazer team designed what they called the 'formula first session task', a task that every client system had to perform by default between the first and second session. 'Between now and the next time we meet, we would like you to observe so you can describe to us next time, what happens in your (pick one: family, life, marriage, relationship) that you want to continue to happen'. (de Shazer, 1982). This standardized intervention invited the client to look beyond his problems. Later this formula was transformed into the so-called *continuation question,* only to be used when appropriate; 'In spite of all of your problems, what are the things in your life that are so important that you want them to keep happening?' This question was later refined into: 'What are the things in your life that are so important that you want to keep *doing* them?' Changing the word 'happening' into 'doing' indicates a more active involvement of the client, a subtle but significant change. Repeatedly asking the question 'What else?' helps the client to go into detail. Very early on, the de Shazer-team developed the habit of taking a break in the session, often at the point when they felt that the above interventions had generated enough material to give the client a positive message. Upon returning to the consultation room from behind the one-way mirror, the therapist offered a summary message full of compliments about what the clients were already doing well in their lives. The purpose of giving as many compliments as possible was to encourage the client to keep doing what is going well despite his problems and to create hope that further change for the better is possible.

The de Shazer-team discovered that complimenting their clients on what they were doing well in their – otherwise problematic – lives invited and encouraged them to take small steps towards a better life. Moreover, this line of questioning leads the client away from his problem fixation and focuses the attention on possibilities. The exception-to-the-problem concept led in 1984 to the idea of differentiation, i.e. there is more in life than black (*I am consumed by my overwhelming problems*) and white (*I live a perfect life full of constant happiness*).

From this emerged the technique of *scaling questions*. For example: On a scale where 0 stands for the moment your problems were almost overwhelming, and where 10 stands for 'now everything is perfect again', where are you now? In 1988, the *miracle question* was invented as a technique that allowed the client to create, in an as-if mode, a future in which his problems were solved. Later, in 1994, in his book *Words Were Originally Magic*, de Shazer specifies: 'All the miracle question is designed to do is to allow clients to describe what it is they want out of therapy without having to concern themselves with the problem and the traditional assumption that the solution is somehow connected with understanding and eliminating the problem'. Here is a representative formulation of that question: Imagine you go to sleep and while you sleep, it is as if a miracle happens. In that miracle, all the problems that you told me about are solved so that they no longer bother you. How would you notice that this change has happened when you wake up? By asking what he would do differently after the miracle, the therapist helps the client to generate possible solution scenarios.

With regards to goal setting, in that same book, de Shazer clarifies: 'For the therapists to expect clients to know at the beginning of therapy exactly where they want to go is unrealistic; if they did, they probably would not need therapy'. de Shazer even specifies: 'For this reason we *do not find it necessary* to contract with clients (a) for a specific number of sessions or (b) for *specific goals* or (c) to measure progress on specific goals'.

In summary, SFT is characterized by – but not limited to – the recursive application of the following four techniques:

- Look for exceptions to the problem and expand those exceptions.
- Ask one or more scaling questions in every session.
- In every session ask the miracle question.
- Give as many compliments as possible.

Limitations of the approach

- Steve de Shazer and Insoo Kim Berg toured the world with training and consulting programmes and thereby created a worldwide solution-focused movement. The innovative techniques of the scaling questions and the miracle question became the icons for which the approach is renowned. All too often, the simple but not easy solution-focused approach was oversimplified by well-meaning novice therapists and trainers, for the (so-called) sake of transferability. Unfortunately, the icons became buzzwords to which the approach is all too often reduced. In some circles of practitioners, SFT downgraded into an arrangement of techniques that gained prominence over the rich epistemology that is hidden in the SFT approach.

Again, the model became leading and not the needs nor the resources of the client. It is obvious that this simplification is not what the rich epistemology of the solution-focused approach is about, nor what Steve de Shazer and his team thought and taught.

- Although the ecosystem played an important role in the approach, the actual work was done predominantly with individual clients.
- Talking about the client's goals happened indirectly, instead of simply asking the client for his goals. In one published transcript (1994), after the session has been going on for 10 minutes, de Shazer comments: 'So far, so good. We have a beginning picture of what it is she wants from therapy'. In de Shazer's posthumously published final book: *More Than Miracles, The State of the Art of Solution-Focused Brief Therapy* (2007), on the topic of goal setting, we read: 'the miracle question is one of the best questions in our repertoire for helping the clients describe how they will know therapy is over and one that consistently provides useful descriptions'. So, nowhere in de Shazer's sources there is room for directly asking the clients what it is that they want from therapy. This indirect method opens room for direct goal setting in later developments of the SFT approach.
- From the axiom that solutions belong to a different logical class than solutions, emanates the practice of neither barely asking nor talking about the problems that bring the client into therapy. If a client feels the need to talk about his problems, the immediate question is: 'What would you like instead?'
- Therapy is seen as a Wittgensteinian language game, or in the words of de Shazer as 'interactional constructivism' by which the parties involved (client and therapist) co-create an alternative reality.
- There are no references to the quality of the working relationship, or to the active elements in the therapy that trigger or provoke change and progress.
- The original SFT model is dealt exclusively with psychotherapy.
- After the deaths of de Shazer and Berg, 'innovations' in SFT were sought only in specific applications: SFT for mentally restricted clients, for gifted children, for ADHD or autism spectrum disorder, for sensitive personalities, etc. Technicality gained prominence over the underlying solution-focused way of thinking and working.

Lessons learned for the development of the envisaged SoFAP-P design

The quasi-protocol-like reduction of the solution-focused approach to the four SFT-techniques is both reductionistic, limiting and simplistic. It goes contrary to Occam's razor: *entia non sunt multiplicanda praeter necessitatem*. The words *praeter necessitatem* are crucial. Things should not be made more complicated than necessary. This implies that cases must be viewed with adequate complexity. There is little to no room for a reductionist simplism that does not consider complicating and complex factors. Instead, interventions can and should be designed and planned in a fluid manner that suits the client, his contextual needs and the back-and-forth flow of change and progress over time.

The ecosystem can be actively involved in therapy rather than remaining background information. *Solution talk* is a powerful tool for changing the client's perspective towards a more adequate future. It opens up access to resources that are available for the client to help him achieve his goals. There is no need for an indirect way of finding out what the client wants from therapy. Goal setting can be made easier and more straightforward by simply asking the client what he wants from therapy.

Ever more attention should be given to active ingredients that promote change in the client's future life and that are activated by the working relationship between the parties. These active ingredients are common to all forms of psychotherapy and psychological assistance approaches: (1) The client feels understood, (2) he experiences authentic attention and (3) respect, and he has (4) hope for change towards a better future. Under the moniker 'non-specific factors', these four active ingredients will become more important in the further development.

It happens that it is necessary to intervene in the real life of the client, especially when he does something that can be harmful to him or others. Even if this is not strictly considered to be part of the psychotherapeutic process, professional ethics, deontology and plain common sense sometimes necessitates such interventions.

2.1.7 Extended solution-focused therapy (extended SFT)[4]

The innovative techniques of the scaling questions and the miracle question became the icons for which the approach is renowned. Unfortunately, the icons became buzzwords to which the approach is all too often reduced. This simplistic implementation lacked the sophistication and subtlety of the original SFT approach developed by de Shazer cum suis. Using the solution-focused adagio 'change works best on the foundation of what already works well', Cauffman enriched the SFT with insights from the Ericksonian practice: The focus on the client's particular situation, challenges and resources (possibilities) was brought in line with the needs for change (the goals) of the client.

This resulted in Cauffman's book *The Solution Tango* (2006). Furthermore, the Erickson family gave him permission to publish *The Canoe Diary*[5] of Dr. Milton H. Erickson (2016), a famous manuscript that had been referred to for four decades without anyone being able to read it. This Canoe Diary is a coming-of-age document in which the boy in Milton Erickson foreshadows the later famous Dr. Erickson.

Cauffman's Ericksonian innovations and improvements are integrated into the traditional SFT approach and will be referred to as extended SFT[6]. It can be summarized in the following seven statements:

1 *Client-centred instead of theory- or model-centred*
A strict adherence to the four SFT-techniques is no longer necessary. Yet, they are still useful when used sparingly and at the right time. When is the right time? When the practitioner believes that the use of the techniques adds value. The same goes for all insights, techniques and interventions that stem from any model of psychological change facilitation that classically are at the core of how practitioners intervene. Instead of putting the theoretical model in the lead, extended SFT puts the client in the lead, the client with his resources and his goals.

2 *Beyond psychotherapy and into the world*
Extended SFT broadens the scope of traditional SFT in such diverse professional application areas as therapy, coaching, management, consulting, education, group intervention, family business, mediation and even pastoral counselling. In fact, wherever humans and their ecosystems interact for the purpose of growth in every possible sense of the word, the extended-SFT approach can be used as a tool.

3 *The working relationship is the engine for change*
From the very beginning of an intervention, it is the task of the practitioner to establish the most constructive working relationship possible. During the intervention process, this working relationship activates the non-specific change factors and therefore needs constant attention and monitoring. These variables that drive change are activated in and through the working relationship. The non-specific factors that are common to all successful interventions are implied in the answers to the next questions:

- *Do I feel understood?*
- *Do I get the appropriate authentic attention?*
- *Do I feel respected as a person?*
- *Do I get the perspective that change for the better is possible?*

In other words, for the client to experience 'good' therapy/coaching/facilitation, it is necessary that he feels understood, receives an appropriate amount of authentic attention and respect while hope blossoms that positive alternatives to his problems are in reach. The 'I' in the four questions clearly is the client. These questions underscore the importance of the client centredness and emphasize that change is brought about by and within the working relationship.

4 *The seven-step dance*
The interaction between the parties, client and professional service provider is like a dance with a limited number of steps that have unlimited combination possibilities. This is possible because the seven steps are *process* interventions, while the client, his ecosystem, his goals and his resources offer the *content* of the conversation. Each step in the dance is an *activity* to be performed together with the client. It starts with making contact (step 1) since the working relationship is the driver for change. After having explored the context (step 2), the client is asked for his goals (step 3), we listen for resources (step 4) and offer

relevant compliments (step 5). When in trouble, people tend to think in black-white terms and, in order to not drown in a sea of misery, we offer differentiation. This can be done by offering differentiating questions, like: When was the problem the most difficult? How did that stop? Are there moments that your situation is more bearable and what do you do differently then?, or by using scaling questions. For example, how do you feel right now on a scale of 0 to 10, where 0 is very bad and 10 is good enough? (step 6). Problems per definition belong to the past. Problems that do not exist today are no problems (yet). Solutions on the contrary belong to the future. The future orientation (step 7) of extended SFT underlines this given.

5 *Beyond the individual towards the client's ecosystem*
The members of the ecosystem are actively engaged by either inviting them to participate in the intervention process or by talking about their potential influences. The client's ecosystem may include the following points:

   a relevant third parties: family, friends, classmates, teams, organizations …
   b beliefs: religion, convictions, political insights, mental fallacies …
   c micro environmental elements: neighbourhood, living circumstances, finances, …
   d macro environment elements (especially when working in a business context): general economic developments, pandemics, ecological changes and/or disasters, …

6 *Goals are indicators for the direction of the change*
After exploring the context and the ecosystem that is most relevant to the client, goals are immediately set: 'What do we need to talk about so that this conversation will be useful to you?' In this goal-setting question, forward-looking is embedded and creates a future orientation.

In addition, when one defines goals as wishes for change, they can be translated into challenges. As mentioned earlier (in Section 1.1), the solution-focused way of thinking and working approaches the concept of a problem as a wish for change that can be outspoken or tacit. By asking the right questions, the practitioner helps the client translate his problems – in casu wishes for change – into challenges. A challenge then is a goal that has become so desirable that the client is willing to put a lot of effort into it.

7 *Three mandates*
The scope of the original SFT approach was limited to psychotherapy and therefore speaks only of a therapeutic mandate. When working in professional contexts beyond psychotherapy in sensu stricto, it is useful to conceptualize additional mandates from which to intervene.

There are three mandates that are always at work simultaneously, albeit constantly alternating. Depending on the specific situation, one mandate is in the foreground, while the others remain in the background. The mandate of leadership alternates with the mandate of coaching and facilitating which alternates with the management mandate that deals with the stewardship and structuring of the intervention process. This topic will be discussed in Section 3.4, where the validity range of the SoFAP-P design is dealt with.

This concludes the seven most important innovations and improvements made to the traditional SFT approach to create extended SFT. The renewed approach claims to be applicable to all fields where interactive influence is exerted and where changes, development and growth are wished for.

The extension added to the traditional SFT approach makes extended-SFT suitable to deal with interventions in situations that range from individuals, families and groups to organizational systems. It also gives room to work on topics where the interactional influence is an adjuvant to the process, for example business and organizational coaching and consulting, working with the complexities of family businesses and coaching teams.

The extended-SFT approach deals with stochastic change processes that have successive stages of progress and setbacks over an extended period. During that period, objectives and circumstances change such that the intervention process must be constantly calibrated. This requires a dynamic sequence of interventions that is iterative as well as recursive: You do one intervention after the other, gauge the results of it on its usefulness and if necessary, you revert to previous interventions that are recursively related to the way the situation has developed. This results in a loop of improvement that is in contrast with the unidirectional diagnosis-root cause-action chain.

FROM EXTENDED-SFT TO SoFAP-P

Extended-SFT is the most advanced addition to the solution-focused approach to date. Our goal now is to further complement this newest version of SFT by removing redundancies and filling in gaps discovered in research on the evolution of the prior models. In particular, we want to make improvements by providing an alternative to the rather linear approach of existing solution-focused treatments.

This development is motivated by the experience-based assumption that seasoned solution-focused practitioners actually work in a more recursive, iterative and circular manner as suggested by extended-SFT.

Parallel to this, we aim to ground the solution-focused approach scientifically by using the DSR methodology. The result should be a validated SoFAP-P design (a Solution-focused Applied Psychology Protocol, grounded on a DSR methodology) that can be considered the successor of extended-SFT.

Note that words like 'therapy' or 'coaching' do not show up in that title.

2.1.8 On the limitations of the reviewed applied psychology theories

Although the evaluated approaches have major application differences, their accumulated limitations reveal certain common roots of their most essential shortcomings.

Within psychoanalysis and the psychodynamic approach, as well as behaviourism and CBT, the client is regarded as a patient, characterized by the description of his problem (or illness). The patient must be treated according to a standard protocol of interventions.

A shortcoming of humanistic psychology is that it pursues ideal goals that are not only very vague (self-awareness, self-improvement and self-actualization), but moreover must be the same for every person.

In family systems therapy, one or more individual family members become 'identified patients' as a result of a malfunctioning ecosystem. Here the focus of attention is not on the intrapsychic (mal)functioning of an individual but on the repetitive patterns of interaction within the dysfunctional family systems.

These approaches are marked by an unbalanced methodological focus, in which too much time is invested in diagnosing (read: classifying) a problematic situation, rather than resolving it. This is done with such conviction that one cannot help but be inclined to think that these underlying diagnoses are mostly sought and formulated in support of the presuppositions underlying them.

Because of this problem-oriented perspective, the complexity of mental problems often is reduced to an excessive degree. Similarly, the linearity of the process of *anamnesis-diagnosis-therapy-prognosis* oversimplifies and thus obscures the situation of the client. No catalogue of psychological flaws can do justice to the singularities of the individual mind, just as the myriad of each person's aspirations can never be captured in an exhaustive list. Like a limiting diagnosis, ill-defined, universal goals are equally unfit to be projected onto the client who, despite elegant general theories, remains an individual with unique personal needs. Squeezing a client into such general moulds inevitably leads to blindness to possibilities and resources that can help the client find a practical solution to the problem.

Proponents of the solution-focused school were aware of the shortcomings of the problem-oriented view. Although they recognized that over-analysing a problem usually resulted in an unbalanced focus on past experiences and historical context, they almost completely avoided talking about the reasons that made a client seek their help.

At the same time, however, the interventions of the early solution-focused practitioners were such that the conversation would only indirectly touch on the goals of the client. Most existing approaches (except for family systems therapy) focus on the intrapsychic and pay attention to the rather negative influence of the ecosystem. The solution-focused approach did take this social ecosystem into account. Yet in the early solution-focused practice, this social ecosystem was mostly discussed but almost never actually involved in the SFT sessions.

All these constraints, by definition, impede the client's path to his goals and therefore imply a lack of efficiency in the use of time, money and other resources.

Next step:
It is the extended-SFT that we want to further detail and validate using a DSR methodology (see Section 2.3).

In this way, the extended-SFT approach constitutes the main input for the scientific design of the envisaged solution-focused applied psychology protocol, which goes under the moniker SoFAP-P.

2.2 Points of attention and lessons learned for developing SoFAP-P

The applied psychological theories discussed in the previous section concluded with detailed *limitations* and *lessons learned* for the design of our envisioned solution-focused applied psychology approach. In this section, an overview on both aspects is given in more generic terms. In order to achieve that, identified *limitations* have been summarized and reformulated into resource- and future-oriented points of attention with the objective of leaving behind the limitations of preceding theories. The condensed *lessons learned* are embraced to capitalize on them in the quest for the new approach.

2.2.1 Points of attention (PAs) for the design of SoFAP-P, derived from limitations of preceding theories

PA-1: Most approaches show an unbalanced methodological focus. They pay more attention (= time and energy) to past experiences and to the historical context of the client, than to his present situation and his wishes for change. This goes at the expense of exploring possible future options to bring the desired changes closer.

PA-2: The emphasis in problem-oriented approaches is on the detailed description of problems and corresponding hypothesized causes. These descriptions and the language in which the professional usually converses with the client are problem oriented. This easily results in a situation where there is (too) little attention paid to finding a solution to solve the client's problem.

PA-3: Client's problem descriptions typically result in classifications of diagnoses[7] and typologies of mental problems and disorders. Such classifications, like DSM V, have the advantage of being convenient, although they can also easily lead to confusion and simplifications that leave little or no room for the complexity of human life, with all its serendipities, unexpected, unfathomable and unpredictable twists and turns.

PA-4: The causal linearity from *anamnesis* and *diagnosis* to *therapy* and *prognosis* obscures the complexity of each client's life, oversimplifies the situation that causes the problem and thereby reduces the opportunity for robust and sustainable solutions.

PA-5: The linear problem-oriented theories (from anamnesis to prognosis) evaluated show an unbalanced stakeholder focus: The emphasis of attention mainly goes to the client as an individual, even if the treatment format is the couple, the family or a group. Other stakeholders in the client's ecosystem are seen as more peripheral.

PA-6: To conclude: In general, problem-oriented approaches suffer to a greater or lesser extent from a lack of efficiency in the use of time, money and other resources.

2.2.2 Condensed lessons learned for the design of SoFAP-P

LL-1: Abandon analytic classifications of mental problems; focus instead on integrated holistic solutions (which may be implicitly multi-dimensional and multi-faceted).

LL-2: The client's goals and resources should be the centre of attention. The paradigm the practitioner uses to guide his interventions is no more than a tool in the client's facilitation process. So don't let the method be leading, but the client.

LL-3: Useful client goals are practical, realistic, achievable, can be phrased in behavioural terms (*What will you do/think/feel different if ...*), and they preferably go from small to large.

LL-4: Refrain from the linearity of anamnesis, diagnosis, therapy and prognosis; work iteratively, circularly and recursively instead.

LL-5: Start from the client's present situation as it relates to his momentary goals and then develops a future orientation.

LL-6: Incorporate the client's actual ecosystemic context directly and explicitly in the approach.

This means involving all relevant stakeholders in the client's ecosystem in such a way that they can contribute additional resources for the client and that they can benefit from the progress of the client or both.

LL-7: First focus on potential solutions and then iterate intermediate steps to create a robust, self-learning, client-specific solution methodology.

LL-8: Solutions can be: (1) outcomes, results, (2) process effects (since thoughts change actions and vice versa), (3) combinations of 1 and 2.

LL-9: Solutions belong to the future, while problems belong to the past. The emphasis should be towards constructing possible solutions and desired outcomes. Instead of concentrating on the (*why* of the) problems in the past, the focus of the practitioner should be on the desired outcome: *What do you want to accomplish tomorrow and next week?*, *What could be the first little step to achieve this?*

These nine *lessons learned* provide appropriate clues for the design of the envisioned solution-focused applied psychology protocol (SoFAO-P).

Tailor-made guidelines prevail over a standard protocol

Transcending the common practice of the linear anamnesis-diagnosis-intervention-prognosis chain leads to a gradual abandonment of the primordiality of the classification of mental health problems and allows for a profound client-focused orientation. Therefore, it is desirable that in the SoFAP-P approach this linear, one-directional chain is replaced by a focus on the client's desire for change, which the practitioner helps to translate into practical and feasible small steps that lead to sustainable solutions.

Positive changes usually do not occur instantaneously but rather gradually and incrementally. Relapses are (often) part of the iterative process that benefits from a recursive methodology that is facilitated (and if necessary guided) by the professional.

Focusing on possible future solutions that align with the client's goals initiates the growth process. Then the SoFAP-P approach iterates between small incremental steps towards the development of self-learning competencies by the client.

In many cases, the most effective way to elicit robust solutions appears to be to include relevant members of the client's ecosystem so that they can contribute additional resources or at least be transformed into stakeholders who can benefit from the progress of the client.

In their practical manifestation, the SoFAP-P epistemology and associated methodology should be developed more as a basic attitude rather than as a toolbox of technical interventions. Since problems, goals, challenges, resources and the ecosystem are unique for each client, the SoFAP-P design should not be based on a linear, deterministic, fixed-step approach. Each SoFAP-P intervention must be tailored as precisely as possible to fit the situational need. This implies, among other things, applying the most effective mix among the mandates of leadership, facilitation and coaching and management.[8]

2.2.3 On the lessons learned from the reviewed applied psychology theories

In the classical field of therapeutic applied psychology, individual problems were (and still are) considered and categorized as symptoms of an illness from which the 'patient' must be relieved according to a standardized protocol. Therefore, as a first step towards improvement, it is essential to become aware that the analytical classification of psychological problems as the sole guide to helping a client is inefficient and ineffective.

This awareness implies moving away from the linearity of the linear 'history-diagnosis-therapy-prognosis' chain and making room for an iterative or – when necessary – recursive and circular course of treatment.

This realization also helps the professional to focus instead on an integrated approach that takes the client's specific situation as a starting point and then focuses on the client's goals and his means of achieving those goals (a.k.a. his resources, included the resources of his client system which preferably is involved in the process).

Moving beyond protocolized and standardized treatment does not mean that one must invent a totally new model with every new client or new situation. What is called for is an approach that is grounded in a conceptual framework with inner logic. In other words, the thinking behind the thinking, which tailors each intervention to the needs and possibilities of each situation, must be internally coherent rather than just doing something in a chaotic way. The pitfall of rigid 'one-size fits all' protocols should be avoided and replaced with an approach that follows a unique path in each case.

Particularly, the lesson that was drawn from the limitations of behaviourism and CBT taught that therapeutic effectiveness can be increased when ideas of agency, growth, mindset, inter-relational influences and the importance of emotions are taken into account.

Hence, the importance of the non-specific factors that were explained in the section on *extended-SFT* in Section 2.1.

The concepts that guide the humanistic psychological approach – self-awareness, self-improvement, self-actualization – are so vague and ill-defined that they are difficult to translate into the client's daily life. Helping the client translate some of these concepts into goals that are then formulated in terms of the useful goals checklist (practical, realistic, achievable, in behavioural terms and from small to larger) provides easier starting points for progress.

Furthermore, any newly suggested approach should incorporate directly and explicitly the actual context in which the client lives. This stance includes the acceptance of the problems that the client brings forward and avoids a counterproductive problem phobia. Put simply, the problems are – at least temporarily – part of the client's context and as such must be considered (without allowing them to monopolize the practitioner's vision or remove hope that positive change is possible).

More importantly, the stakeholders in the client's ecosystem should be actively involved. The original family system model can be greatly improved by simply giving each member of the client's ecosystem sufficient room to express their own goals.

Whilst the adage 'solutions belong to the future while problems belong to the past' would not have surprised the proponents of the early solution-focused approach, Steve de Shazer was not in the habit of explicitly asking the client for his goals.

As we already mentioned, talking about the client's goals happened indirectly in early solution-focused practice.

SoFAP-P puts the focus on the client's goals in a more straightforward manner with questions such as: *What do we need to talk about today so that this conversation will be useful to you?* or *What do you want to accomplish in the coming weeks?*

Another lesson learned from the early solution-focused approach revealed that at times its proponents were more solution-focused than client-oriented. Put simply, there was a tendency to focus more, and sometimes even exclusively, on the path towards solutions, and this stance could lead to clients who felt not understood because they felt that their problems were swept aside. A practitioner who is careful not to succumb to such optimistic tunnel vision will therefore consciously try to assume an attitude, which is best suited to the needs of the client.

Finally, solutions are difficult to mark out in absolute terms, but they can be characterized as a positive change in the client's situation or in the client's thoughts (or a combination of both). As these changes usually don't occur instantaneously or gradually, without any relapses, an approach that aims to build towards solutions would benefit from an iterative or recursive methodology that the client learns to internalize as the process goes on.

2.3 Field problem, design objective and the design science research methodology

The envisioned SoFAP-P design aims to support practitioners in their ambition to address clients' challenges successfully.

This section will explain why and how DSR methodology is used to scientifically design and validate the approach.

The first part of this section (2.3.1) outlines the design objective, the resulting methodological choices and the research strategy for this study. It then clarifies why a design-oriented methodology was chosen (Section 2.3.2). Next, the approach to collecting research data is explained and specifies the data analysis and research activities to be conducted (Section 2.3.3).

2.3.1 From field problem to design objective

Field problem

In general, problem-oriented applied psychology has been researched more often, more widely and more in depth than solution-focused applied psychology (see also Section 2.1). This is to a large extent the reason – as evident from interviews and testimonies – that solution-focused practitioners in debate with their problem-focused colleagues often have difficulty making the relevance and results of their way of working plausible to them. Given that situation in the field of applied psychology, we choose to define the relative lack of validation of solution-focused applied psychology as our field problem.

Given the breadth of such a study, we further want to limit the field problem in the following way:

the lack of validation of the way of working
that solution-focused practitioners apply
when helping clients to address their challenges.

Concepts and terms should be precise tools. Therefore, here follows a clarification of how the words *problem*, *solution* and *challenge* are used in this study. With the term *problem*, a situation, emotion, thought or combination thereof is indicated that is hindering one's functioning and that one wants to get rid of. Given the field problem, we are not in search of root causes but are interested in how the practitioner explores together with the client what he or she would like instead of the problem. This exploration usually leads to the formulation of a goal: something the client wants to accomplish, which will help him of her have a better, more fulfilling or at least easier life. A problem has arisen in the present or past. A goal lies in the future. Solution-focused practitioners ask questions that help the client translate goals into *challenges*, for example: *What do you need in order to reach X?* Challenges therefore are drivers towards a solution. A *solution* is considered here a (temporary or permanent) situation, emotional and/or cognitive state or a combination thereof that is regarded as 'good enough to live with'.

Design objective

Given the aforementioned field problem and based on exploratory ad hoc discussions with (academic) theorists and solution-focused practitioners, we decided to contribute to the elimination of the field problem by designing a scientifically grounded applied psychology method that solution-focused practitioners can use to help clients address their challenges.

In further ad hoc exploration of this intention with practitioners and theorists, two conditions certainly emerged that the design must meet if it is to have a chance of success in practice and thus reduce the field problem:

- the productivity of the use of the design had to be high (given the current high demand for applied psychological support and the limited resources for it), and
- the environment of the client (his material and immaterial context) had to be an important variable in the design to both avoid falling into the trap of intrapsychological assumptions and keeping a broad and realistic view on the challenges that the client faces in real life.

The objective for a design that, when applied, contributes to the elimination the field problem can now be formulated as follows:

To provide a validated and tested
solution-focused applied psychology protocol
to help clients in a productive way
to address their challenges.
The protocol should consider the client's actual context
from the start.

As indicated in Section 1.1 in the note on the term 'protocol', here again we want to emphasize that 'protocol' does not imply a standardized procedure or a uniform 'one-size-fits-all' method.

We continue with some explanatory notes on the terms *productivity* and *actual context*.

In organizational science, productivity is seen as the product of effectiveness and efficiency (Stack, 2016). Effectiveness implies achieving the intended goal and efficiency indicates working with the least possible use of resources such as time, money and other means. Thus, a productive outcome means that the intended goal (for example, a client who can take on a particular challenge) is reached, with the use of the least conceivable number of resources.

So *in a productive way* also implies that the intended goal is achieved. The protocol we are looking for cannot sustain the claim of *productivity* if the existence of a solution is not presupposed. In other words, a valid result of the design objective requires methodologically a solution-focused approach.

If the existence of a solution is not presupposed, we are dealing with a limitation. In that case, a *solution* is not possible and therefore should not be pursued. Learning to cope with the consequences of the limitation, then, is the only alternative.

As far as the *actual context* is concerned, the assumption is that – no matter what – helping will be less successful if the client's ecosystem is not explicitly and directly (= from the beginning) incorporated in the process.

So the search must be for a protocol that provides a direction to any practitioner who wants to help clients with their challenges, and who accepts or is convinced that this cannot be done productively without considering the environment in which the client now lives, loves and works. To use the benefit of *short language*, from now on we will refer to this environment as *the client's actual context*, which represents the current environment of the client, tangible and intangible, including the behaviour and interaction patterns of the stakeholders in place. The terms client's actual context and client's ecosystem are used interchangeably.

Given the formulated design objective, it is logical and sensible to explicitly formulate the following three support questions (SQs) to be answered by empirical research:

SQ1: What are the characteristics of a solution-focused applied psychology approach, as opposed to a problem-oriented approach?
SQ2: What is an appropriate area of application for a solution-focused applied psychology protocol to address challenges?
SQ3: What are productivity characteristics of the client-practitioner interaction, in a solution-focused applied psychology protocol to address challenges?

The answers to these questions will support the process of designing the solution-focused applied psychology protocol and will help us to formulate relevant design principles and design propositions.

2.3.2 The research approach

The protocol we aim to design is intended to support practitioners working in the general domain of human interactions, where the mission is to influence others and facilitate change processes to help clients to address their challenges productively. This design which – according to the field problem definition above – must take the client's actual context into consideration will be presented in Chapter 4.

To be able to do that, we have synthesized theory and empirical practice, which is reported in Chapter 3.

For the development and scientific validation of the envisioned design, we choose to make use of a design methodology. Given the design objective, we consider the DSR methodology, to be the most promising one.

Design science research (DSR)

The DSR methodology is still under development, as is the case for most scientific design approaches. The protocol for applying DSR is still converging, mainly based on applications of the method in concrete field studies and in design-oriented PhD research. However, a DSR methodology book that summarizes the state-of-the-art is still lacking. In this sense, it is a developing methodology to which our research also wishes to contribute.

DSR is a discipline-independent strategy for the knowledge-intensive solving of field problems. It is motivated by the researchers' desire to understand what these problems are, in what context they occur, and what outcomes certain actions in the problem area might lead to. Data-driven input-output analyses usually cannot provide sufficient solutions to these field problems.

So, a DSR project is guided by a particular category of field problems or challenges and aims to design and test a generic set of actions that yields interventions to address the problem or challenge at hand. The purpose of design is always to improve what already exists. This is in accordance with Herbert Simon's frequently quoted statement: *Everyone designs whom devises courses of action aimed at changing existing situations into preferred ones* (Simon, 1969).

In summary, this research aims to create prescriptive knowledge by developing design propositions that support solving defined challenges in a client's ecosystem.

van Aken and Andriessen (2011) mention four differences between DSR and traditional hypothesis testing research:

1. The research is driven by the desire to solve a field problem. Usual research is driven by a question; DSR research is driven by a problem statement or design objective.
2. The research is conducted from the perspective of an *involved actor* with the desire to gain knowledge to improve. This contrasts with usual research that focuses on knowledge for the *uninvolved observer* with the aim of understanding existing reality.

3 The research is – in methodological terms – solution-oriented, aimed at producing knowledge about interventions that professionals can apply to solve the type of problem posed.
4 The criterion, by which a design or intervention theory is judged, is its pragmatic validity. This concerns the question whether applying the proposed intervention will indeed lead to solving the chosen field problem. In other words: It is not about the truth of the knowledge presented, but about the effectiveness of applying that knowledge.

van Aken and Andriessen further state that there are two possible approaches to describe, explain and solve problems in the field. On the one hand, there is a focus on understanding field problems. That understanding should then make it easier for practitioners to come up with workable solutions. On the other hand, there is the possibility of design-oriented research that has its defining focus on the attempt to categorize problems and then aims to design solutions for *a class* of field problems. It is this last way of executing design science that we need to apply in this study, given our design objective mentioned above. That choice is in line with what Keskin and Romme (2020) state that 'design-oriented research has … been proposed as a way to bridge the gap between theory (i.e. rigor) and practice (i.e. relevance), to produce scientific knowledge while solving complex and relevant field problems'.

The aspiration to ground the SoFAP-P design largely on case histories and testimonials from practitioners reflects the DSR methodology geared towards the development of design propositions, derived from literature, empirics and evaluated experiences of the designing researchers. DSR is chosen because in that methodology, the emphasis is on design propositions to solve empirical problems, to improve real-life situations and to create relevant prescriptive knowledge. The orientation of DSR is much less focused on analysis and explanation of causes (Denyer, Tranfield, & van Aken, 2008) and is more geared towards improvement.

The paradigm of the design sciences is inspired by Simon's *The Sciences of the Artificial* (1996), in which he explores the fundamental differences between the natural sciences and the sciences of the humanities. Simon proposed a science of design that was not only limited to the physical and technological domain but also encompassed the social field. Since then, the idea of design research as a scientific methodology has also been adopted by various non-technical disciplines. Design research as a methodology in the social sciences differs from that in technical disciplines because of the characteristics of the problem area. In the physical or technological domain, very complex projects are usually repeatable with a high degree of precision. This makes a technical-rational approach to design possible (Schön, 1983). Problems with an important social component, on the other hand, are 'dynamic situations consisting of complex systems of changing problems that interact with each other' (Ackhof, 1979). Yet, using the *United States Constitution* as an example, Simon illustrates that large-scale design in the social field can be successful when the boundaries of human rationality are taken into account. Because of the 'dynamic situations', it is impossible to produce generic designs for the social domain. However, it is possible to generalize designs – making them transferable – beyond the specific contexts in which they have been evaluated (Gioia, Corley, & Hamilton, 2013).

Based on this idea, van Aken (2004), and later Denyer et al. (2008), refer to 'the distinction between explanatory sciences (Simon's natural sciences but also disciplines like sociology and economics) and design sciences (most of Simon's sciences of the artificial)'. Design science is characterized by:

- Research questions driven by an interest in field problems;
- An emphasis on the production of prescriptive knowledge, connected to interventions and systems to produce outcomes that are essential to solving field problems; hence a design science is more focused on knowledge *to improve* than on knowledge *to explain*.
- A justification of research products grounded largely on pragmatic validity: Do the actions based on this knowledge produce the intended outcomes?

Design science methodology is suitable since 'the mission of design science is to develop knowledge that professionals can use to design solutions for their field problems' (van Aken, 2005). Design science produces prescriptive solutions that are tested and grounded in practice, having pragmatic validity. The design delivered, will have a level of abstraction that allows it to be used for a specific class of field problems. The individual user needs to customize the design developed into a solution for his specific field problem that belongs to the class of problems at hand. Design science assumes patterns in human systems. These patterns do not have causality as in clockwork systems (Boulding, 1956), but they demonstrate sufficient causal potential to convert them into causal outcomes (Pawson & Tilley, 1997).

Using a design-oriented methodology fits the aim of this research project to contribute to both scientific knowledge and to support practitioners. Furthermore, a design-oriented methodology is not only applicable to specific situations, but also to processes that develop over time. This is why the DSR methodology is chosen for the development of the intended solution-focused applied psychology protocol. After all, the development of the client and his ecosystem can be accommodated in this methodology.

The CIMO-construct

As said before, this research aims to combine theoretical knowledge and field understandings into an approach that can be used by applied psychology practitioners.

In DSR, *knowledge-to-explain* is used to develop *knowledge-to-improve* by scientifically analysing practical, real-life field challenges and processes. Much of this knowledge is shaped in so-called design principles and design propositions. These are solution-oriented guidelines for a specific class of problems or challenges: the 'real helps' of entrepreneurial thought and action (Romme & Reymen, 2018; Sarasvathy & Venkataraman, 2011).

According to van Aken and Andriessen (2011), a *design principle* is a general directive to be used in a certain context but not applicable yet unless translated into a concrete action in the specific situation, whereas a *design proposition* is considered a possible solution directly to be applied in a certain context.

A fully developed repertoire of DSR-based actions can be described using the CIMO-logic. This logic (Denyer et al., 2008) includes four elements:

- What is happening and where, what is the challenge? (Context)
- What are the possible actions or interventions that can be taken?
- How do the proposed interventions lead to the desired effects? (Mechanisms)
- What results or outcomes can be expected from the actions taken?

Formulating such CIMOs yield design propositions.

In the CAMO-variant (Romme & Dimov, 2021), agency (A) emphasizes the decisive influence that the actor (A) has on the intervention to be applied. The mechanism (M) explains why the intervention of an actor with agency (A) leads to outcome (O) in context (C). In this study, the 'agent' is always and without interference the practitioner, equipped with three mandates to act[9]. We therefor stick to the CIMO-construct of van Aken c.s.

The CIMO-logic has been chosen because it allows for a practical way of describing research findings in design-oriented research. The pragmatic validity of CIMOs makes them a valuable tool for practitioners. Moreover, it provides solution-oriented knowledge on how to solve field problems and increase practitioners' productivity.

When extracting a CIMO from a single case, the context is specific. By extracting similar CIMOs from multiple cases, a generalized CIMO can be constructed. Evaluating resembling interventions in dissimilar cases and then identifying similarities in underlying mechanisms do this.

A developed DSR-based intervention repertoire consists of a generic version of the design, combined with contextualization knowledge to enable the generic version to be applied case-specifically.

For the sake of clarity, we would like to point out that the methodology of DSR does *not* require that the building blocks found in literature and empirical research – such as CIMOs – are explicitly addressed in the design. They are implicitly recognizable in the design, but it is not required to indicate which building block underlies which rule or part of the design. Nevertheless, for those interested: The SoFAP-P design is 'deconstructed' into building blocks in Appendix C.

Limitation regarding the CIMO-logic

In 'mining' CIMOs from practitioners' cases, we decided to focus on making explicit the *experiences* practitioners have encountered in their interactions with clients. This is done to reduce complexity in the description of the CIMOs. The consequence of this is that in most cases, the context, the intervention and the expected result (the output) are more clearly expressed in the wording of the CIMO than the mechanism. This limitation is the reason for formulating a related suggestion for further research in Section 6.1.

α- and β-testing

DSR features two types of field tests to validate the design, called α- and β-testing.

The purpose of the α-test is to present the design to experienced practitioners and receive feedback regarding internal consistency, reliability, validity and usability in order to assess the extent to which the design meets the requirements. The design is theoretically tested by means of interviews, panel discussions, simulation-based conversations, surveys and the like.

According to McKenney and Revees (2012), the α-test comprises *early assessment of design ideas*. The α-test is used to assess the internal structure of – parts of – a design for theoretical soundness and feasibility:

- *Soundness*: Testing the propositions that underpin the design and how these are operationalized in the design. Soundness also concerns the logical coherence of the design.
- *Feasibility*: Conceptual testing of the design for feasibility in practice, answering questions as: To what extent can the design be used and applied in practice? Which elements still need to be considered? Does the design fit into the relevant environment?

Based on feedback gained from the α-test, the design is adjusted.

The β-test can be considered an indirect form of action-based research because the designer does not participate directly in the test (Stam, 2011).

During a β-test, a group of practitioners, preferably not involved in the prior empirical studies, use all or part of the design in practice to discover operational improvements for applying the design. Participating practitioners then are asked to assess the extent to which the application of the design turned out to be valid, usable and productive.

Generalizable knowledge is then inductively extracted to adapt the design.

VAN AKEN ON α- AND β-TESTING (VAN AKEN, 2005)

A key element of a technological rule resulting from academic research is justification. It is obtained by testing the rule in the intended context – at first, during the development of the rule by the researchers themselves through a series of cases, and subsequently by third parties to obtain more objective evidence. Third-party testing counteracts the 'unrecognized defences' of the researchers (Argyris, 1996), which may blind them to flaws or limitations of their rules. This idea is borrowed from software development, where third-party testing is called β-testing – see e.g. Dolan and Matthews (1993) – and α-testing by the software developers themselves.

β-Testing can be seen as a kind of replication research (see e.g. Hubbard, Vetter, & Little, 1998; Tsang & Kwan, 1999), but its design orientation makes that it has more in common with evaluation research of social programs (see e.g. Guba & Lincoln, 1989; and especially Pawson & Tilley, 1997).

The α- and β-testing of technological rules can offer further insight into the intended as well as the unintended consequences of their application, in their indications and contraindications, and in the scope of their possible application: their application domain. For algorithmic rules testing can lead to conclusive proof, or at least to conclusive internal validity.

The more indeterminate nature of heuristic rules – and in management technological rules will often be heuristic – makes such proof impossible, but α- and β-testing can lead to 'theoretically saturated' supporting evidence (Eisenhardt, 1989).

Concluding remarks on the DSR methodology

Given the design objective, DSR is chosen as the most appropriate research method, primarily for four reasons:

- The DSR methodology requires that there is a field problem. In this case: the lack of validation of the way of working that solution-focused practitioners apply when helping clients to address their change processes and challenges.
- Our ambition is to support practitioners in their daily work by providing them with (arrangements of) interventions to find viable solutions to client's challenges. A characteristic of DSR is that it tries to provide generic usable knowledge for actors responsible for dealing with field problems. Therefore, with the help of DSR, it should be possible to produce generic actionable knowledge that is suitable to be tested and applied in our 'problem' context. In this way, the design approach better meets the objective of contributing to a solution of the field problem than the possibilities of descriptive or exploratory research would allow.
- Furthermore, our ambition is to design an approach that does not deviate too much from what experienced and seasoned solution-focused practitioners are already doing, and to ground this scientifically. DSR is suitable for such a

foundation, because DSR allows the experience and beliefs of professionals to suffice as a scientific foundation.
- DSR has an actor (or agent) perspective. It is the actor who takes responsibility. The preliminary interviews we conducted showed that practitioners often believed that the challenges presented to them *could* be addressed. The priority for the professional then becomes to facilitate the client in finding solutions that have the potential to improve the situation, rather than understanding the problem and looking for its origins. This is in line with the way the role of the practitioner is perceived.
- Finally, DSR is based on pragmatic validity. The answer to the question 'does it work?' has a higher priority than 'is it true?'

As mentioned earlier, it is our wish that the outcome of our research – the envisioned solution-focused applied psychology protocol – is relevant from a practitioner's perspective. To prevent the intended design from a lack of significance, these four issues are of interest (van Aken & Andriessen, 2011):

1 *Practical relevance:* The design should be relevant for everyday practice in the field. Too much reduction in the number of variables considered, or a too high conceptual level might risk the practical relevance for real-life use of the design. The rich content of the client's ecosystem should not impede the efficiency of the application of the design, while richness and an appropriate level of complexity should be sufficiently included in the design to achieve the desired results.
2 *Operational relevance:* Professionals must be able to actually apply the design in their practice. To this end, the design presented must be consistent with the way practitioners are used to operate (face validity), and they must be able to quickly become familiar with the recommended design.
3 *Non-obviousness:* This refers to the degree to which the theory behind the design exceeds or complements the commonsense theory already in use. Newly added aspects that practitioners did not previously consider, or given extras to take into account when carrying out their work, should be non-obvious. This requirement for non-obviousness of the design means that if the design is seen as a recurrence of commonly known knowledge, the design is less likely to be adopted by practitioners.
4 *Appropriateness:* The design should be up to date and relevant to contemporary real-life problems in the field.

In developing the design, these four aspects, which determine the significance of the design, were set as requirements that must be met. In this sense, these four aspects form the specifications of the design to be developed.

FAQ: EVIDENCE-BASED PRACTICE AND RANDOMIZED CONTROLLED TRIALS (RCTS) VERSUS DSR

Evidence-based medicine (EBM) was developed to make the quality of interventions measurable, verifiable and replicable based on scientific research criteria derived from the 'hard sciences'. This evolution was of historical importance because it was a step forward from judging care based on personal beliefs, experience and professional reputation. EBM expanded into many other areas of application, so that today we speak of evidence-based practice.

The highest level of evidence within EBM is provided by randomized controlled trials (RCTs), studies in which all variables are held constant so that a causal relationship can be demonstrated between that one experimental variable and the final outcome. The subsequent double-blind design of RCTs further expands the evidence. This research method leads to an average patient with average complaints and ditto symptoms being approached with an average intervention, an intervention that should differ from the control group on only one variable. In psychological and interpersonal problems, this research methodology is not only impossible but also contra-indicated, mainly because the diversity between patients and the context of care practices is not sufficiently taken into account.

After all, there are no average patients with average complaints needing average interventions nor are there average counsellors, coaches or therapists. Double-blind interventions in which neither the practitioner nor the client knows whether an experimental variable is offered are de facto impossible and encounter ethical problems.

Hence, in the field of interpersonal facilitation, counselling, coaching and psychotherapy, evidence-based practice is not the research model of choice, RCTs are difficult to set up and double-blind RCTs are impossible.

DSR offers a scientific methodology that does not aim to explain but to change, to improve. DSR is used to design personalized context-sensitive interventions that fit into a broader protocol. The solution-focused applied psychology-protocol presented here is such a protocol that is aimed at improving the situation of a particular client.

2.3.3 Research activities

Data collection

Designing is the process of determining the requirements that the object has to fulfill, and drafting the design for this object (van Aken, 2011). The core of DSR is to design and validate a solution to a field problem based on learning from experiences. By learning from experience, we mean conceptualizing a solution to the problem and then in a series of tests, adapting and retesting the concept to learn what works and what does not.

Data collection is an essential part of this design process. The data collection can be iterative and exploratory, and it is part of the continuous loop for improvement of the design. Data collection is relevant for several different steps in the design process:

- For problem analysis as well as to gain an understanding of the challenges present in the field.
- To obtain an understanding of the context of the field problems and challenges.
- To establish design principles and propositions from different perspectives of the various stakeholders in the relevant field:
  - User requirements; the ease of use for practitioners
  - Functional requirements; like technical capabilities
  - Prerequisites and preconditions
  - Design limitations; accessibility, state of professional skills and knowledge.

In the design process executed, there were several times and ways for data collection. Data were collected during the literature review, through case analyses, an opinion survey, interviews and simulation-based conversations with practitioners.

With the help of the cases and the conversations with practitioners, the field experiences of the professionals were made explicit. Next, the consequences of their experiences were incorporated in the design in statu nascendi, and then the practitioners' opinion was asked again about the thus improved design. This turned out to be an iterative process that took several rounds.

Research activities

In order to achieve the research objectives, we carried out the following research activities. Although the research steps are listed in order, the process was iterative. Characteristic of these iterative steps have been the continuous incorporation of new data and insights into the design.

The research activities conducted were as follows:

- *Literature review*, based on key words in the design objective.
- *Networking:* Structured networking with practitioners who applied solution-focused psychology techniques or who had sympathies for this way of working. The relevance of the design objective was also explored with this group.

Furthermore, they were asked to generate ideas about the requirements the design should meet and about their wishes for the design.
- *Interviews,* using semi-structured protocols. Before each interview, the available information about the working context of the practitioner was reviewed. These preparations stimulated the efficiency and effectiveness of the interviews. After each interview, the following steps were taken: transcribing the interview, identifying key-issues from the interview and processing new insights into the interview protocol that is to be used in the next iterative round.
- *In-depth studies:* In-depth studies of a number of cases, which have occurred in different contexts, followed by cross-case analyses.
- *Simulation-based conversations:* On several moments during the iterative design process, the state-of-the-art design was discussed and evaluated with practitioners and scientists. The dominant inputs for these talks were concept-CIMOs, in casu the (developing) building blocks of the design.

Analysis of all these collected data eventually resulted in a first draft design of the solution-focused applied psychology protocol.

This first draft was then improved in several iterative rounds by subjecting it to α- and β-testing. α-Testing involves testing the design theoretically in interviews and simulation-based conversations with practitioners. Based on the evaluation of these talks, the design is then improved. β-Testing involves the same process, but on the basis of a practical, real-life application of – part (or parts) of – the design.

The final SoFAP-P design is presented in Chapter 4.

In general, in DSR, the first design is about 80% right. After the first iteration, the design generally climbs to 90% correctness. With the second iteration, 95% is reached and 100% coverage is never achieved. After two or three iterations, methodological saturation usually occurs. This is also how it went during the development of the SoFAP-P design.

As usual, only the final version of the design is presented (Chapter 4). The previous versions remain implicit.

The validating α- and β-tests are discussed in Chapter 5.

To conclude: The design process in DSR is not a mechanistic exercise in which the design follows logically from the inputs gained but is characterized by *synthesis-evaluation iterations* that involve *a creative leap* as the result of *a* process of abduction[10] (van Aken & Andriessen, 2011). The iterations are not an exclusively cognitive process but they are 'situated' in the social work context of the researcher. These ongoing situated interactions between the researcher and the object of study during the design process are in alignment with Simon's (1996) definition of an artefact as *a meeting point – an 'interface' in today's terms – between an 'inner' environment, the substance and organization of the artefact in itself, and an 'outer' environment, the surroundings in which it operates.*

> **FAQ: WHAT IS THE DIFFERENCE BETWEEN ACTION RESEARCH AND DSR?**
>
> - Action research is usually a 'one case' approach, but through triangulation it can be analysed in different ways. However, the results of such action research cannot be generalized.
> - Even if a number of cases in the same domain are examined using action research, the action research methodology does not provide methods for generalizing across cases.
> - DSR is aimed at *improving*, instead of *explaining*. Therefore, the result of DSR is always a design of a protocol, intervention or arrangement of interventions to address real problems that arise in the empirical field.
> - Two defining characteristics of DSR are CIMOs and the α- and β-testing. There are no equivalents in action research (in the α-test, the design is tested theoretically using interviews, panel discussions, simulation-based conversations and surveys. Drawing on the evaluation of the α-test results, the design then is improved. In the β-test, the same happens, but then on the basis of a practical, real-life implementation of – a part (or parts) of – the design).

Notes

1. Throughout the book, we have made no distinction between *he* and *she*. Where it says *he*, you can read *she* and vice versa.
2. In the systemic literature, the term 'identified patient' is used.
3. NLP today is often seen as a pseudoscience. From the vast literature on this topic we want to refer to the 2006 research article of Norcross et al. in *Professional Psychology: Research and Practice*: Discredited psychological treatments and tests: A Delphi poll. ....
4. This study was conceived, conducted and written in co-creation by both authors. For the sake of objectivity, this section on *Extended SFT* was written by Weggeman alone.
5. https://miltonericksoncanoediary.com
6. The building blocks of the Extended-SFT approach are meticulously detailed in Cauffman's book: *Creating Sustainable Results with Solution-Focused Applied Psychology* (Routledge, 2023). That book is intended as an instructional guide when one wants to study and learn the intricacies and practical aspects of the SoFAP approach.
7. Merriam-Webster: The word and concept of diagnosis comes from the Greek διαγιγνώσκειν (diagignoskein, *to know, to discern* and *through*) and according to Merriam-Webster (2016) means: (1) the act of identifying a disease, illness or problem by examining someone or something. (2) A statement or conclusion that describes the reason for a disease, illness or problem.
8. Also see Section 2.1, under *Extended-SFT*, point 7, and paragraph 3.4, ad. SQ-2 (*Support Question 2*), under *depth* of the approach.
9. See Section 2.1, the seventh characteristic of the extended-SFT approach.
10. Abduction is a way of reasoning in which a possible explanation for an (unexpected) phenomenon is chosen as the correct one. The explanation is then a sufficient condition,

but not a necessary one. Other explanations are possible. The term was coined and first used by the American logician and philosopher C.S. Peirce.

By weighing different abductions with respect to probability, inference to the best explanation arises: the most probable explanation is chosen as the correct one. This usually produces a better result than random selection, but is less reliable than induction or deduction.

Source: https://nl.wikipedia.org/wiki/Abductie_(philosophy).

3
EMPIRICAL GROUNDING OF THE SoFAP-P DESIGN

In this chapter, in Section 3.1 the results are presented of a limited literature review that complements the lessons learned from the different schools in applied psychology evaluated in Section 2.1. The next two sections, 3.2 and 3.3, contain the results of empirical research among practitioners. This was done using interviews and case analyses. Based on the results of these studies, the three support questions posed in Section 2.3 are then answered in Section 3.4. Finally, Section 3.5 summarizes the collection of empirically found building blocks and CIMOs that underlie the SoFAP-P design outlined in Chapter 4.

3.1 Lessons learned from professional and scientific literature

In most research on testing explanatory hypotheses, it is common to first determine what the gap in literature is, given the research question. This requires an extensive, almost exhaustive review of at least the recent scientific literature. Since DSR is aimed at designing and validating tools and protocols that can be used to address a class of field problems, the literature review component of a design research approach usually is more limited: There is pragmatic, but targeted 'shopping' in the scientific and professional literature to find clues for previously formulated design requirements and design limitations.

Given the successive directions in applied psychology already discussed in Section 2.1, this explains why the extent here can be limited.

LL-10[1]: *Stimulate a client-driven or steered approach, instead of a client-oriented or focused one.*

To give the client a more central, navigating role in the relationship with his practitioner, it is essential for the practitioner to adapt a style of conversation that corresponds to the wishes, goals and learning style of the client. These learning

DOI: 10.4324/9781003404477-3

styles contain stage directions on which intervention style has the most chance for success. Specifically, this means that the practitioner should assume an emphatic, friendly and attentive caring attitude in 46% of the cases. In 39% of the cases, it is better for the practitioner to use his expertise to clarify the client's functioning by adopting an insight-oriented stance. In 15% of the cases, the practitioner should treat the working relationship as a cooperation in which client and practitioner are equally invested, a collaborative alliance (Bachelor, 1995).

LL-11: *Pay attention to three major tendencies that prevent clients from being open to a solution-focused applied psychology approach: (1) no intrinsic motivation to change, (2) 'resistance' to change and (3) translating mental issues into physical problems.*

Firstly, some clients have no intrinsic motivation but are referred to psychological services by a third party. Solution-focused Therapy (SFT) has designed a respectful and pragmatic way to cope with these so-called mandated clients.

Secondly, de Shazer (1984) showed that client resistance does not exist: Anything a client might do or say can be seen as a directive, instructing the practitioner how the client would like to be helped. Therefore, what used to be defined as resistance to change, Extended-SFT translates into a stage direction in which the client (without being aware of it) offers the practitioner additional information leading to helpful interventions.

Thirdly, the (false) distinction between physical problems and mental health is widely accepted in many societies. In some cultures (e.g. more oriental countries) and some subcultures (e.g. professional sports), mental problems are frowned upon to the extent that they are 'translated' into physical problems. This explains why many patients would rather undergo a medical scan than opt for a psychological approach.

LL-12a: *Integrate the exploitation of non-specific therapeutic factors seen from the client's point of view, into the facilitation approach (instead of regarding them as a welcome by-product).*

Non-specific factors that are common[2] to all successful interventions are implied in the answers to the next questions:

- *Do I feel understood?*
- *Do I get the appropriate authentic attention?*
- *Do I feel respected as a person?*
- *Do I get the perspective that changes for the better is possible?*

As early as 1936, Samuel Rosenzweig argued that: 'It is justifiable to wonder whether the factors that actually are operative in several different therapies may not have much more in common than have the factors alleged to be operative'. In other words, successful therapies have more to do with the factors that are common in the way the different therapies operate than in the way their underlying theories differ. For decades, this insight was left aside while all effort went into developing more models with increasingly complex, sometimes even exotic, intricate operating assumptions. It was only since the beginning of the 90s that researchers became interested in the consequences of Rosenzweig's ideas. Until then this discussion was absent in the literature. Even today, research around non-specific therapeutic factors remains remarkably undiscussed in psychotherapeutic articles (Duncan, Miller, Wampold & Hubble, 2010). The vast majority of authors remain preoccupied with model- or method-specific insights and interventions. The lesson learned here is to refrain from considering the non-specific factors as epiphenomena of successful interventions but instead want to embrace Rosenzweig's ideas, possibly to such an extent that the non-specific factors move to the heart of the approach.

LL-12b: *Integrate the exploitation of the non-specific therapeutic factors seen from the practitioner's point of view, into the facilitation approach.*

By viewing the non-specific factors from a different angle, Jerome David Frank and his daughter-collaborator Julia B. Frank (1991) were able to rephrase those common factors and add subtle informational cues to help practitioners design psychological facilitation interventions. As a result, facilitation interventions that activate the non-specific factors in an effective way:

- contain an emotional and confidential relationship with a person who is trying to help,
- take place in a setting of which the client believes that the help offered is professional,
- give a credible explanation for the client's symptoms, and
- offer reliable procedures to cope with these symptoms.

Lambert (1992), in his phrasing of the common factors, says that four non-specific factors are responsible for changes caused during psychological facilitation:

- 40% of the client changes are due to client-factors and extra therapeutic variables.
- 30% of the changes is determined by the quality of the relation between client and professional.
- 15% of the changes are driven by the client's hopes and expectations, and
- 15% of the changes can be attributed to method-specific interventions.

The percentages Lambert mentions are not mathematically measured realities, but they are the result of a deliberate and reasoned assessment.

No less than 40% of the change caused by therapy sessions is ascribed to client factors, such as openness, perseverance, trust, optimism and a warm family on the one hand and extra-therapeutic elements on the other. These are events, in which the client links his inner strength to coincidences, such as a new colleague at work, moving to another town, a prize in the lottery and new neighbours. In short, 40%

of the therapeutic outcomes are provided by factors completely beyond the control of the therapist.

Overall, 30% of the results are attributed to the therapeutic relationship and more specifically: to a positive perception of this relationship. This can be reinforced when the client plays an active role during therapy. In this way, the therapist can make a difference by promoting the agency factor in his clients.

Furthermore, 15% is attributed to the client's expectations about the outcome of his treatment: i.e. the placebo effect which occurs because the client's self-healing capacities (including his resilience) are activated, as is the trust the client has in his treatment and therapist.

Finally, only about 15% of the results achieved with clients are attributed to model- and method-specific techniques, while therapists spend so much time, energy and money acquiring those techniques.

Many academics and therapy gurus make it their life's work to (further) specify their own model or method. An undefined part hereof can probably even be traced back to the previous factor, namely the active placebo effect it has on the client, caused by the trust the therapist has in his own model.

When summarizing this body of research, it is assumed that 70% of the changes attributed to therapy have something to do with factors over which the therapist has little or no control: 40% client-factors and extra-therapeutic variables, +15%, being half of the therapeutic relationship and +15% client's hopes and expectations (the placebo-effect). This adds up to 70%. Of the remaining 30%, 15% can be assigned to model/method-specific interventions and the other half to the quality of the therapeutic relationship. When considering that a huge part of the 15% of the model-/method-specific varieties is attributed to the therapist's confidence in his own actions, and when linking this to the client's perception that the therapist knows what he's doing, the contribution of the model-/method-specific techniques seems almost negligible.

In his meta-analytic study, highly esteemed in scientific circles, Wampold (2001) states that the best case scenario is that only 8% of therapeutic outcomes can be assigned to model-/method-specific contributions. He concludes: '*Decades of research in psychotherapy haven't given us the slightest evidence that any specific ingredient is necessary for change*'.

This introduced ordinary aspects of human interactions into the realm of psychotherapy and stripped the practitioner of his almightiness.

LL-13: *Put the effect of psychological and inter-relational facilitation techniques into a more differentiated perspective by asking differentiation questions (including scaling questions).*

The generic scaling question goes like this: 'Imagine if I asked you to give a number on a scale where the starting point, the zero, stands for X (to be filled in according to the specific situation) and the 10 stands for Y (ditto), then where are you now'?

LL-14: *Allow the therapeutic relationship to develop into a therapeutic alliance.*

Only since the development of Extended-SFT (see Section 2.1), did the significance of the therapeutic relationship become an important insight and even a tool in psychological facilitation, therapy and coaching. Before that time, the quality of the working relationship appears to have been seen as an epiphenomenon that arose – as if by itself – from the interaction between the client and the practitioner. It became increasingly evident that the quality of the working relationship is crucial for success. Moreover, practitioners, experts and researchers discovered that, to increase the effectiveness of their interventions, it was important to bring the client's goals into the equation. After the expert asks the client about his goals and helps the client translate his goals into the useful goals checklist (see also Section 3.2, BP-2), both parties deploy their working relationship to achieve the goal together. The client and the practitioner forge an alliance in which the client provides his resources, and the practitioner provides his expertise.

3.2 Best and bad practices applied by solution-focused practitioners

During many years of collaborating with thought leaders and experts in the fields of psychotherapy, cybernetics, epistemology, hypnotherapy, systems thinking, linguistics, swarm intelligence and, of course, solution-focused practice, Cauffman as a researcher had the opportunity to spend countless hours co-teaching, learning from, studying and discussing with those experts. These contacts broadened, contradicted, tested, challenged, confirmed or falsified (in whole or in part) and at least sharpened the views of the participating researcher and author of this book.

From that groundwork, the following *Best* and *Bad Practices* (from here on *BP* and *BaP*, respectively) for the envisioned SoFAP-P design were distilled.

BP-1: Transform the working relationship with the client into an alliance
A relationship reflects a connection, while an alliance is a bond between parties that share a common goal. The psychological practitioner therefore must consider the goals of the client and construct his working relationship into an alliance with the client that is geared towards this goal. The practitioner and his expertise are the tools to help the client help himself.

BP-2: Set goals in an active manner
Instead of merely accepting whatever goals the client comes up with or whatever goals the practitioner extracts from his model or method, it is necessary to actively ask questions to help the client set his goals and to help him translate them into a list of useful objectives that can serve as a checklist. Useful goals are practical, realistic, achievable, can be phrased in behavioural terms (*What will you do different if ...*) and preferably go from small to large.

BP-3: Set goals in a continuous manner
Goal setting in psychological facilitation differs from goal setting in a mechanistic working field where goals – however difficult to reach – still are rather simple:

You set your goal at point B and find the shortest way from A to get there. Once you reach point B, all is solved. In psychological facilitation, the client is helped to translate his goals into challenges. Once a partial goal is achieved, this change becomes the context for a follow-up challenge until the *mother of all goals* is reached: The client is helped to help himself reach his own goals by using his own resources. In brief, goal setting is not a fixed-state intervention (you once set a goal and that is it) but an active, iterative and recursive process.

BP-4: Concentrate on the client's resources and possibilities

Use the idea and accompanying question: *What is going well (enough) despite the problem?* to focus – both the client's attention and the practitioner's perspective – on the resources that can be used to take steps forward toward a desired future.

BP-5: Use the Minimax Decision Rules

Our empirical research among practitioners has shown that most of the experts appear to apply, implicitly or explicitly, the following four basic rules in their work:

- *Rule 1*: If something is not broken (a.k.a still works), do not repair it but show respect and appreciation for what still works.
- *Rule 2*: If something does not work, or no longer works, or does not work well enough after trying it for a while, stop, learn from it and do something else.
- *Rule 3*: If something works well, well enough or better, keep doing it and/or do more of it.
- *Rule 4*: If something works well, well enough or better, then offer it to or learn it from someone else.

This list of basic decision rules can be used as a checklist. Whenever a particular intervention does not work, the checklist can be consulted to see what was overlooked, not given enough attention or was given a too exclusive focus.

Whenever a practitioner has the impression that his interventions are not catching on, there is a good chance that he sins against one or more of these basic rules. Maybe he is overlooking a rule, maybe putting too much emphasis on a rule or maybe the practitioner is switching between rules too quickly without giving it a chance to catch on. If this is the case, the Minimax Decision Rules[3] are used to adjust the interventions.

'Minimax' stands for using minimal effort as a practitioner while attaining maximal output and change for the client.

Where best practices exist, it is only normal that one encounters Bad Practices. The main pitfalls here appear to be the therapist's convictions and theories.[4] The therapist may be so attached to them that they can be a hindrance to the client. A couple therapist who has recently taken a course in communication therapy may become convinced that couples can only function well, if they communicate clearly and transparently, for example by letting each other finish their sentences. One of the interviewees mentioned a case of an elderly couple, where the wife says 'cra ...' and the husband immediately adds 'she means crayons sir'. If the (beginning) therapist insists on strictly obeying the theoretic rules of clear communication, he must correct the husband. If the (seasoned) therapist really listens to the clients, it is evident that he should not intervene for the simple reason that the communication between the partners, albeit rather idiosyncratic, functions well.

In the long tradition of the problem-oriented applied psychology models and methods, many insights (or rather, beliefs and convictions) became so engrained that they seem to obviously represent the only correct intervention mode.

BaP-1: Give primacy to a theory, model or method over the idiosyncratic needs and possibilities of the client.

BaP-2: Delve into speculations about the *why* of what goes wrong.

BaP-3: Have an obsessive focus on the past.

BaP-4: Limit the desired goals to the mere absence of problems.

BaP-5: Treat the working relationship as an asymmetric one in which the client is the source of all difficulties and the practitioner is the all-knowing expert.

To avoid getting stuck in unshakeable convictions about what is or is not a BP or a BaP, continuous reflection is as important as the ongoing testing of the effect of our interventions against the clients' reactions. The client's reactions are guiding but not necessarily determining. It can happen that both client and professional become blinded by a conviction while this inhibits further development.

3.3 Design propositions (CIMOs) derived from client cases

For this study, 25 cases were collected from which – in accordance with the DSR-approach discussed in Section 2.3 – CIMOs[5] could be distilled that act as building blocks for the envisioned SoFAP-P design.

In terms of the DSR methodology, in 'mining' CIMOs from practitioners' cases, the focus was on making explicit the experiences the practitioners had encountered in their interaction with the client. This implies that in most cases, the context, the intervention and the expected result (the Output) are more clearly expressed in the wording of the CIMO than the mechanism. This limitation is the reason for formulating a related suggestion for further research in Section 6.1.

Appendix A contains the 25 cases ex ante. For each case, it is indicated where within that case the antecedents for a particular CIMO are located. Most CIMOs are based on multiple indications that occur in several cases.

Both researchers did the mining of CIMOs from the cases separately and independently, with the design objective (see Section 2.3.1) on the table. After that, differences between them were discussed together. Those differences for which consent could not be reached were presented to applied psychology practitioners. As a result of a dialectical debate, some draft-CIMOs then were rejected and others were added to the list of agreed CIMOs. Here, that list of agreed CIMOs, derived from the cases, is presented in an annotated form.

The title of each CIMO is derived from the intervention (I) contained in it. Hence, the CIMO-titles have the character of an imperative: They tell you what to do.

CIMOs 1–3 contain the context markers that set the scene on which the rest of the interventions will take place.

CIMO-1: *Establish contact to build a client-practitioner alliance*
From the first contact, establish, ensure, maintain and constantly update the best possible contact with the client. In this way, a constructive relational basis is created for accomplishing the joint effort in psychological facilitation. This is equally true when you work with clients as when you work to facilitate and optimize the working relationship between other parties. To optimize the client-practitioner alliance requires an active effort, initiated by the practitioner who constantly fine-tunes his interventions to the needs and the style of the client. This alliance is the contentless interactive tool that primes and contextualizes the basis for all subsequent interventions. In short: contact is the motor for change.

CIMO-2: *Distinguish problems versus limitations to enhance effectivity*
To avoid disappointment or disillusionment, the practitioner must determine at the start of the working relationship, whether the client's complaints are the result of a problem or a limitation. A limitation (such as difficulties inherently caused by age, background, disability, physiological and physical defects or past events) cannot be solved by any conceivable action. Problems are defined by their possible solutions. Whenever a limitation is treated as a problem, failure is inevitable. To avoid failure and focus on successful interventions, one must make this vital distinction.

However, by recognizing a client's limitation as such, the practitioner can – thoughtfully and emphatically – prime the idea that acceptance of the given situation may open a door towards a solution. Then the working relationship can focus on coping with the consequences of the limitation, which can indeed be defined as a problem.

CIMO-3: *Explore the context*
No problem occurs in a vacuum. This implies that the context in which the client lives is always of significance. Most, if not all clients come to their first session with a problem that they have already carefully articulated for themselves, convinced as they are that an accurate formulation of the problem and its causes is necessary to reach a solution. This well-meant misconception not only limits the thinking of the client but restrains the (novice) practitioner's scale of possible interventions if he follows that preconceived line. This pitfall must be avoided by asking context-exploring questions that elicit information about the client and his context: 'Please tell me something about yourself. How old are you? Yes or no in a relationship? What kind of work do you do? Etcetera'. Furthermore, the practitioner can ask the client to tell something about the relationship with his family (or neighbours, friends, colleagues etc.) and then look for resources in these constellations. These questions show that the practitioner is more interested in the person behind the client than in his problems. The context influences and is influenced by whoever and whatever happens to play a part in it. This mechanism is summarized as follows: *Problems are not solved by adding more information, but by reshuffling what we already know* (Wittgenstein, 1953).

CIMOs 4–6 show how to deal with goal setting, the obstacles when no intrinsic motivation is present and how to handle this.

CIMO-4: *Direct the conversation towards a goal*
The working relationship between client and practitioner must be distinguished from a mundane social conversation. Since the psychological facilitation process is a professional encounter with a purpose, you must steer this process in a direction where the practitioner employs his expertise to help the client verbalize what he wants to accomplish and what his goals are (instead of just describing his problems). The question that invites the client to verbalize his goals is: *What do we need to discuss today so that this conversation will be useful to you?* Whatever the client responds, his answer can always serve as a directive for the practitioner for the next question. As the response guides the follow-up questions, the goals of the client become co-constructions of both parties, obviously with the client at the centre.

CIMO-5: *Circumvent absent intrinsic motivation.*
Whenever a mandated client does not feel intrinsically motivated to engage in a facilitating conversation, he might assume a rather defensive attitude as is common when working with mandated clients. This means that the client shows no immediate goals for himself. Then, the practitioner can help the client to circumvent this obstacle by asking a question: *What do you need to talk about so that you don't have to come here anymore?* With this question, the practitioner shifts the attention from the absent motivation of the client to the wishes of the referring party. If the client is prepared and/or able to formulate a goal that he supposes to be the goal of the referring party or, at least, a goal that will help the client get rid of the pressure of the referring party, the practitioner obtains a mandate to work towards a solution (even though it is not the solution, the referring party might have had in mind).

Two parties are involved in person, while the third party is only virtually present: A practitioner, B client and C absent referring third party. A asks B a question that invites B to get into the head of C with the result that B might be willing to work on a goal that C demands of B. For example, Practitioner A asks client B the following question: *If I could ask your partner/friend/colleague/co-worker/boss (=C) his opinion about the situation, what do you think he would answer me?*

CIMO-6: *Focus the client's attention on accepting responsibility and accountability for the client's own actions*
If a client blames a third party for his problems and shows that he is not (yet) willing or able to assume accountability, the task of the practitioner is to help the client to adopt a more constructive attitude that facilitates taking responsibility. This can be done by directly asking: *What can/would/should you (try to) do differently?* This question primes the idea that such an attitude change is possible and focuses the client's attention towards a positive and more active direction.

CIMOs 7–10 comprise solution-building questions that contrast with problem-oriented questions that are geared towards the search for causes, what happened in the past and reveal the fitting root causes and diagnoses. In contrast, the solution-focused approach uses questions with a totally different purpose: prime the client to think in a solution-focused way ('Problem talk creates problems; solution talk creates solutions' – de Shazer[6]), activate the alliance with the practitioner by offering the client a central position in his own growth process, regain access to his resources and elicit forward-looking goals. The generic version of a solution-building question is constructed around the phrases 'What still works?' 'What is different?' and 'What would you do instead?'. The upcoming CIMOs reveal special uses of this generic version.

CIMO-7: *Ask solution-building questions*
If the client is able and/or willing to answer these questions, pathways to possible solutions emerge immediately. Even if the client is not able and/or willing to provide answers or if he simply disregards the questions, the mere asking of these questions primes the attention of the client on possibilities that are implied in the questions.

CIMO-8: *Activate resources*
The resource orientation that is so characteristic of the solution-focused approach is founded on the axiom that every human system, be it an individual, a family or a group of any constellation, always has resources at its disposal, even in times of trouble. Resources are defined as every available tool that can be used to achieve goals, create solutions and support growth, well-being and contentment. Asking the appropriate questions will unveil the available resources so that the client can apply them to obtain his goals.

CIMO-9: *Ask the pre-session change question*
The first encounter with a client offers the opportunity to mark the solution-focused approach. To begin with, it is helpful to indicate that the client has taken a first step towards change simply by accepting to enter into a working relationship, and therefore change is indeed possible. After having done some work on the alliance, the practitioner asks the client if there are some things which have already changed for the better since the appointment was made. Weiner-Davis et al. (1987) have shown that 40% of clients say that nothing has changed, or that the situation has deteriorated. Yet it is positive that this client took the step towards help. The remaining 60% of clients, however, react surprised and go on to tell what has changed for the better. For these clients, there is a greater chance that solution-focused facilitation will be successful. In any case, for these clients, the facilitation process starts off with a head start.

CIMO-10: *Ask continuation questions to activate resources*
Clients who indicate the need to dwell upon their problem state are helped with the question*: In spite of everything, what things go well enough for you to want to keep them?* This question shows recognition for the client's difficulties yet invites him to look beyond his problem-focused perspective. This continuation question primes the idea that there is always something positive in a person's life (large or small) and makes the client aware of resources he has at his disposal.

CIMOs 11–13 are interventions that direct, facilitate acceptance of positive changes and uncover resources while acknowledging the client's struggle.

CIMO-11: *Offer positive feedback by giving compliments*

When the client shows constructive change and onsets of growth, the practitioner supports this movement by giving positive feedback on things the client does well. This feedback strengthens the working relation between client and practitioner and stimulates the client to do more of what works well.

CIMO-12: *Give advice in the guise of a question*

Whenever the client has set himself a workable goal but does not know how to apply his resources to reach it, the practitioner does well to advise the client. Advice is best given in the form of a question. This works because it gives the client ownership of the solution, even if the practitioner suggests this solution. Mark the contrast with the classic *Do as I say because as an expert I know better*. Asking a suggestive question implies that the practitioner trusts that the client has the resources to use (parts of) the suggestion. Thus, the practitioner acknowledges the client's expertise by handing him responsibility to use his own resources.

CIMO-13: *Ask the coping question in case of serious distress*

When the client says to be in dire straits, it is of little use to try and contradict him with rational arguments. It is far more useful to ask the question: *If you feel the situation to be so utterly difficult, how do you cope?* This question not only shows recognition for the client's difficult situation but, most importantly, implies that the client has resources that keep him going. Simultaneously, the question includes a compliment that cannot be rejected because it is implied in the question.

CIMOs 14–16 identify interventions that help the client to get access to resources.

CIMO-14: *Ask the question: What have you tried thus far?*

This question contains a powerful tool to – again – hone the working relationship and to help the client (better) access to his resources.

With the question *What have you tried thus far?* the practitioner implicitly compliments the client on his past efforts, even if they were not successful. The answer offers information on the coping style of the client, whilst eliciting information on strategies that proved (un)useful in the past. It often happens that these old strategies can be used after a minor revision.

The information that comes from the answers to this question also uncovers the client's resources.

CIMO-15: *Ask for exceptions to the problem*

The questions *Were there moments when your situation felt more bearable?* or *Were there moments when you were unaware or less aware of the problem? What did you do differently then?* contain the implicit assumption that exceptions to the problem exist. When a client is overwhelmed by his problems, this information often is closed off for him. These questions and their implications help the client understand that exceptions to the problem do occur and that they are related to the client's behaviour. Follow-up questions then reveal details about the partial solutions that emerge during the exceptional moments. The follow-up question *What did you do differently?* suggests an internal locus of control and this reinforces the client's self-efficacy. The effect of an internal locus of control coupled with increased self-efficacy might lead to a self-fulfilling prophecy that propels the client forward.

CIMO-16: *Ask the usefulness question*
Whenever the practitioner has the impression that his facilitation is not resulting in sufficient progress or that feedback is needed, he should ask the client the following question: *Is it useful when we talk like this?* This intervention is as powerful as it is elegant and serves to invite the client to view the working relationship from a meta-perspective. The question simply elicits useful feedback from the client while answering does not require specific intellectual capacities. In this sense, the question can even be used in conversations with children or people with a mental disability. The goal of this question is to offer the client the chance to give feedback on his own facilitation process which puts him in the centre of the alliance.

CIMOs 17–19 include interventions that help clients shift from stifling black-and-white explanations to differentiating viewpoints that allow for greater agility in dealing with the situations they face.

CIMO-17: *Offer a relativistic perspective*
When clients have the impression that they are in deep trouble, they often tend to think in black-and-white terms, which petrifies their vision. Then the practitioner must help them find nuances to counteract this dismal viewpoint. Giving rational counterarguments rarely yields results. To elicit the desired perspective, ask questions or make comments that suggest a more relative perspective. Examples include questions or comments, as follows: *Wouldn't it be good to sleep on this? Are you sure you're not exaggerating? The soup is never eaten as hot as it comes out of the bowl. Tomorrow is another day.* And so on. One must, of course, be careful to phrase these remarks respectfully and avoid the possibility that they could be interpreted as cynical, trivial or demeaning.

CIMO-18: *Ask differentiating questions*
When the client is stuck, the practitioner can ask differentiating questions, as follows: *Are there moments when you are less burdened with the problem?* or *Have there been moments when it was even worse than it is now?* or even *When do you feel slightly better?* These questions will help the client to look at his problem from another perspective and focus his attention on the things in his (work) life that are going well or better. The client's answers will lay the foundation upon which he can build change in a constructive direction.

CIMO-19: *Use scaling questions*
To facilitate differentiation in all kinds of different contexts, use scaling questions. The generic scaling question goes like this: *Imagine if I asked you to give a number on a scale where the starting point, the zero, stands for X (to be filled in according*

to the specific situation) and the 10 stands for Y (ditto), then where are you now? Whichever number the client gives, you first ask what is in the given number and subsequently you use follow-up questions to elicit more and more details.

Besides questions that invite differential thinking and nuances, scaling questions are useful tools because they prime the idea that change is possible: Any number on the scale serves as a metaphor for change and immediately influences the perception of the client. In this way, any answer to a scaling question already brings the process of change in motion.

Several types of scaling questions have been designed to fit with the specific situation at hand. First, an overview of the questions is presented and some examples are given.

Different types of scaling questions

The number of scaling questions you can think of is endless, because the content of the X and Y is different for each client; for each situation, several major classes of scaling questions can be distinguished[7]:

a the scale of difference
b the scale of progress
c the scale of hope for change
d the scale of motivation
e the scale of usefulness
f the scale of confidence
g the scale of well-being

The different types of scaling questions are presented in this order because it is the logical way to use them during a conversation or in a full facilitation process. The situation determines which scale to be used, and in which order. Sometimes just one type needs to be used, sometimes more and sometimes – when the client is already functioning in a differentiated way – the use of a scaling question is not relevant at all.

CIMO-19a: *The scale of difference*

Imagine, on a scale of 0–10, where the 0 represents 'the moment you decided to pick up the phone and make an appointment' *and the 10 represents* 'that's how it's going now', *where are you already?* This scale can be combined with CIMO-9: Ask the pre-session change question.

CIMO-19b: *The scale of progress*

Imagine a scale that goes from −10 to 0, where −10 stands for 'the hardest situation you've ever experienced' *and 0 for* 'not everything is solved, but I can get by', *where are you now?*

Note the difference between the following questions and choose the most appropriate version to promote change. *Where are you now? Where are you already? Where are you just now?*

CIMO-19c: *The scale of hope for change*
On a scale of 0–10, where the 0 represents 'I have no hope that any change is possible for me' *and the 10 represents* 'I am hopeful that, with the right effort, I can make a positive change', *where do you stand now?*

CIMO-19d: *The scale of motivation*
On a scale where 0 represents 'I am in an impossible situation and I have zero motivation to do anything about it' *and 10 represents* 'no matter how difficult it is, I am willing to do anything to address my problems', *where are you now?*

CIMO-19e: *The scale of usefulness*
We have already discussed many things in our conversation. Imagine a scale where the 0 stands for 'this is completely useless, this doesn't benefit me at all' *and the 10 for* 'this really benefits me, this is very useful for me', *where are we now?*

This scale can be combined with the usefulness question from CIMO-16.

CIMO-19f: *The scale of confidence*
On a scale where 0 stands for 'I have absolutely no confidence in myself to address the issues in the right way' *and 10 stands for* 'I am confident that I have everything I need to get out of this', *where are you now?*

CIMO-19g: *The scale of well-being*
Once the client has made sufficient progress working towards solutions, he will probably be interested in raising the bar and focusing on his well-being and self-efficacy. Indeed, when the original difficulties and challenges lose their blinding effect, a scale of well-being can be presented: *On a scale from 1 to 10, where 1 stands for* 'I should learn to be more content with my life instead of complaining about little things that in the end don't really matter', *and 10 stands for* 'perfection does not exist and I accept that, but I am happy with what I have', *where do you stand right now?* This question might surprise clients who have a history with psychotherapy and coaching that limits itself to 'cure', in the sense of getting rid of problems, and where the well-being of clients is overlooked.

CIMOs 20 and 21 contain future-orienting questions as an important marker that focuses the client's attention on the desired future rather than on analysing past problems.

CIMO-20: *Use future-orienting questions*
Future-orienting questions – for which the basic goal-setting question (*What do we need to discuss* today *so that this conversation will be useful to you?*) in CIMO-4 often is the opening question – are: *What would you like to see different and how will you notice that? What will be the first signs that you are making a little progress toward what you want to achieve?*

The mechanism in a future-oriented question is that the client's answer describes what will be different in the future and converts these answers into feelings, thoughts and actions that are different today. In other words, the client projects answers into the future and in his detailed description of how things will be different, the client 'retrojects' possible alternatives into today's reality.

CIMO-21: *Use the miracle question*
If a client is stuck in his problem-oriented worldview, a positive, imagined perspective might be suggested by asking the miracle question. This question comes in many forms. It can be introduced as follows: *Suppose that, while you are sleeping, a miracle happens which solves all your problems (just enough so that they no longer bother you so much). How would you notice that it is as if a miracle happened for you?* The use of the word 'suppose' and the subjunctive gives the client a detached, dissociated, objective – yet subjective – view of an accomplishment, which thereby contains an expression of his hopes and desires (Erickson & Rossi, 1979). Subsequently, by asking follow-up questions, ways can be found to apply the client's solutions of the imagined future into the present.

Together with the 6 Points of Attention (see Section 2.2), the 14 Lessons Learned (see Sections 2.2 and 3.1) and the 10 Best and Bad Practices (see Section 3.2), the 21 CIMOs are the building blocks for the envisioned SoFAP-P design, to be presented in the next chapter.

3.4 Answering the three support questions

From the design objective (presented in Section 2.3.1) three support questions have been derived:

SQ1: What are the characteristics of a solution-focused applied psychology approach, as opposed to a problem-oriented approach?
SQ2: What is an appropriate area of application for a solution-focused applied psychology protocol?
SQ3: What are productivity characteristics of the client-practitioner interaction in a solution-focused applied psychology protocol?

Based on what we have learned from literature (Section 3.1), working with experts (Section 3.2) and CIMOs as derived from client cases (Section 3.3), these three support questions now can be answered:

3.4.1 Characteristics of the SoFAP approach (SQ1)

Solution-focused applied psychology refers to the overarching approach that acts like an operating system versus concrete interventions and methods that are like applications.

The following overview provides a summary of solution-focused applied psychology essentials. These are the eight core features of the envisioned solution-focused applied psychology protocol presented in Chapter 4.

Problems become possibilities

In the solution-focused approach, problems are only of interest as far as they provide clues to the possible solutions. Although problems can be overwhelming, there are always moments when the problem is not there or when the problem is less severe or slightly different than at other times. In other words, the state of a (mental) problem is dynamic and this dynamic is the cause of temporary absence of the problem or exceptions to the problem. These absences and exceptions are of great interest because they indicate that there are partial solutions that can be enlarged into broader solutions.

The solution-focused practitioner asks: 'What still works well (enough) in spite of the problems you are facing?' The working hypothesis here is that there are always possibilities: practices worth continuing with and behaviours that still work despite everything.

Image of Humankind

The *Image of Humankind* behind the solution-focused applied psychology protocol is based on the following assumptions:

- Every human being and every human system is fully equipped to cope with life;
- Human systems (individuals, families, teams, companies etc.) always have resources at their disposal that they can use to reach their goals;
- However dire the situation may seem, there are always practices that are worthwhile to keep doing;
- There are always practices and behaviours that still work positively in spite of the problem;
  Change works best on a foundation of what works well.

Resource orientation

In solution-focused work, one continuously concentrates on the available resources that the individual, couple, family or larger system can use to move forward in life. A resource can be anything: not only background, intelligence, work, relations, friends, family, money and environmental factors but also convictions, experiences, skills, knowledge and so on. Many artefacts and intangibles can function as a resource to draw strength from. A half-bottle contains exactly the same reality as a half-empty bottle. Yet, seeing the bottle as half-full is a resource that enhances your chance of survival in the desert. A loss, however sad, inevitably contains the possibility of a new development.

Thinking in terms of resources will be so pivotal in the SoFAP-P design that it could have just as well been named *resource-focused working*.

Future orientation

Problems help to understand the past. Solutions help to live the present and shape the future. Therefore, the solution-focused approach offers a wide range of interventions that channel attention towards the construction of possible future solutions. Instead of focusing on the (why of) problems in the past, the SoFAP-P design must concentrate on desired outcomes: 'What do you want to accomplish tomorrow and next week?' 'What could be the first small step in that direction?'

Goal orientation

The solution-focused approach focuses on the goals of the clients and not on the paradigm that the experts adhere to. These client goals need to be in accordance with legal, medical and deontological restraints as well as best practices.

Useful goals are practical, realistic and realizable, can be formulated in behavioural terms ('What will you do different if …') and preferably go from small to large.

In contrast to conventional methods with a focus on diagnosis, root causes and subsequent treatment, the search for a solution-focused applied psychology protocol stems from the idea that clients benefit most from a goal-oriented approach

Questions take precedence over explanations

Questions help to shape the answers given and vice versa. Asking appropriate solution-building questions will uncover resources that can be used to build solutions towards the goals of the client.

When offering suggestions or even specific directives that are justified by a management mandate, it is best to phrase them in the form of a question. In this way, the client becomes the owner of the answer, which increases the chance that the client will act on it.

Minimax decision rules

Based on BP-5[8] (Best Practice), solution-focused professionals are invited to constantly strive to achieve maximum effects with minimum effort. To reach this Minimax effect, the following solution-focused applied psychology decision rules apply:

- *Rule 1*: If something still works, do not repair it but show respect and appreciation for what still works.
- *Rule 2*: If something does not work, or no longer works, or does not work well enough after trying it for a while, stop, learn from it and do something else.
- *Rule 3*: If something works well, well enough or better, keep doing it and/or do more of it.
- *Rule 4*: If something works well, well enough or better, then offer it to, or learn it from someone else.

This list of basic decision rules can be used as a checklist. Whenever a particular intervention does not work, the checklist can be consulted to see what was overlooked, not given enough attention or was given a too exclusive focus. If this is the case, use the checklist to adjust the interventions.

See Appendix B for a detailed explanation of these four decision rules.

Solution talk

Language is our most important tool. Listening and talking are the main components of 'languaging'. The cooperation between the practitioner and his clients is aimed at helping the clients to create an alternative reality to their problem state.

Problem talk: 'What is the problem and why?'

Solution talk: 'What still works well despite the problem?' 'What would you like *instead* of the problem?'

3.4.2 Area of application (SQ2)

This second question is answered on two dimensions that are called the width and depth of the protocol.

Width

The empirical application of scientifically validated psychological insights, called applied psychology, means *the use of psychological methods and findings of scientific psychology to solve practical problems of human behaviour and experience* (Britannica, 2021). This form of psychology is used, among other things, for study and career advice, in recruitment and selection, consumer marketing, coaching, organisational consulting, leadership development and, of course, in mental health care. Facilitating change in and among people is the scope of the envisioned SoFAP-P design presented in Chapter 4. The way we want to deal with this is founded on two essential solution-focused notions: exceptions to the problems (there is no problem that is always to the same extent, in the same form and in all circumstances, the same) and the working hypothesis that – however dire the situation may be – there are always things that (still) work well. This last notion brings one immediately to the idea that human systems always have resources at their disposal. All of this is reflected in how the intended SoFAP-P design has an alternative way of defining the nature and scope of problems: An individual and/or interrelational problem represents a wish for change that with the help of solution-focused questions can be translated into a challenge.

Imagine a client who says: *I am insecure*. After acknowledging the clients' feelings, the practitioner (e.g. a psychologist) can ask questions like: *Are there moments when you feel less insecure? What is different then? What still works well despite your insecurity? What would you like instead of your insecurity? What will be the first small steps that tell you that your sense of security is growing?*

Imagine colleagues from different departments in a company, working on a common project who say: *We are getting nowhere. Due to our conflicting interests and approaches, we are not able to cooperate efficiently. It even happens that we argue with each other.* After acknowledging each teammate's perspective, the practitioner (e.g. a professional coach) can ask questions like: *Are there moments when you are cooperating slightly more efficient? What is different then? What still works well despite your conflicting interests? What would you like instead of your bickering? What will be the first small steps to replace your arguing with more constructive communication?*

Caveat

To avoid the pitfall of seeing the solution-focused approach as a panacea for everything, one needs to be aware of one major exception: Problems that cannot be reformulated as a challenge are declared to be unsuitable to be the subject of the envisioned SoFAP-P approach. For problems that present themselves as of a psychological and/or inter-relational nature (or can be interpreted as such), but behind which there is a major (neuro)physiological defect, the mere application of psychological or inter-relational interventions is not useful (enough). A striking example: For many decades, gastric ulcers were seen as stress related and required psychological treatment. Barry Marshall and Robin Warren won the 2005 Nobel Prize for Medicine for their discovery that gastric ulcers were due to the bacterium *Helicobacter Pylori* and can be cured with antibiotics. The existing industry of psychological treatment programs to deal with 'stress related' ulcers immediately went extinct. Other examples of problems that cannot be reformulated as challenges and are therefore less suitable to be the subject of the intended SoFAP-P approach are psychological and/or psychiatric problems with a predominantly neurophysiological background. Some examples are vital depression and manic-depressive psychosis. Without specific medication, psychotherapy offers no sustainable cure. Talking with the patients to whom one gives medication is necessary, not so much as therapy per se, but more as mental support and to promote compliance in taking the pills.

Fortunately, there are many more psychological and/or inter-relational problems that can be reformulated as challenges than those that cannot, so this limitation is relative.

Depth

For the solution-focused applied psychology protocol aimed at, the depth of applicability depends on the use of the practitioner's various mandates. Each mandate structures what can and should happen in the interaction between client and practitioner. It is crucial to realize that the specific authority to intervene attached to each mandate is not self-evident.

This means that the practitioner does not 'own' authority independent of the client and by the mere fact of being the practitioner. On the contrary, such authority must be earned in the interaction between the client and the solution-focused practitioner. The client's willingness to grant a mandate to the practitioner is based on the client's perceived quality of the interaction and thus of the working relationship between them.

The following three essential mandates are always operating simultaneously:

- **A leadership mandate** allows the practitioner, on the basis of his professional expertise, knowledge and experience to take the lead in the interventions. In the leadership mandate, the practitioner decides which questions to ask, which answers to follow up and which answers to disregard. This mandate also decides who is to be invited from the client ecosystem and in what order. The leadership mandate is a two-way street. This means that the practitioner can only offer his leadership to clients who want to follow him, and vice versa. This manifests itself, for example, in questions such as, 'Correct me if I am wrong'. 'Do I understand you correctly when you say X?'
- **A management mandate** which gives the professional the authority to make appointments with the client, including planning and monitoring meetings and recording commitments and homework agreements. In other words: The practitioner executing a management mandate acts as a process manager at that moment and thus assumes stewardship of the process. The management mandate also includes the continuous updating of the state-of-the-art professional knowledge and expertise of the practitioner.
- **A mandate as a coach and facilitator** gives the practitioner the authority to create a context in which the client is empowered to help himself to reach his goals by making use of his resources and possibilities.

Through skilful use of the three mandates, a solution-focused applied psychology protocol can be deployed to help client systems achieve deep change in very different circumstances. The content always comes from the client's situation, while the intervention process is driven by the professionals.

These three mandates are always and simultaneously at work. Depending on each situation, one of the mandates is in the foreground, while the others are more in the background. Solution-focused work means that the practitioner continuously must switch between these three mandates. The leadership mandate directs those switches by determining how and when to apply the other two mandates. After all, it is the practitioner who decides – based on expertise, experience and awareness of the current situation – whether to intervene as a coach/facilitator, manager or leader.

Hereby the *width* and *depth* of the intended SoFAP-P design are explained and delineated. A more detailed demarcation of the scope of the envisaged solution-focused applied psychology protocol is given in Section 4.2. There the indications and contra-indications for application of the design are listed.

3.4.3 Productivity characteristics (SQ3)

As far as the term productivity is concerned, we stick to the view of Stack (2016) given in Section 2.3.1 and repeated here for convenience:

> *(...) productivity is seen as the product of effectiveness and efficiency. Effectiveness implies achieving the intended goal and efficiency indicates working with the least possible use of resources such as time, money and other means. Thus a productive outcome means that the intended goal (for example: a client who can take on a particular challenge) is reached, with the use of the least conceivable number of resources.*

Solution-focused practitioners are inclined to aim at obtaining maximal effects with minimal efforts for their clients (Prior, 2021). To reach this, solution-focused practitioners tend to constantly evaluate their actions qualitatively and quantitatively, asking themselves questions like: *Does this intervention work well enough? Should I use this intervention more or less frequently, with a longer or shorter lead time? Am I qualified enough to apply this intervention? Am I giving enough space to what the client brings in?*

This constant and ongoing calibration with the client, his systemic context and his goals guide the practitioner's interventions towards a co-created alternative reality as the result of an iterative, recursive process with an – ultimately and hopefully – cumulative positive effect.

According to de Jong and Berg (1998), productivity (efficiency × effectivity) of the practitioner's interventions depends to a large extent on his linguistic skills. This means, among other things, adapting the level of his language (in terms of nuances and sophistication) to the level of the client. As known, in solution-focused applied psychology, the cooperation between the professional and the client is geared at helping the client to create an alternative reality. That reality is 'made' in language (Miller & McKergow, 2012). The result will only be successful if the language used is rich enough to create a reality that offers perspective.

Productivity is then achieved when, in a relatively short period of time, the client feels that he is understood, receives authentic attention, feels respected and is offered a perspective that gives him hope for change (the four non-specific factors from Lesson Learned 12a, see Section 3.1).

In addition, it can easily be said that the solution-focused approach takes less time on average – and is therefore more efficient – than the problem-oriented approach, because no time needs to be spent on diagnosing the problem and analysing its historical background and root causes. Time is also saved because positive results show up earlier and are more sustainable over time.

When the SoFAP-P design was for about 80% ready, an opinion survey among professionals and academics was conducted as part of the α-testing of the design (see Section 5.1) in which they were asked to give their opinion about the relevance of the building blocks of the design (see Appendix A for the survey). To answer

SQ3, in the opinion survey, six statements were included to be assessed in order to support a comparative evaluation of the *efficiency* and *effectiveness* of problem-oriented applied psychology versus solution-oriented applied psychology.

By means of questions E-1 and E-2 (see below), it was tried to obtain comparative opinions only from practitioners who are familiar with both the problem-oriented approach and the solution-focused approach.

In the end, 70 respondents met that criterion and the averages and standard deviations of their scores on the 4 comparative E-3 questions are shown below.

ON THE EFFICIENCY AND EFFECTIVENESS OF THE PROBLEM-FOCUSED VERSUS SOLUTION-FOCUSED APPROACH

E-1: I am familiar with problem-oriented applied psychology approaches.

$\bar{X} = 3.83 \quad \sigma = 0.92 \quad n = 105$

E-2: I am familiar with solution-focused applied psychology approaches.

$\bar{X} = 4.25 \quad \sigma = 0.75 \quad n = 77$

If you scored 4 or 5 on question E1 and 4 or 5 on question E2, then go to the 4 E3 questions.

If you scored 1, 2 or 3 on E1 or E2, then you are now done with this survey.

In view of the intended interpretation of the two key concepts in question E3, first operational definitions were provided of the terms *efficient* and *effective*:

- *Efficient*: in the most economical way, a way that costs relatively little time and little money.
- *Effective*: achieving the intended goal, meeting the targets set.

E-3a: With the same case and comparable practitioner expertise, problem-oriented applied psychology is generally more *efficient* than solution-focused applied psychology.

$\bar{X} = 1.89 \quad \sigma = 0.81 \quad n = 70$

E3-b: With the same case and comparable practitioner expertise, solution-focused applied psychology is generally more *efficient* than problem-oriented applied psychology.

$\bar{X} = 4.13 \quad \sigma = 0.72 \quad n = 70$

> E-3c: With the same case and comparable practitioner expertise, problem-oriented applied psychology is generally more *effective* than solution-focused applied psychology.
>
> $$\bar{X} = 2.13 \quad \sigma = 0.83 \quad n = 70$$
>
> E3-d: With the same case and comparable practitioner expertise, solution-focused applied psychology is generally more *effective* than problem-oriented applied psychology.
>
> $$\bar{X} = 4.01 \quad \sigma = 0.81 \quad n = 70$$

From the results of questions E-3a and E-3b, it can be concluded that solution-focused applied psychology is in general considered to be more *efficient* than problem-focused applied psychology.

At the same time, it can be concluded from questions E-3c and E-3d that solution-focused applied psychology is in general to be considered more *effective* than problem-oriented applied psychology.

It can also be noted that the difference between both approaches on *efficiency* is greater than on effectiveness. In other words: Solution-focused working is generally more effective than problem-oriented working, but it is above all more efficient.

And with that, SQ3 has been answered. The answer will help us to formulate relevant design principles and design propositions.

Further subquestions regarding the productivity of the solution-focused approach concern:

a the sustainability and durability of the effects of the solution-focused facilitation process,
b the occurrence of relapses and how to proceed when they do emerge,
c and to some degree: the extent to which the solution-focused approach is evidence based.

Subquestion a: There is little or no research available that helps to quantify the sustainability and durability of the effects of the solution-focused approach. What is left are impressions and beliefs that come from the experience of practitioners who are experts in the solution-focused approach.

They generally report that the solution-focused approach works better, has longer-lasting positive effects and the approach is applicable to challenges in a variety of situations. *Works better* means that fewer sessions are needed to produce a wished-for outcome, meaning the client reaches his goals faster. *Last longer* means that the sustainability of the positive effects has prolonged durability: What has improved is the tendency to keep improving. *Better* and *longer* can be understood to be the result of the fact that the solution-focused approach works towards the goals of the client and makes use of the client's resources instead of working towards the practitioner's goals, which is to strictly follow the expert-chosen model.

Subquestion b: As far as relapses are concerned, the common understanding is that in contrast to traditional problem-oriented models where relapses are seen as declines in progress, the solution-focused approach defines relapses as part of the learning process towards healing and self-efficacy. When relapses occur, they invite solution-building questions like: *What have you learned from this experience? When did it stop and what little difference did you notice then?*

Subquestion c: Is the solution-focused approach evidence-based? The answer is affirmative. A broad summary of existing research supports this claim:

- From 120 studies, of which 23 are RCTs (randomized control trials), all show positive outcomes; 12 RCTs show results that were superior to the existing treatments (McKeel, 1996).
- A total of 36 of 45 comparative studies show significantly better results for solution-focused work (McDonald, 2011).
- Effectivity studies on n = 5.000 cases show a success ratio above 60% with an average of 3–6 sessions needed (McDonald, 2011).
- Two meta-analytical reviews conducted on 43 studies show that, compared to traditional approaches, the solution-focused approach achieves the best results in terms of personal behaviour change (McKeel, 1996).

3.5 Summary of building blocks for a solution-focused applied psychology protocol

At the end of this empirical chapter, an overview is given of the knowledge gained from the studies conducted for our intended SoFAP-P design.

The overview consists of 6 Points of Attention (PA's from Section 2.2), 14 Lessons Learned (LL's from Sections 2.2 and 3.1), 10 Best & Bad Practices (BP's & BaP's from Section 3.2) and 21 CIMOs (from Section 3.3).

PA-1: Most approaches show an unbalanced methodological focus. They pay more attention (= time and energy) to past experiences and to the historical context of the client, than to his present situation and his wishes for change. This goes at the expense of exploring possible future options to bring the desired changes closer.

PA-2: The emphasis in problem-oriented approaches is on the detailed description of problems and corresponding hypothesized causes underlying these problems. These descriptions and the language in which the professional usually converses with the client are problem oriented. This easily results in a situation where there is (too) little attention paid to finding a solution to solve the client's problem.

PA-3: Client's problem descriptions typically result in classifications of diagnoses and typologies of mental problems and disorders. Such classifications, like

DSM V, have the advantage of being convenient, although they can also easily lead to confusion and simplifications that leave little or no room for the complexity of human life, with all its serendipities, unexpected, unfathomable and unpredictable twists and turns.

PA-4: The causal linearity from *anamnesis* and *diagnosis* to *therapy* and *prognosis* obscures the complexity of each client's life, oversimplifies the situation that causes the problem and thereby reduces the opportunity for robust and sustainable solutions.

PA-5: The linear problem-oriented theories (from *anamnesis* to *prognosis*) evaluated show an unbalanced stakeholder focus: The emphasis of attention mainly goes to the client as an individual, even if the treatment format is the couple, the family or a group. Other stakeholders in the client's ecosystem are seen as more peripheral.

PA-6: In general, problem-oriented approaches suffer to a greater or lesser extent from a lack of efficiency in the use of time, money and other resources.

LL-1: Abandon analytic classifications of mental problems; focus instead on integrated holistic solutions (which may be implicitly multi-dimensional and multi-faceted).

LL-2: The client's goals and resources should be the centre of attention. The paradigm the practitioner uses to guide his interventions is no more than a tool in the client's facilitation process. So don't let the method be leading, but the client.

LL-3: Useful client goals are practical, realistic, achievable, can be phrased in behavioural terms ('What will you do/think/feel different if …') and they preferably go from small to large.

LL-4: Refrain from the linearity of anamnesis, diagnosis, therapy and prognosis; work iteratively, recursively and circularly instead.

LL-5: Start from the client's present situation as it relates to his momentary goals and then develop a future orientation.

LL-6: Incorporate the client's actual context directly and explicitly in the approach.

This means involving all relevant stakeholders in the client's actual ecosystemic context in such a way that they can contribute additional resources for the client or that they can benefit from the progress of the client or both.

LL-7: First focus on potential solutions and then iterate intermediate steps to create a robust, self-learning, client-specific solution methodology.

LL-8: Solutions can be: (1) outcomes, results, (2) process effects (since thoughts change actions and vice versa), (3) combinations of (1) and (2).

LL-9: Solutions belong to the future, while problems belong to the past. The emphasis should be towards constructing possible solutions and desired outcomes. Instead of concentrating on the (*why* of the) problems in the past, the focus of the practitioner should be on the desired outcome: 'What do you want to accomplish tomorrow and next week?', 'What could be the first little step to achieve this?'

LL-10: Stimulate a client-driven or -steered approach, instead of a client-oriented or -focused one.

LL-11: Pay attention to three major tendencies that prevent clients from being open to a solution-focused applied psychology approach: (1) no intrinsic motivation to change, (2) 'resistance' to change and (3) translating mental issues into physical problems.

LL-12a: Integrate the exploitation of non-specific therapeutic factors seen from the client's point of view, into the facilitation approach (instead of regarding them as a welcome by-product).

LL-12b: Integrate the exploitation of non-specific therapeutic factors seen from the practitioner's point of view, into the facilitation approach.

LL-13: Put the effect of psychological and inter-relational facilitation techniques into a more differentiated perspective by asking differentiation questions (including scaling questions).

LL-14: Allow the therapeutic relationship to develop into a therapeutic alliance.

BP-1: Transform the working relationship with the client into an alliance.

BP-2: Set goals in an active manner.

BP-3: Set goals in a continuous manner.

BP-4: Concentrate on the client's resources and possibilities.

BP-5: Use the Minimax Decision Rules.

BaP-1: Give primacy to a theory, model or method over the idiosyncratic needs and possibilities of the client.

BaP-2: Delve into speculations about the *why* of what goes wrong.

BaP-3: Have an obsessive focus on the past.

BaP-4: Limit the desired goals to the mere absence of problems.

BaP-5: Treat the working relationship as an asymmetric one in which the client is source of all difficulties and the practitioner is the all-knowing expert.

CIMO-1: Establishing contact to build the client-practitioner alliance

CIMO-2: Distinguishing Problem versus Limitation to enhance effectivity

CIMO-3: Exploring the context

CIMO-4: Directing the conversation towards a goal

CIMO-5: Circumventing absent intrinsic motivation

CIMO-6: Focus the client's attention on accepting responsibility and accountability for the client's own actions

CIMO-7: Solution Building questions

CIMO-8: Resource Activation

CIMO-9: Pre-session change question

CIMO-10: Continuation question to activate resources

CIMO-11: Offer positive feedback, (or: giving compliments)

CIMO-12: Give advice in the guise of a question

CIMO-13: Coping question

CIMO-14: What have you tried thus far?

CIMO-15: Exception questions
CIMO-16: Ask the usefulness question
CIMO-17: Offer a relativistic perspective
CIMO-18: Differentiating questions
CIMO-19: Scaling Questions
CIMO-20: Future orienting questions
CIMO-21: Miracle question

For the design of the solution-focused applied psychology protocol that we will present in the next chapter, all items listed in this summary will be used as building blocks. The more than 50 items (6 PAs, 14 LLs, 10 B(a)Ps and 21 CIMOs) should not be seen as constraints, but – in accordance to DSR methodology – together, they constitute a multidimensional space within which creative design can take place.

Notes

1 See Section 2.2 for the first nine Lessons Learned.
2 That is why the non-specific factors are also known as common factors.
3 Appendix B specifies the details of the Minimax Decision Rules.
4 Kottler and Carlson (2003).
5 For ease of reading, we repeat in one sentence what the acronym CIMO stands for: If you want to achieve in *this* Context, *this* Output, then it offers advantages to perform *this* Intervention that is supposed to work on the basis of *this* mechanism.
6 Personal communication during a training.
7 See: *Creating Sustainable Results with Solution-focused Applied Psychology: A Practical Guide for Coaches and Change Facilitators* (Cauffman, 2023) for more practical applications and examples.
8 See Section 3.2.

4
SoFAP-P

A Solution-Focused Applied Psychology Protocol

This chapter presents the solution-focused applied psychology protocol in text as well as summarized in the form of a flowchart (a fixed version that can be printed and a dynamic version that can be used for study or teaching). SoFAP-P as an arrangement of interventions is constructed using the building blocks from the previous chapters and is described in three major movements. Each movement has several components and the often consecutive, iterative and sometimes recursive paths through the movements are intended to lead to a cumulative change process. The text and flowchart version of SoFAP-P can be used for designing, testing, evaluating and fine-tuning any intervention geared to facilitate change for the client. The chapter concludes with indications and contra-indications for a justified use of SoFAP-P and tests the design against the predetermined specifications it should meet.

4.1 SoFAP-P, an arrangement of interventions

The design has an overarching structure consisting of three major movements.[1] Within each movement, there is a substructure of components that guide the flow of the intervention process within that movement. This flow is guided by what happens in the working relationship between the practitioner and the client system.[2]

The flow can follow the logic of the developing intervention in which either the five sequential components (Movement 1) or the different types of working relationships (Movement 2) are the driver. The intervention flow ends with Movement 3 where the outcome of the process is evaluated.

This flow is rarely linear but jumps both within each movement and across the different movements. Within each movement, the flow can jump from one component/working relationship type to another as a result of the continuously

FIGURE 4.1

evolving situation. As depicted in the SoFAP-P flowchart, sometimes it is necessary to retrace previous steps or move back to a previous movement.

Often successive steps are applied sequentially and iteratively, and recursively if necessary, allowing for all kinds of variations and ramifications in the intervention process. It may be necessary to return to earlier steps and make subtle changes in them. Then the flow becomes recursive. Yet, since the creation of a reality is a constantly unfolding process, there is no possibility of returning to the exact initial state (πάντα ῥεῖ).

The succession and accumulation of interactive and recursive steps leads to a change process of a cumulative nature.

It is important to keep in mind that, even if the formal working relationship is ended, the SoFAP-P process can remain operational within the client or client system. This happens when the client has *learned to learn* during the intervention process so that he continues to implement the internalized change process and thus becomes his own solution-focused practitioner.

READING GUIDE

Scanning the above QR code, one will find a static visualization of the SoFAP-P flowchart that can be printed for ease of use while studying the process. The QR code at the end of this chapter presents a dynamic version of the SoFAP-P flowchart that shows the different moves in a sequential order.

The design is structured as follows:

In **Movement 1**, the flow of the intervention runs across several logically connected components. The process starts with preparing the solution-building

SoFAP-P 77

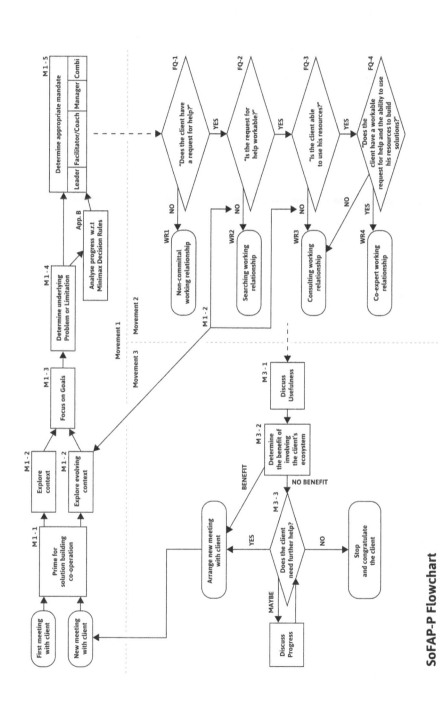

SoFAP-P Flowchart

FIGURE 4.2 *App.B* between M1-4 and M1-5 refers to Appendix B: *The Four Minimax Decision Rules in Detail*

cooperation, by making contact (M1-1). Then the context in which the client system functions is explored (M1-2). When that is sufficiently done, the focus shifts to the goals of the client (M1-3), differentiates problems from limitations and decides the appropriate mandate from which to intervene, while continuously monitoring the minimax basic decision rules to obtain maximal efficiency.

The continuous review of the interventions against the minimax rules (see Appendix B) also fosters maximum effectiveness. Movement 1 additionally involves a choice about which mandate or combination of mandates[3] is most appropriate at that time.

Movement 2 distinguishes four distinct types of working relationships that are defined by the answers to four fundamental questions (FQ). Does the client have a request for help, are his goals workable, does he have access to his resources and is he able to use his resources to make progress. In other words, the four types of working relationship are delineated by his willingness to ask for help, the nature of his goals, the access to his resources and the ability to use his resources. The names that go with each different type of working relationship are mnemotechnical aids that help to remember the different positions on the flowchart. These positions describe the quality of the working relationship with the client at that moment in time regarding the specific problem at hand. The four positions are as follows: a non-committal (WR1), a searching (WR2), a consulting (WR3) and a co-expert working relationship (WR4). Constant evaluation will cause the dialogue to move iteratively and/or recursively between the four types of Movement 2.

Movement 3 describes the components in use when the ongoing working relationship is ended for that session and a new one is planned or when the working relationship comes to a full stop. Two specifications are useful here: (1) The full stop can be the result of a successful facilitation process or when the process fails to become useful. (2) The actual ending of the working relationship, namely no longer meeting each other, does not necessarily mean that the change process within the client or client system is not taking place. However, the practitioner no longer plays an active role in that case.

Valid for all three movements

The different steps of the *Seven-step-dance*[4] describe what happens in the interaction between client and practitioner. These seven steps form, as it were, the 'basso continuo' on which the ever-changing, developing, sometimes recurring, yet always unfolding melody of the intervention, process is based. The steps are active during the intervention process in all three movements.

To conclude

The SoFAP-P design offers multiple moments when the client is complimented for using his resources to make progress towards his goals. This essentially implies a future orientation, as evidenced, for example, by the goal-setting question: *What do we need to talk about so that this conversation* will *be useful to you?* The miracle question is the iconic future-oriented technique that has made the solution-focused approach famous: *Imagine that, while you sleep, it is as if a miracle happens, and in that miracle the things that are bothering you are resolved just enough so that your life becomes easier again. How will you know? What will you do differently?*

The protocol also offers multiple moments when differentiating or nuance-inducing questions can be used to help the client pry himself loose from a black-and-white fixation. This sometimes takes the form of a scaling question.[5] Scaling questions all have the following generic formula: *Imagine if I asked you to give a number on a scale where the starting point, the zero, stands for X (the starting point, to be filled in according to the specific situation to be nuanced) and the 10 stands for Y (the guide point), where are you now?* For the sake of brevity, scaling questions will be formulated as follows: [*0 = starting point, 10 = guide point*].

The next section explains the sequential movements through the SoFAP-Protocol, along with all the possible interventions that can be applied. Loops between the different parts and movements are likely. They show that the SoFAP-Protocol is an extremely fluid and flexible tool with unlimited variation possibilities.

Movement 1: Structuring the SoFAP-P intervention process

Following the rules described in M1-1, the working relationship should be primed as a cooperative relationship that is geared towards building solutions with and for the client. Then, the different process components are activated, following the order in which they are presented in the next paragraphs or sometimes simultaneously. Questions[6] are asked that invite the client to provide information that help explore the context (M1-2), and the client is asked for his goals (M1-3). Distinguishing between problems and limitations (M1-4) avoids embarking on a mission impossible that tries to solve the unsolvable. This distinction simultaneously opens the realm of possibilities while accepting the (consequences of) the limitations. How to cope with the consequences of a limitation is a problem for which a solution is possible. Based on this informative interaction, it can be decided which mandate to activate and how to alternate between the three mandates.

M1-1: Prime for solution-building cooperation

From the very first meeting with the client, prime the interactional style in such a manner that the resulting working relationship is one of collaboration. Create and sustain a client-practitioner working alliance by applying the following rules:

DO NOT	*DO*
Allow your own style to dominate the conversation	Focus on the client's way of thinking and speaking
Use jargon	Speak plainly and simple, yet concise and precise

DO NOT	DO
Pretend to know better or best	Demonstrate cooperation: work *with* the client
Act with professional neutrality that the client feels as aloofness	Show engagement and commitment
Hurry	Go slow
Act pushy or pedantic	Behave in a polite, considerate, courteous and inviting manner
Act inquisitive and on the outlook for all that went wrong	Be appreciative of everything the client offers that can be used to make progress
Act as the distant professional	Be authentic in the focused attention to the client

Thus, priming the working relationship as a solution-building collaboration increases the likelihood that the client feels both understood and invited to buy into the solution-building process. This building of a constructive working relationship, along with the components that will follow next, creates a context in which the client assumes ownership of whatever proposals originate during the facilitation process.

M1-2: Explore the context

M1-2.1: When the client is met for the first time, ask for contextual information about the ecosystem of the client: *Would you be so kind as to tell me something about yourself? How old are you? Do you have a partner? Children? What work do you do?*

Not only do these questions have easy answers, but their main purpose is also to prime that the practitioner is more interested in the client as a person than in (the causes of) the problems.

M1-2.2: As of the second meeting, ask *What is different since the last time we met?*

M1-2.3: Additionally, questions can be used as follows: *Can you tell me more about that? Can you give me a concrete example? What else can you tell me so I can better understand the situation?* or: *Is there something I forgot to ask that is important for this matter* to deepen and broaden the scope of the conversation.

M1-3: Focus on goals

Since SoFAP-P is goal-oriented, make sure to ask the client what *his* goals are.

M1-3.1: When first meeting the client, ask the general goal-setting question (which also introduces a future orientation): *What do we have to talk about so that our conversation will be useful to you?*

M1-3.2: Ask appropriate follow-up questions that help the client formulate his goals according to the checklist for useful goals: practical, realistic, realizable, observable in behavioural terms and preferably from small to larger.

M1-3.3: At the right time, ask *Is it useful when we talk like this?* to elicit feedback from the client on the evolution of and in his facilitation process. This feedback then can be used to feed forward the next question and/or intervention.

Use the question-and-answer cycle M1-3.1 till M1-3.3 in every session to subtly guide the facilitation process. Thus, a loop of incremental improvement is created.

M1-4: Distinguish between *problem* and *limitation*

The client's responses to questions M1-2 and M1-3 provide clues as to whether his difficulties are the result of a *problem* (for which a solution could be possible) or a *limitation* (for which no conceivable solution is possible).

M1-4.1: When it can be noticed that the client is not aware that he is dealing with a limitation, ask *Do you really think that it is possible to change X?* This question primes a negative answer so that the client discovers the impossibility himself and therefore is more apt to be open for an alternative.

M1-4.2: If the client accepts the X as a limitation, ask *Would you be interested to learn how to deal with the consequences of limitation X so that it will bother you less?* This question directs the client's attention to things that can be solved incrementally.

M1-5: Assume the appropriate mandate

The solution-building intervention process that is the core of SoFAP-P requires flexibility in the mandates from which the practitioner intervenes. The practitioner must take the lead in terms of professionalism and effectiveness (leadership mandate), invite the client to allow and accept the offering of facilitation and support interventions (facilitation mandate) and assume the management mandate to make sure the process is planned, controlled (*of:* reviewed) and transparent. Based on the information the practitioner gets from the client in response to components M1-2, M1-3 and M1-4, the practitioner decides which mandate has priority and which mandates are temporarily in the background.

Concluding notes on Movement 1:

- M1-4 and M1-5 are often implicit in the conversation without the need for explicit mention.
- The five-component cycle is the overarching structure of Movement 1.
- The *Seven-step-dance* is always operational in the background during the iterative and recursive interventions in all movements.

Movement 2: Differentiate between types of working relationships

The answers to the four FQ reveal the nature of the working relationship (WR), which provides a clue to the corresponding useful arrangement of interventions.

FQ-1: Does the client have a request for help? If no: Apply the arrangement of interventions that is suitable for the *non-committal working relationship*.

FQ-2: Is the request for help workable? If no: Apply the arrangement of interventions that is suitable for the *searching working relationship*.

FQ-3: Is the client able to use his resources? If no: Apply the arrangement of interventions that is suitable for the *consulting working relationship* for clients who have a workable need for help but who are not able to use their own resources.

FQ-4: Does the client have a workable request for help and the ability to use his resources to build solutions? If yes: Apply the arrangement of interventions that is suitable for the *co-expert working relationship*.

FUNDAMENTAL QUESTION-1:

Does the client have a help request for the goals he expresses in response to question M1-3?
- **Yes:** → go to FQ-2
- **No:** → go to WR1.

WR1: Non-committal working relationship

The practitioner encounters the client because the client was obliged by a third party to meet the practitioner without himself having a request for help. Even though there is no request for help from the client, or in other words that the client has no wish (yet) to enter a change-oriented working relationship, there is minimal contact. This minimal contact is the starting point for the following general arrangement of interventions:

- Do *not* insist on offering help.
- Show appreciation for whatever there is to appreciate.
- Offer information (if useful).
- Highlight good intentions of the referring party.
- Take time to develop an alternative request for help ('*What do you need to do differently so that you no longer must come here?*').
- Point out the consequences when the client refuses to ask for help.
- Take your time.

FUNDAMENTAL QUESTION-2:

Does the client articulate a workable request for help?

A workable request for help is formulated as practical, realistic, achievable, observable in behavioural terms and from small to larger.
- **Yes:** → go to FQ-3
- **No:** → go to WR2.

WR2: Searching working relationship

The client has a request for help but formulates his goals in such a way that this request for help is unworkable. Unworkable goals are theoretical, unrealistic, unachievable, vague, and/or very large. This can be overwhelming for the client to such an extent that he feels hopeless and helpless.

In such case, the following arrangement of general interventions is appropriate:

- Show recognition for the difficulty of the situation.
- Compliment the client on his motivation.
- Stimulate the client's own responsibility.
- Ask questions that help the client to translate his unworkable goals into workable terms.
- Focus on what still works well.
- Look for exceptions to the problem.

This general arrangement may be supplemented with the following more specific (suite of) interventions, depending on the specific situation.

WR2-1: If the client shows helplessness or insists that his life is a total wreck and that everything must change totally and immediately, accept his statement, show recognition for his difficulties and compliment him on the fact that he took the step to ask for help.

WR2-2: If the client formulates his goals in vague, impractical or absolute language (*I don't know, I want to be happy, I want to be perfect*) or if he lists too many goals at once, ask solution-building questions that help the client specify, concretize, differentiate and prioritize the constituent elements of his goals.

WR2-3: If, in response to goal-setting question M1-3.1, the client formulates his goal negatively *I no longer want X*, then ask what he would like instead and follow up with ensuing questions that will elicit more concrete details about what he might do himself to create changes.

WR2-4: If the client blames a third party for his problems, accept this without arguing and help the client to adopt a more constructive attitude that facilitates taking responsibility. This can be done by asking *What can/would/should you (try to) do differently?*

WR2-5: Ask the pre-session change question: *Has anything changed between the moment you decided to come here and this conversation?* The practitioner meets clients for the simple reason that they have made the effort to contact him. If there is some time lapse between the session and the moment the meeting was scheduled, this pre-session change question can yield useful information while simultaneously priming the client that change, however small, is possible. *Has anything changed between the moment you decided to come here and this conversation?*

WR2-6: Ask continuation questions. If the client is not able to formulate his goals but gets stuck in a description of all that goes wrong, accept this, and then ask continuation questions: *Which things are going well enough for you to want to keep them?*

WR2-7: Assign the continuation-task. If the client is not able to give an answer to the continuation question during the session, offer the following task: *Until our next meeting, at the end of each day, write down what little things happened that day that went well so that you want them to happen again.*

WR2-8: Ask exception questions. If the client gives the practitioner a detailed description of how his problems blacken his entire existence, ask questions that probe for exceptions: *Are there moments when your situation feels more bearable? Are there moments when you are not or less bothered by the problem? What do you do differently then?*

WR2-9: Ask relativizing-questions. Offer a relativizing perspective by questions as follows: *Do you really think these matters are so black-and-white? Wouldn't it be wise to sleep on it?*

WR2-10: Ask differentiation questions. If the client has an exceptionally negative outlook on life, ask differentiating questions: *Can you remember moments when it was a little different? When was it a little better than now? Does it happen that you feel less stressed?*

WR2-11: Apply scaling questions. Black-and-white thinking by the client can be addressed by asking scaling questions for which we already discussed the generic formula in the introduction of this chapter. Scaling questions can be applied to exceptions (on a scale where the 0 stands for *it stays always extremely difficult with no exception at all* and 10 stands for *not perfect but sometimes things ease up just enough to be able to cope*. Or for pre-session changes where on the scale 0 stands for *nothing changed at all* and 10 stands for *these little things seem to be different compared to how it was before I took this appointment and today'*.

Any answer to a scaling question already brings a process of change in motion. Scaling questions yield the best results if you follow these steps:

1   Ask the client for permission to ask a question.
2   Introduce a numeric scale, defining the endpoints.
3   Ask the client where he stands on that scale.
4   Accept any given number.
5   Repeat the given number, affirming it with a compliment: *A 3, fine.*
6   Ask what has changed, which resulted in the client's numeric answer.
7   Accept and affirm the answer by repeating or rewording it.
8   Invite the client to describe in detail all that has changed as is implied in the given number: *And what else?*
9   Widen the perspective by asking triangular questions: *What would your [friend, partner, family members, team members, boss, etc.] say if I asked him the same question?*
10 End with: *What could be the smallest next step?*

WR2-12: Ask future-orienting questions. *What do we need to talk about so that our conversation will be useful to you? What might be the first small sign that will* tell you some improvement is possible? How will you know that our work together is sufficiently successful so that you can cope on your own?

WR2-13: Apply the miracle question. This iconic question helps the client to translate his unworkable goals into terms of the useful goal checklist: *Suppose that, while you are sleeping, a miracle happens which solves all your problems to such an extent that you can cope with them and take small next steps forward. But you don't know that because you were sound asleep. How will you notice these differences when you wake up?*

Does the sequence of arrangements lead the client towards a workable goal?
Yes: → go to FQ-3
No: → go back to M1-2,
and further explore the context and possible goals hidden in the folds of this additional information and see if an alternative iterative process from that point on can be started.

If this yields no result, stop the facilitation process.

FUNDAMENTAL QUESTION-3:

Is the client with a workable request for help able to use his resources?
Yes: → go to FQ-4
No: → go to WR3.

WR3: Consulting[7] working relationship

The client expresses clear and workable goals that fit nicely within the useful goals checklist, but he indicates that he has no access to his resources to do so.

In this case, the client typically says *I want to change X, but I do not know how to do it. Can you help me?* This message contains a stage direction that the practitioner must decode as follows: *I know what I want different in my life, but I have (temporarily) lost access to my resources to do so. Please help me (re)discover my resources and how to use them so I can address my problem.*

This refers to the basic assumption in SoFAP-P that, however dire the situation seems, there are always resources available. The client explicitly asks for help or advice, so the practitioner can activate the leadership mandate to do so.

In such case, the following arrangement of general interventions is appropriate:

- Offer positive support and show recognition.
- Find out what the client has tried before that was successful.
- Offer advice in the form of a question, a suggestion, or a suggestive question.

This general arrangement can be supplemented by the following more specific (suite of) interventions activated in the accompanying questions. Each response can be expanded by follow-up questions.

WR3-1: Look for resources in the past or in other situations: *Have you encountered similar problematic situations in the past? What was helpful then?*

WR3-2: Use small steps as starters for incremental change: *What have you tried that was a little bit helpful?*

WR3-3: Ask the confidence scaling question: on a *scale where 0 stands for no confidence at all that any progress is possible and 10 stands for being confident that you can get rid of the things troubling you, where are you now?*

WR3-4: Ask further context-clarifying questions (like M1-3.1) that invite the client to look for resources by asking questions about the client's (partial) successes, his ability to cope, and by exploring the different contexts in which the client lives: *What have you tried thus far? Have you tried anything that had a positive effect, however small? How did you cope with these or similar problems in the past? What worked best in similar circumstances?*

WR3-5: Explore different contexts by asking about the client's relationship with his family, neighbours, friends, colleagues etc. and pay attention to resources in those contexts.

WR3-6: Use triangular questions that elicit information about the non-present members of the system: *What would your partner, friends, family, co-workers, boss etc. say if I asked them about your strengths?*

WR3-7: Apply an appropriate selection of the questions WR2-5 till WR2-13.

WR3-8: Ask the coping question: *If the situation is as bad as you say it is, how do you cope?*

WR3-9: When a client is totally unable to think of anything remotely positive, ask the special *find-a-treasure-in-a-quagmire* question in which the gravity of the perceived problem state is first accentuated and then the question is put forward how this absolute low ended or at least became bearable: *When was your problem at its very worst? How did that soften or stop and what was different then?*

FUNDAMENTAL QUESTION-4:

Does the client have a workable request for help and the ability to use his resources to reach his workable goals?
  No: → go to WR3
  Yes: → go to WR4.

WR4: Co-expert working relationship

The client has a workable request for help, and he can use his resources to find solutions. In that case, the following arrangement of general interventions is useful:

- Encourage the client to do more of what he is doing because what he does works.
- Refrain from showering the client with knowledge, ideas and convictions about what he should do next but step aside and encourage the client to keep going on his self-found path; apply the minimax decision rules (see Appendix B).
- Show broad appreciation for everything the client does that puts and keeps him on his path of progress.
- Offer every possible tool to the client that will help the client help himself and preferably do this by using (suggestive) questions.
- Ask the question *What have you learned?* to implicitly give credit for the progress to the client himself and answering this question gives ownership of the answer to the client.
- Ask the question *How will you use these successful strategies in future circumstances?* to project what the client has learned into the future when the practitioner is no longer present nor needed.
- Once the client has found successful solutions for his goals, there is an opening to focus on the client's attention to his well-being. Ask the question: *Now that you have solved the problems that were hindering you, what makes you happy and content?*

Concluding notes on Movement 2:

- The position that the working relationship occupies on the flowchart is dynamic and in constant flux. In the same session or over the course of different sessions, the working relationship may be of a different type on Theme A than on Theme B.
- All types of working relationship are equal and there is no qualitative discrimination between them.
- The different types are to be used as benchmarks that indicate which interventions will be the most useful at that time for that theme.
- It is pointless to try to force the course of the intervention process from WR1 to WR4, as if the co-expert working relationship is the ultimate finality.
- Over the course of a facilitation intervention, the iterative and recursive nature of Movement 2 across types culminates in Movement 3.

Movement 3: Continuation and evaluation

When Movements 1 and 2 have run their due course, the time comes to make the bridge to Movement 3.

M3-1: To open Movement 3, ask the *usefulness question* to elicit an evaluation from the client on the cooperative process: *Is it useful what we are discussing? Is it useful to you what we have been discussing so far?*

If the client answers negatively:

- ask the question: *What we should discuss* instead *so that the conversation will be useful to you?* To gather as much detail as possible, ask the follow-up question: *What else?*

If the client answers positively:

- ask the question that invites the client to provide details by asking: *What is it that is so useful to you?* To gather as much detail as possible, ask the follow-up question: *What else?*

M3-2: Under the following conditions, it is useful to suggest inviting a member (or multiple members) from the client's ecosystem to take part in the facilitation process: *Is it a good idea to invite person X or Y, or X and Y to join you in the effort to deal with your problems in a more satisfying manner?*

Conditions that indicate when additional participants are useful:

- when third-party clarification on (aspects of) the situation is appropriate and helpful;
- when additional resources stemming from the client's ecosystem are needed;
- when members of the client's ecosystem need to be informed so they can understand, acknowledge and support the process the client is undergoing;
- when potential obstruction against changes may pose within the client's ecosystem;
- when the members of the client's ecosystems need to make changes themselves;
- when the inter-relational processes between all client-system members are in need of change.

M3-3: Movement 3 is about the answer to the following question: Does the client need further help from the practitioner?

Yes: → Organize a subsequent meeting with the client that brings the intervention cycle back to the beginning of Movement 1 and initiates the next level.

Maybe: → The client and/or the practitioner are not sure that further help is useful.

This can happen in two instances for which different tools are helpful:

Instance-1:

Parties indicate that no or not enough progress has been made yet. Then, ask the scale of progress: On a scale where the 0 stands for *I have not made any progress* and the 10 stands for *I have made fair progress so that I can move on*, where are you now?

- If the client answers 0 or maximum 2, go to WR3-8: the coping question.
- Whatever other number the client gives, ask what is in that number because that invites the client to describe his small steps forward.

Instance-2:

Parties feel low confidence that progress is possible. Then, ask the scale of confidence (WR3-3): On a scale where the 0 stands for *I have no confidence at all that I can do anything useful* and the 10 stands for *I have total confidence that I can do what is necessary to make progress*, where are you now?

- If the client answers 0 or maximum 2, go to WR3-8: the coping question.
- Whatever other number the client gives, ask what small signs of confidence reside in that number.

> M3-3: Movement 3 is about the answer to the following question: Does the client need further help from the practitioner?
> **No:** → Stop.

Both parties agree that the client has learned to build his own solutions, or, more precisely, that the client has learned to learn to build solutions by himself. Since the finality of every facilitation process is to help the client help himself, this response marks the end of the collaboration. To maximize the chances that the client keeps his own solution-building process going without the practitioner present, it is useful to compliment the client extensively for his efforts and give him full credit for his progress.

4.1.1 SoFAP-P flowchart guidelines

As the professional practitioner becomes more experienced and, thus, more proficient in the use of the approach, along with his continuous development as a person and practitioner by gaining deep knowledge in his professional field, the flowchart tool will be used in a more 'compressed' or 'streamlined' way. This means that the practitioner develops the ability of parallel processing and multi-tasking. The practitioner more and more masters the ability to handle different aspects of the solution-focused approach at the same time. This can be compared to driving a car: as a beginner, it is difficult to take notice of all the different variables (handles,

90 SoFAP-P

FIGURE 4.3

pedals and the moving environment) and act accordingly by synchronizing. As an experienced driver, one can drive a car by handling all the different variables simultaneously while having an interesting conversation with a fellow passenger. As a seasoned practitioner, you can establish contact with a client while at the same time exploring the relevant context in which the client lives and collecting first ideas about his goals and resources. What is at issue here is the simultaneous (i.e. non-linear) use of relevant tacit knowledge (Polanyi, 1966) by the seasoned practitioner.

The novice will have more need to follow the relevant route through the empirically grounded flowchart as closely as possible. After all, given his limited experience, he will want to rely on codified knowledge and will seek to avoid any appearance of magic or charlatanry. He only needs to be constantly aware that the flowchart presented is a tool to help streamline interventions and not a mandatory standardized one-size-fits-all linear protocol.

4.1.2 Dynamic representation of the SoFAP-P flowchart

Scanning the above QR code provides a dynamic version that can be used as a teaching or case study didactic tool.

4.2 Indications and contra-indications for using SoFAP-P

Organization science has greatly benefited from the contingency theory as formulated by Jay Galbraith (1973). The theory is based on two assumptions: *There is no one best way to organize*, and *Any way of organizing is not equally effective*.

For the relevance of SoFAP-P in a specific situation, analogous contingencies are valid:

1 There is no best applied psychological approach.
2 Not every applied psychological approach is equally effective.

This means that there is little choice but to try to provide indications and contraindications for using SoFAP-P on logical grounds and based on experience. This is a common way in DSR to deal with Galbraith assumptions. We do so in this chapter.

In the classic cause-effect chain, one needs to define the root cause of the problem so that the expert can define the appropriate interventions to alleviate the problematic effects. This implies that, for every category of problems, there exists a well-defined intervention tool. This requires that an exact indication is needed to connect the dots among problem, cause, intervention and effect. The operational procedure therefore is a problem-oriented anamnesis that analyses all possible aspects of the problem, including a hypothesis about its root cause, so that the cause-effect chain is put to work, resulting in an intervention that removes or, at least, mollifies the root cause. The question of which indication fits what problem is tantamount in this approach.

The solution-focused approach has a delicate relationship with the thorny issue of (contra)indication. This stems from a different approach to the indication-question. We will discuss here general indications, two contra-indications and some pseudo-contra-indications for using SoFAP-P.

4.2.1 Indications

Snowden (2005) distinguishes four types of systems. Applied to the situation at hand, they are described as follows:

1 *Simple systems*: clearly ordered with recognizable cause-and-effect relationships;
2 *Complicated systems*: ordered with hidden but strong cause-effect relationships that can be discovered through systematic investigation;
3 *Complex systems*: narrowly ordered with clusters of weak cause-effect relationships;
4 *Chaotic systems*: not ordered, no useful cause-effect relationships can be discovered.

In the material domain, one often finds *simple* systems like a fountain pen and *complicated* ones such as a combustion engine. Deterministic, generally applicable interventions can be used to solve problems in these two types of systems.

When dealing with a *chaotic* system, no generic intervention knowledge can be developed and validated. Experienced practitioners who are equipped with suitable tacit knowledge and sound intuitions must then tackle problems through trial and error.

In the social domain, systems are usually *complex*. Human behaviour is influenced by a dynamic cluster of weak mechanisms, loosely coupled connections, *strange attractors*[8] and the like, in which the relative importance of each of these factors can vary at different speeds over time, depending among other things on the – generally not static – context. As a result, in the case of complex systems, it is hardly possible to work with deterministic formulas or with linear protocol-like step-by-step schemes. Here iterative, recursive, circular, cumulative methods are required.

Therefore, an indication for the use of SoFAP-P is the desire and ability of a practitioner to intervene in a complex (social) system. For simple and complicated systems, SoFAP-P is over-dimensioned; for chaotic systems, the method is insufficient.

Furthermore, even in lapidary terms, an indication for a solution-focused intervention is of course the presence of a solution-focused practitioner, i.e. a professional who is well versed in the solution-focused way of thinking and working. This expertise allows the practitioner to translate, or more accurately, to help the client translate his problems into wishes for change that can be converted into challenges. To provide this help, there is no need for a cause-and-effect chain in which all the details are unambiguously delineated and can be remedied point by point.

More specifically, SoFAP-P is indicated, meaning useful, effective and efficient when the client:

- agrees to develop a working relationship with a solution-focused practitioner,
- is able and/or willing to formulate a goal,
- is open to acknowledging his own resources that can help him to obtain his goal, and
- is prepared to do the necessary work.

From a practical point of view, SoFAP-P is ideally suited for situations where time- and monetary resources are limited. After all, the solution-focused approach was originally designed to keep the suffering of the clients as short as possible and to help the clients obtain as swift and sustainable results as possible.

SoFAP-P assumes that working on wishes for change and challenges does not need to be connected to problems. The application of SoFAP-P works equally when dealing with problematic situations as with pure challenges, e.g. high potentials and clients who have personal, relational and/or work-related career problems and for whom growth as a person and progress in their well-being is desired. The indication also applies to doing systemic interventions that deal with relational structures and organizational issues that transcend the individuals involved.[9]

In short, the general indication for a SoFAP-P intervention transcends classical diagnostic classifications and overrides divisions in individual intervention models or schools.

4.2.2 Contra-indications

The solution-focused approach is no panacea that pretends to work anywhere, anytime and for everything. There are contra-indications or, more stringently speaking, situations in which it makes no sense to try solution-focused interventions like SoFAP-P that aspire to remedy the problematic or challenging basic condition the client is in.

1. The most general contra-indication is a client who is completely unable to either communicate or enter a constructive working relationship. Examples include persons so severely intoxicated that – temporarily – no connection is possible with them, persons in a florid psychotic state that totally engulfs them and patients who have lost the ability to be in the world, i.e. comatose, unconscious or in a state of mental and/or physical incapacity or disability that makes human connection (nearly) impossible.

    Yet, within the limits of these contraindications, the possibility for solution-focused interventions like SoFAP-P arises. As Chris Iveson[10] (2015) sharply states: *The 'rule of thumb' in Solution-focused practice is to ignore unusual or inexplicable behaviour (provided no risk of harm is involved) and carry on asking (solution-building) questions while listening for those answers (or fragments of answers) that can be built upon with further questions. This makes it perfectly possible to work successfully with clients under the influence of drugs or alcohol, who are psychotic (but still prepared to answer questions) or suffering physical conditions such as Alzheimer's Disease.*

2. A second major contra-indication is to be found in cases where the psychological, relational and communicative abilities are hampered by neurophysiological disturbances. In those cases, the priority lies with an intervention in the underlying substrate to rectify the underlying neurophysiological causality. A person, who unexpectedly starts acting out violently, may be the victim of a brain tumour. An elderly person with early signs of dementia (sudden and partial forgetfulness, an inexplicable emotional unbalance, acting out behaviour that does not fit with his normal behaviour repertoire ...) may suffer from pseudo-dementia which can cover a 'masked depression'. These patients need an intervention in the underlying causal problem first (removal of a tumour, antidepressants) and psychological assistance second.

3. Situations where it is simply not appropriate and even illegal to apply psychological interventions. When confronted with illegal acts, unethical behaviour that is hurtful and/or harmful to others or to oneself etc. In sum, contraindications that are stated in the deontological codes of the professional.

4.2.3 Pseudo-contra-indications

Some situations may initially appear to be contra-indications at first, until after careful consideration one discovers that there are opportunities to intervene. Some of these pseudo-contra-indications reflect misunderstandings that exist around the solution-focused approach. On the one hand, it is often thought and said that solution-focused practice is an exclusively verbal intervention (talk therapy) and therefore the client must be linguistically fluent, show adequate imagination and have verbal creativity. On the other hand, a misunderstanding about solution-focused interventions is that they require a minimum intelligence and a rationally emotionally balanced inner life as a common basis from which interventions can work. When these conditions are not met, using SoFAP-P seems impossible. Quod non. Some examples clarify this. When working with deeply mentally handicapped persons who have no access to verbal language, one can find out which non-verbal interventions make an impact. If you figure out what sounds, music, fabrics, cuddle toys give the best response, you can use those tools for the best possible results. Communication with deaf-mutes can be done by sign language. Communication with deaf-blind people can be done through touch. Persons with limited imagination skills and creativity require simple, straightforward language.

In conclusion, SoFAP-P helps to design interventions that go beyond the conventional division of indications and the associated dispute between (therapeutic or facilitative) schools.

In summary: The solution-focused applied psychology protocol approaches clients' problems as challenges that they can solve by using their own resources to achieve positive results towards their desired goals, independent of problem-focused indications and specific model-driven beliefs.

4.2.4 The SoFAP-P design up to specification

As mentioned earlier, it is our wish that the result of the design research is relevant from a practitioner's perspective. To achieve this, it was indicated beforehand (at the end of Section 2.3.2) that the final design must comply with the following four specifications:

1 *Practical relevance:* The protocol should be relevant for everyday practice in the field.
2 *Operational relevance:* Professionals must be able to actually apply the protocol in their practice.
3 *Non-obviousness:* This requirement means that if the design is seen as a recurrence of commonly known knowledge, the protocol is less likely to be adopted by practitioners.
4 *Appropriateness:* The approach should be up to date and relevant to contemporary real-life problems in the field.

These four specifications set the significance of the design. They are met with SoFAP-P in the following way.

Practical relevance

The insights, tools, best practices of SoFAP-P and its infinite combinations can be used in all professional domains where human actions, interactions, emotions create meaning. The content of what is at hand comes from the client, his situation, his goals and the corresponding challenges. SoFAP-P is a process-oriented protocol calibrated to the client's needs at that specific time and to the resources and possibilities available to the client. The three mandates (leadership, management and coaching and facilitation) leave room for the practitioner to add professional expertise to the intervention process. Doing this in the form of (suggestive) questions increases the likelihood that the client will add what is offered to his own existing toolkit.

Operational relevance

The CIMOs describe the interventions the practitioner can apply, while the flowchart facilitates the choice of the best possible strategies to support and facilitate the client to find practical ways of creating solutions for his challenges. SoFAP-P provides a validated design-science-based approach for the (beginning) practitioner to learn the different steps in an incremental, recursive and cumulative manner without being limited by a reductionist protocol. The seasoned practitioner will discover ways to co-create the most useful, i.e. effective and efficient, strategy by improvising on the general theme that the client brings forward in combination with the expert's deep knowledge of the professional field in which he operates.

Non-obviousness

SoFAP-P is not a linear, fixed-step-deterministic method but a fluent, ever-changing and adapting way of thinking and working based on sound and tested principles with proven effectiveness. Even if interventions might look like interventions employed in comparable situations, no two intervention processes are exactly the same. Human idiosyncrasy, serendipity, ever-changing contextual factors form waves on the Ocean of Life that, however similar to other waves, are never the same. Banal interventions, like: *It hurts here when I push, doctor, what do I need to do?* Doctor: *No longer push there*, are out of the question. True change facilitation requires creativity and flexibility from the part of the professional and the client, for the simple fact that they are in that co-creative process together.

Appropriateness

Heraclitus Ephesus (ca. 530–475 B.C.) taught us 'Πάντα ῥεῖ' (everything flows) or simply put the only thing that never changes is change itself. The same goes for all professional knowledge. What worked yesteryear might not work tomorrow. It is

FIGURE 4.4

therefore only obvious that a true professional must try to keep up with the evolution in his professional field and as much as possible with changes in the world in general. Circumstances that bring the client to the practitioner are subject to the same eternal flux and the practitioner can only be useful when he has his finger on the pulse of that change. Ideally, professionals working in the field of change facilitation should look over the horizon of the future to spot incoming changes as much as possible, in order to be as ready as possible for whatever comes their way.

We refer to the companion book, *Creating Sustainable Results with Solution-focused Applied Psychology: A Practical Guide for Coaches and Change Facilitators* (Routledge 2023), for an in-depth practical guide to facilitate adding the intricacies of solution-focused thinking and working to practitioners' existing expertise. Scanning the QR code above gives you access to a synopsis of the book.

Notes

1 The term *movement* is used here to suggest that the concepts we describe in this chapter are like a musical movement: fluid rather than static, ever-changing yet essentially the same, elusive yet well-defined, like reality.
2 When we use the term *client*, we always refer to *the client in his relevant context* and we do not refer to the internal psychological or intrapsychic mechanisms that are operational within the client himself. Moreover, the client can be an individual, a couple, family, team, organization as a whole, i.e. a client system.
3 See Section 2.1 *Extended-SFT*, Statement 7.
4 In Statement 4 of the Extended-SFT wave (see Section 2.1), the interaction between the parties – client and professional service provider – is likened to a dance with a limited number of steps that have unlimited combination possibilities. The seven steps are the components whereby each step in the dance is an *activity* to be performed together with the client. It starts with making contact (1), exploring the context (2), goal setting (3), uncovering resources (4), complimenting (5), offering differentiation (6) and future orientation (7).

5 See CIMO-19 in Section 3.3 on scaling questions.
6 By asking questions, you prime the notion that the client is central in the facilitation process, that he needs to work by answering those questions and that the practitioner's task is to facilitate the change process within the client and his system instead of coming up with ready-made solutions.
7 Merriam-Webster (2016) defines *consulting* as 'Providing professional or expert advice'. In WR3, the client consults the change agent for help to (re)access his resources that can be used to address his workable problems.
8 Unlike the randomness generated by a system with many variables, chaos has its own pattern, a peculiar kind of order. This pattern is known whimsically as a *strange attractor*, because the chaotic system seems to be strangely attracted to an ideal behaviour – Gary Taubes, *Discover*, May 1989 (Merriam-Webster, 2016).
9 Cauffman's (2022) book, *Developing and Sustaining a Successful Family Business, A Solution-Focused Guide*, is the first book to apply the solution-focused applied psychology approach to family businesses.
10 Founding member of BRIEF, an independent training, therapy and consultation agency in the practice of solution-focused brief therapy based in London, UK, in Burgstaller (ed.), 2015.

5
VALIDATING SoFAP-P

According to design science research (DSR) methodology, the first draft of the SoFAP-P design was improved in several iterative rounds by subjecting it to α- and β-testing. α-testing involves testing the design theoretically with practitioners, using interviews, simulation-based conversations and an opinion survey. Based on the evaluation of the α-testing, the design is then improved. β-testing involves the same process, but on the basis of a practical, real-life application of – a part or parts of – the design.

The final SoFAP-P design was presented in Chapter 4. The validating α- and β-tests are discussed in this chapter.

(For more background on α- and β-testing as a component of the DSR methodology, see Section 2.3.2).

5.1 Validating the building blocks of SoFAP-P, based on a survey among solution-focused practitioners (α-testing)

In order to validate the SoFAP-P design at the α-test level, in April and May 2022, an on-line opinion poll was released on the building blocks of the SoFAP-P design. The survey was conducted among practitioners and scientists who have both knowledge and experience related to problem-focused as well as solution-focused applied psychology. Respondents came from the network of both authors and were invited by them personally or through Louis Cauffman's newsletter for practitioners who took his training courses, master classes and seminars over the past decades.

All in all, each question was answered by an average of 73 respondents with the range going from 66 to 77.

The purpose of the opinion survey is to obtain quantitative information on the extent to which knowledgeable practitioners agree with the building blocks, used

DOI: 10.4324/9781003404477-5

to construct the SoFAP-P design: *points of attention, lessons learned, best and bad practices* and *CIMOs*.

The assumption in this indirect test of the design is that if the building blocks can rely on sufficient face validity from practitioners, the chances are that the structure created with these building blocks will thus provide sufficient confidence.

The different types of building blocks were offered interchangeably in the questionnaire in order to reduce the effect of a possible bias per type (questions with the same number but split into a, b, c etc. were held together).

A 5-point Likert scale (1932) was used for scoring, ranging from strongly disagree to strongly agree.

At the end of the survey, six questions were included about the effectiveness and efficiency of solution-focused working; the E-questions. These questions helped to answer support question 3, (see Section 2.3.1 for the question and Section 3.2 for the answer).

The on-line opinion survey was developed using Google Forms (see Appendix D for an example of a digital page in the Google Forms format) and contains 81 questions, also listed in Appendix D, with for each question the mean score, standard deviation and number of respondents.

The survey was open for five weeks and a reminder was sent after three weeks.

Respondents were asked to provide an email address if they would like to receive a PDF of the chapter presenting the survey results in due course.

INTRODUCTION TO THE QUESTIONNAIRE

Dear Colleagues,
Dear Solution-Focused Cognoscenti,

Anyone who has studied the work of Steve de Shazer knows that Steve was a researcher at heart.

Since his passing in 2005, many applications have been added to the rich solution-focused catalog.

However, a scientific foundation for the approach is lacking. As a result, solution-focused working threatens to remain limited to the domain of pure practice. This is of course fine, but this merely practice-oriented way of working means that many colleagues, especially academics, do not find their way to it, or only by accident, or worse: that the solution-focused approach runs aground on unfounded prejudices.

To change this situation, we are engaged in a study that explores a scientific foundation for the solution-focused approach. In doing so, we use the DSR methodology, a tool that has been tested and recognized in other fields of science.

> Today we kindly invite you to help make this research a success by completing the attached survey.
> We will be happy to send you a PDF with the results if you leave your email address at the end of the survey.
> Here is the link to the survey that contains all the questions:
> *(followed by an internet link)*
> Many thanks for filling out and helping us.
> In the name of the further emancipation of the solution-focused approach,
> Warm regards,
> Louis Cauffman & Mathieu Weggeman

Evaluation of survey results

The survey contains 81 questions of which 75 are about the building blocks and 6 about the presumed productivity of the solution-focused approach in casu about its effectiveness and efficiency; see Section 3.4.

All 75 building blocks of the SoFAP-P design can rely on sufficient face validity

This is the main conclusion of the α-test. All 75 building blocks score higher than 3.00 on the 5-point Likert scale used, of which 70 score higher than 3.50.[1] According to common practice, it was stated that if a building block would score higher than an average of 3.00 it would be considered to have sufficient face validity.

Furthermore the standard deviation[2] (σ) is < 1.00 for most building blocks. For 11 of the 75 statements, σ is slightly larger than 1: 6x < 1.10, 4x < 1.20 and 1x 1.60.

This concretely means that for each building block there are only a few respondents whose assessment of the content of the building block differs substantially from the average assessment. In other words, the low standard deviations obtained here mean the presence of a strong consensus on the content of each building block.

All CIMOs are equally relevant

CIMOs are the most specific and therefore the most influential building blocks for SoFAP-P. Because the frequency is known (see Appendix A) in which each CIMO occurs in the studied cases ex ante, the relationship can be determined between the CIMOs about which there is the most agreement and the frequency in which those CIMOs occur empirically. The assumption here is that the CIMOs about which there is the most agreement are also the ones most often found in practice.

The average agreement score of the seven CIMOs occurring 11–22 times in the 25 studied cases is 4.29 (this does include the two highest scoring CIMOs: CIMO-3 with $\bar{X} = 4.48$ and CIMO-8 with $\bar{X} = 4.46$).

The average score of the seven CIMOs in the middle group (occurring more than 3 and less than 9 times) is 4.16.

The seven CIMOs occurring in only one to three cases have an average agreement score of 4.17.

These results falsify an eventual assumption that the most commonly agreed CIMOs are also the ones that are most often encountered in practice. This is because the average agreement scores for high- and low-frequency CIMOs do not differ significantly. Ergo, each CIMO can be considered as important as a building block for the SoFAP-P design as any other CIMO. In other words, all CIMOs are equally relevant.

CIMO predicting the future task has been removed

From the cases presented in Section 3.3, originally a CIMO was derived that read as follows:

> *When a client cannot find anything positive, nor moments when things are a little better or different in his daily life, he may be able to find solutions by performing the task of predicting the future.*

During the pre-test of the questionnaire with some professionals in the field, it was found that this CIMO generated relatively much confusion. That confusion was caused in part by a lack of clarity about the difference of the CIMO compared to CIMO-21 and -22, which were judged to be less ambiguous. This may be because the *Predicting the future task*-CIMO gives the client an assignment, while CIMO-21 and -22 are about direct intervention by the practitioner.

CIMO-21: To help the client disengage from staying stuck in the past, ask questions that allow to 'retroject' possible solutions from the future into the reality of today.

CIMO-22: If a client is stuck in his problem-oriented worldview, a positive, imagined perspective might be suggested by asking the so-called miracle question. Suppose that, while you are sleeping, a miracle happens which solves all your problems (just enough so that they no longer bother you so much). How would you notice that it is as if a miracle happened for you?

Therefore, it was decided to drop the *Predicting the future* CIMO.

Noteworthy extremes

Regarding LL-11

Of the five items with $\bar{X} < 3.50$, three of them relate to Lesson Learned-11 (LL-11), divided into 11a, 11b and 11c where LL-11a and LL-11b also have an $\sigma > 1{,}00$: 1.14 and 1.13, respectively.

LL-11: There are three major tendencies that prevent clients from being open to a solution-focused applied psychology approach:

- LL-11a: no intrinsic motivation to change;
- LL-11b: 'resistance' to change;
- LL-11c: translating mental issues into physical problems.

Extra vigilance is therefore required in *Movement 2* of SoFAP-P when applying FQ-1, for LL-11 is one of the five building blocks on which question FQ-1 is based, (see Appendix C).

Regarding PA4-b and LL-12b3

The remaining two items with $\bar{X} < 3.50$ are PA-4b and LL-12b3.
PA-4b has a negligible deviation from the 3.50 criterion with a score of 3.43.
LL-12b3 scores $\bar{X} = 3.32$ and is one of four LL-12bs where the three others have an $\bar{X}$ of 3.97, 4.08 and 3.84.
PA-4: The causal linearity from *anamnesis* and *diagnosis* to *therapy* and *prognosis* obscures the complexity of each client's life, oversimplifies the situation that causes the problem and thereby reduces the opportunity for robust and sustainable solutions.

- PA-4a: obscures the complexity of each client's life;
- **PA-4b: oversimplifies the situation that causes the problem;**
- PA-4c: reduces the opportunity for robust and sustainable solutions.

LL-12b: Facilitation interventions that activate in an effective way the non-specific factors, mentioned in the previous question:

- LL-12b1: contains an emotional and confidential relationship with a person who is trying to help,
- LL-12b2: takes place in a setting in which the client believes that the help offered is professional,
- **LL-12b3: gives a credible explanation for the client's symptoms,** and
- LL-12b4: offers reliable procedures to cope with these symptoms.

Therefore, to avoid useless lapidary explanations that might have a perfume of quackery, it is best to refrain from offering such explanations, it is recommended that restraint be exercised in applying the reasoning mentioned in LL-12b3.

Regarding the four types building blocks

The 75 building blocks covered in the questionnaire consist of 10 points of attention, 31 lessons learned, 13 best and bad practices and 21 CIMOs. These four types of building blocks are, in that order, increasingly specific and therefore ever more influential on the design that is constructed with them.

It is also the order in which the building blocks were created: First came the points of attention and the lessons learned, which are primarily based on descriptions in the literature of schools and practices in psychology. Next came the best and bad practices and finally the CIMOs. These last two types of building blocks are based on empirical research that consisted of interviews with practitioners and the analysis of client cases.

What we see in the survey results is that the degree of agreement with the 75 presented statements in the survey, on average increases as they belong to a 'higher' type of building blocks:

- Points of attention: $\bar{X} = 3.73$
- Lessons learned: $\bar{X} = 4.05$
- Best and bad practices: $\bar{X} = 4.19$
- CIMOs: $\bar{X} = 4.21$

This fact justifies the assumption that as the knowledge of the researchers, necessary for designing the approach they have in mind, increases, so does the appreciation of the building blocks they created. Of course, this is not a startling conclusion, but it is nice to see that what we logically expect is actually confirmed by the data.

Outliers

Lesson Learned-12a3 has the highest agreement score of all 75 building blocks: $\bar{X} = 4.77$, and the second lowest standard deviation: $\sigma = 0.54$.

LL-12a3:
A non-specific factor that is common to all successful interventions:
I feel respected as a person

Best Practice-5c has the second highest agreement score of all 75 building blocks: $\bar{X} = 4.70$, and the third lowest standard deviation: $\sigma = 0.58$.

BP-5c:
Minimax Decision Rule 3:
If something works well, well enough, or better, keep doing it and/or do more of it.

Best Practice-5a has the third highest agreement score of all 75 building blocks: $\bar{X} = 4.69$, and the lowest standard deviation: $\sigma = 0.53$.

BP-5a:
Minimax Decision Rule 1:
If something still works, do not repair it but show respect and appreciation for what still works.

You could say that if you must make a very concise summary of no more than half an A4 sheet showing how to do SoFAP-P concretely, it must include LL-12a3, BP-5a and BP-5c.

104 Validating SoFAP-P

5.2 Validating the application of SoFAP-P based on cases ex post (β-testing)

For the β-test,[3] four ex post[4] cases have been used. After each case, the route followed by the practitioner is indicated with a red line in the relevant section of the SoFAP-P flowchart. The fact that this proved to be possible in a necessary and sufficient manner in each of the four ex post test cases provides a positively valued β-test result.

However, a note of relativization is in order: One must be aware that real-life situations do not follow the strict order indicated here by the red route line. Real life is 'messier': Steps and movements in the case can jump from movement to movement, sometimes back and sometimes parts of (sub)movement are skipped.

5.2.1 Case – Keep your friends close, and your contractors closer[5]

(Cauffman, 2007)

[M1-2] Bill, a facilities manager responsible for the coordination of technical building projects in an oil refinery, is constantly frustrated. He complains to his employees that the contractors, and particularly their respective subcontractors, are not keeping their promises. Consequently, the building projects are chronically behind schedule. From fear of losing face, he doesn't talk to his boss about these problems. The problem comes to a head when the work on a special production unit doesn't finish in time, causing the whole production line to be stopped with big financial losses consequently. At that point, Bill is put on the spot by the management. The production manager and the financial manager are furious. They order Bill into their office: 'What the %&$*!* is happening, Bill? You never tell us anything. We just have to guess how things are going in your part of the organisation. And now you shut down production without warning us. This can't go on any longer.' [M1-5/Manager] When Bill tries to defend himself by blaming the contractors, the management reminds him that he is the one who is paid to get things done on time. The management agrees to give him another chance. They appoint Bruce, an experienced project manager, as Bill's supervisor. 'You seem not to be able to get things straightened out on your own, Bill. You have been working hard in the past, that's why we aren't firing you on the spot. But our patience is wearing thin. We no longer accept that you keep us uninformed about progress. You accept help now or you are out.' It should be no surprise that Bill doesn't welcome this move from the management, but he has no choice but to accept. [M1-4]

In their first meeting, Bill tells Bruce: 'I don't see why my management is after me like that. I have been working extremely hard and have done everything possible. To me, the fact that they're forcing you upon me seems more like a punishment than support. Mind you, I have nothing against you — you are just following orders. I don't see what you can do for me unless you have a magic trick to make sure that the contractors get their work done on time.' [FQ-1/WR1]

Bruce is immediately aware that Bill is not asking for help on how he can proceed differently to appease the management and accepts that Bill is stuck in his focus on the unwilling contractors. This is clearly a non-committal relationship. Bruce realizes that entering a discussion is useless so, instead, he decides to give Bill the chance to vent some of his frustrations.

Bruce: 'OK, Bill, you and I are not going to change the world, let alone the contractor's behaviour. Why don't you first explain your viewpoint to me, then we can investigate how you can use your skills to improve your management of the situation.' [M1-1] →[M1-2]

    Bill relaxes a bit and, insisting that it wasn't his fault that the projects were behind schedule, he offers a litany of explanations and excuses. 'I have done everything in my power to make the contractors do their work on time. You surely agree that I can't go after them with an Uzi. Constantly yelling at them doesn't work either. That just invites them to make up even more lame excuses that would cause even more problems for our company. The contracts I give them are already as clear and as strict as legally possible. In this business, you have to understand, Bruce, that you need to give people some leeway, or you find nobody who is willing to accept the job. Whenever I finally contract a certain party that will do the job, I just don't have the time to sit down with them and talk it through with them. Once they take a job, the contractors are on their own — it is their responsibility to do a good job, not mine.'

Bruce: 'How do you communicate with your management during these processes?'
Bill: 'Are you kidding? I don't even have time to talk to the contractors, let alone time to talk to the management about how I proceed. I leave them alone and they leave me alone — everyone to their own work.'
Bruce: 'So, if I understand correctly, what you are telling me is that, once the contracts are drawn up, you have blind faith in the outcome.'
Bill: 'Well, basically that's it, yes. Isn't that normal? I mean, when I say that I will do something, I just do it. I don't see why my contractors shouldn't behave in the same way. And I totally do not see why my management wouldn't trust me on this. But apparently, they don't trust me or we wouldn't be talking now.'

    Bruce now goes for the second (appreciative) part of the intervention: 'There is a lot that is still going well, Bill, despite the problems. You have earned a good reputation within this company. Most of your projects are on time, even if it's often a close shave. The fact that your management is worried and sent me over to work with you intrinsically means that they don't want to lose you. Plus, amid storms, you have been able to maintain a positive attitude toward your contractors. However difficult your job is, you keep going at it.' [FQ-2/WR2]

    Feeling supported, Bill relaxes some more and becomes a little less defensive. Then Bruce goes for the third part of the intervention: 'What is it that you could do differently so that your management no longer feels that you and I need to talk about this?'

Bill: 'If I could get all my contractors to do as they promise, I wouldn't have to talk to anybody at all. But I guess that that's a fairy tale.'

Bruce: 'Correct, and fairy tales sometimes happen but it is best not to count on them happening. What about your management? What could you do differently, so that they would no longer be breathing down your neck?' [M1-5/Leader]→ [M1-5/Facilitator/Coach]

Bill: 'Well, maybe I should cover my back a little bit more. As it goes now, I only do my best to get the contractors aligned, but there will never be a full guarantee there. Up to now, I have only taken care of putting the entire project into the planning software so that the contractors have an overview. I will of course keep doing that but maybe it would be good if I gave more feedback to my management about what's going on in the process. [FQ-2/WR2] If things spin out of control, then they at least know this straight away. What do you think, Bruce?'

Bruce: 'Seems like a good idea. Any thoughts on how you could combine that with giving/getting more feedback to and from your contractors? It would be nice to kill two birds with one stone, don't you think?' [M3-2]

Bill: 'That would be perfect but how on earth could that be done?'

Bruce: 'It is obvious that you haven't much time, yet you will probably need to make some time to get more time. I know that your department is using planning software. Do you see any possibility of putting together reports from this software?'

Bill: 'Sure, whatever you put in can be shuffled into almost any report one can think of. Ah, it's dawning! Since I put every assignment into this planning software, I can easily create two different reports from it. One could serve as an implementation guide for the contractors and another could go to management so that they can follow what is happening.' [FQ-3/WR3]

Bruce: 'Excellent idea, Bill, excellent. Would it be feasible to take your idea one little step further? When you assign a contract, might it be a good idea to fix a meeting with the contractor and go through your implementation plan step by step? [M1-1] That way you can involve the contractor from the very beginning. The report of this meeting then can be sent to your management and at the same time it can be used as a continuation protocol.'

Bill: 'That's it. I can use that continuation protocol — must find a better name though — to satisfy my management, it keeps them in the loop. At the same time, it obliges me to talk more to the contractors. [M3-2] Although I have little time, this will save me a lot of time in the long run. You know, Bruce, this brainstorm is really useful to me. And to the company. [M3-1]

Bruce: 'Congrats. Go for it.' [M3-3]

The result of this intervention is that Bill finds a different way to deal with his own management and that he develops an alternative method for dealing with the contractors. [FQ-4/WR4]

Validating SoFAP-P **107**

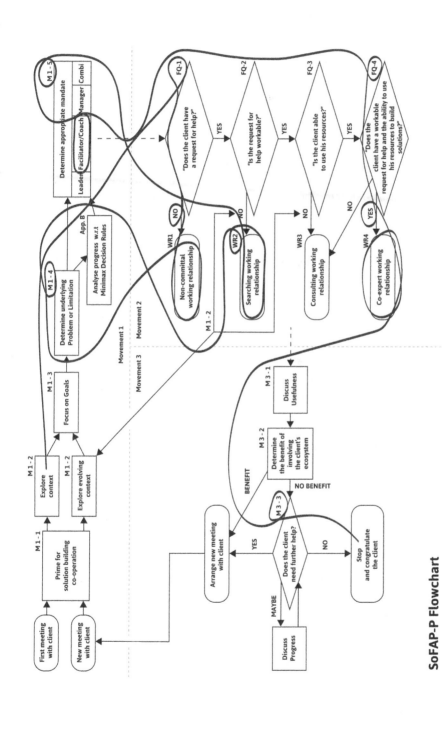

SoFAP-P Flowchart

FIGURE 5.1 Case – Keep your friend close and your contracters closer

5.2.2 Case – The Italian way

(Cauffman, 2007)

Roberta is a successful commercial manager working for a large American multinational company based in Detroit. She works from her office at home in Rome and is responsible for sales for a large part of Europe. [M1-2] She regularly gets into trouble because she has made agreements with some of her customers that were out of line with the general directives, especially on payment terms. Headquarters now insist that she follow the international guidelines on the collection of accounts receivable. The Detroit office has repeatedly told her that they would accept exceptions to those guidelines only after they had been consulted. Ensconced behind her desk and far from the main office, Roberta thinks this is nonsense. She is convinced that the people from headquarters have no idea how the European market, and especially the Italian market, functions. How on earth can she get the Italian customers to pay faster? She would lose the account! Moreover, her customers always pay their bills in the end, and she makes sure that the payments are protected by letters of credit. 'So what's the problem in Detroit?' Knowing that she represents a large European turnover for the company, she feels rather at ease: 'They won't come after me when I ignore their stupid headquarter inflexibility.' [FQ-1/WR1] Unfortunately, her director loses his patience. When Roberta again allows a customer to pay much later, he sends her a registered letter with the message that this is the last warning: 'One more transgression and you will be fired on the spot.' [M1-5/ Leader] Such a formal warning is the last thing Roberta expects. Promptly Roberta calls Tom, the HR director and an old friend, for help: 'Tom, could you help me, and try to explain to my director that the people in headquarters need to be more understanding about the different market situation in Europe and especially in Italy. It is absurd that I'm having this problem with HQ, because I do my best to sell as much as possible. They must acknowledge that I can only keep most of the Italian accounts because I give in to them over the payment issue.' At this point, Roberta has no request for help which puts her in a non-committal working relationship with the company. [WR1]

After consulting with the director, the HR director gives Roberta some bad news: 'Your director tells me that he really appreciates your work. You bring in a lot of revenue. But he is furious and fed up with the way you handle certain things, especially the way you keep overruling the policy on accounts receivable. HQ insists that you follow corporate directives. They urge you to stop making promises to your clients that you cannot keep, because they are against the international regulations. You have to stick to the corporate policy, end of story.' The leadership of the company made it clear that the corporate policy is a limitation with which Roberta will have to deal. [M1-4]

That message sends Roberta off the rails. For two weeks, she feels very insecure and is afraid when the phone rings in case it is one of her 'unauthorized' customers. She considers sending in her resignation but decides that she loves the job; plus, as a single mother, giving up her job is not really possible. She is afraid to call some of her clients so she busies herself with a backlog of administration. After two weeks, she realizes that this can't go on forever and, in desperation, she contacts Tom again: 'Tom, I need your help. I'm in a mess. I've been trying to find another way to work, but I just don't know. Most of my clients are too used to my granting their wishes, I don't know what to do. Maybe I just have to throw in the towel and leave the company.'

The HR director proposes a videoconference with her so they can look for a way out. It is clear to Tom that Roberta is in a searching working relationship: She has a strong demand for help but her goals are unworkable. [FQ-2/WR2] The more she looks for a solution, the more she becomes stuck. During the first videoconference, the HR director brings up every positive aspect of Roberta's work, talks about her successful track record in the company and tells her that the company really is not out to get rid of her, far from it. Tom also stresses the fact that she has to find a way to get her 'unauthorized' customers to accept the company rules on payments. He allows Roberta to vent her ideas and troubles and then asks her the following question: 'Where are you on a scale from zero to ten, where zero stands for "not having any hope at all for finding a solution to your problems" and ten stands for "having enough hope of solving the problem"?' Roberta answers: 'A big fat zero'. [M1-5/Facilitator/Coach]

Tom:	'OK Roberta, what would be the smallest thing that has to change to get you to a one?'
Roberta:	'To start again with full confidence instead of hiding behind my desk and hoping that particular clients don't call.'
Tom:	'Great, Roberta. That is a lot, maybe even too much. What else?'
Roberta:	'You ask difficult questions. I don't know. Maybe I need to take another look at my travel schedule and call some clients — but only those who I know for sure are already following our standard payment requirements.'
Tom:	'Wonderful, Roberta. If you did that, where would you then be on a scale from zero to ten?'
Roberta:	'Hmm. Maybe on a two but I don't know if I would get into trouble again. Sooner or later the unauthorized clients will call again, and I need them because they represent almost a third of my turnover.'
Tom:	'No problem, Roberta, take it easy. You don't need to address everything at the same time.'

Then he gives Roberta the following assignment: 'I would like to ask you to take time between today and our next meeting to look at each workday the night before and predict where you will be on this scale from zero to ten. Write that number down. The following evening you give yourself a number on that same scale that reflects how the day went. See if there is any difference between the number you predicted and the number you write at the end of the day. Also, jot down the things that you think are relevant in this respect. In three weeks, we will discuss this when I am in Italy. Good luck!'

Now that is a fairly vague assignment. The only goal is that there is a chance that it will help Roberta to look for changes in her behaviour as she predicts different numbers. Maybe this will help her to broaden her attention to other things than just the one problem she is stuck with.

When after three weeks, they meet in Rome, Roberta is happy to tell her HR director that she feels a lot better. 'After our call,' she says, 'I summed up all my courage and went to work full speed. I called almost all my "unspoiled" customers and I even made myself call prospective clients. It helped a lot [FQ-4/WR4] By the way, I hope you won't mind that I did not do your assignment.'

In the last three weeks, she has made a good number of sales, all with the standard payment requirements. On top of this, she has also drawn up a proposal for the main office. The title alone is very promising: 'Changes for the Improvement of our Client Relationship.' In this proposal, she has done a detailed and step-by-step analysis on how she will prepare for negotiations with each client in order to get them to pay according to the international guidelines. She clearly states that she will do her best to 'sell' this to her 'unauthorized' clients on the condition that the main office gives her a transition period. She also indicates the length of that transition period for each client. 'That's all I can do,' Roberta tells Tom. 'Now it is up to the main office. If I lose turnover because of this, they have to guarantee that they won't blame me.'

Tom compliments Roberta on her flexible attitude and creativity and promises her that he will do everything he can to support her proposal. He again asks Roberta the scale for hope. She is now at a five.

Some weeks pass. The main office studies her proposal, changes a few minor things and approves. The director sends a fax to Roberta stating that he appreciates her attitude and that he will take responsibility for any lost clients. Roberta is now in a co-expert working relationship vis-à-vis the company.

In retrospect, three months later, only a few clients have been negative about Roberta's new approach, but even those clients appreciated the transition period. One client wrote to Roberta to say that he found it difficult to accept the changes but that he appreciated not being presented with a fait accompli, which would have prompted him to pull out. Of course, some clients are still making special requests, but Roberta is now able to consult with the main office about this in an open way. She is certain to get permission for flexibility in some cases and the main office is confident that they remain in control.

This intervention was designed in such a way that Roberta could learn not to fight a losing battle against company policy – she instead figured out a way to take the corporate rules into account without letting her clients down. [M3-3/Stop] The company learned that it is commercially useful to apply strict rules in a flexible way.

Validating SoFAP-P **111**

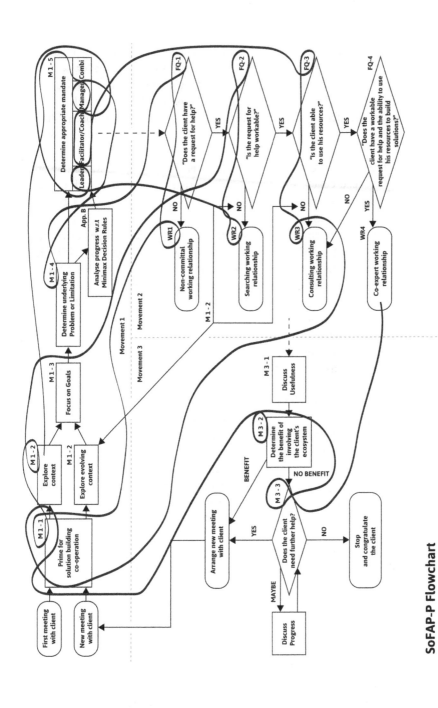

SoFAP-P Flowchart

FIGURE 5.2 Case – The Italian way

5.2.3 Case – The devil is in the details

(based on two cases in Cauffman, 2007)

Bill works as head of a project management team in a bank. He is highly regarded by his colleagues and directors for his excellent work. [M1-2] However, when it comes to coaching his team, he has the feeling that he functions below par. He asks the HR department to help him with this. Denise is assigned to work with him on this topic. She is an expert in coaching individuals. [M1-5/Facilitator/Coach] She is briefed on Bill's status of a high potential in the company, so she knows the context of her session.

Denise calls Bill to make the first appointment and asks what he wants to work on. As an experienced coach, she immediately starts [M1-5/Leader] with a goal-setting question during the phone call. [M1-3]

Bill: 'When coaching my project managers through projects, especially when the going gets tough, I tend to get too involved and lose myself in details. Under time pressure it's very hard for me to refrain from taking over. In high-pressure situations, I simply don't feel confident enough to let them do it all by themselves and I take over and do the job myself. I lose a lot of time and energy by doing this. Plus, I realize that I don't give my colleagues the opportunity to prove to me that they can do it themselves. I know that they are able to do it themselves. They have proved that many times when I am not around. I realize my behaviour is counterproductive. I want to learn to control myself so that I no longer allow myself to fall into this trap.'

Denise: 'Very good, Bill. That is a clear goal you have there. [FQ-2/WR2] Can I ask you to make a little preparation for our meeting? That way we will be able to proceed fast.'

Bill: 'Sure. I expected something like that.'

Denise: 'I would like you to prepare an exhaustive list of what you think you are already doing well. Add to that, what you see your team is doing well. Just take a few minutes a day and jot down what comes to mind. We will meet soon.' [M1-1]

Bill says he will be happy to do this. In their first session, they go over this list together. It is clear to Denise that Bill and his team have a lot of resources and tools available. [FQ-3/WR3]

She compliments him on this and asks: 'What do you think that your colleagues would put on this list if we asked them?'

Bill answers that they would put pretty much the same things on the list as he has done.

Denise: 'Great. Now, Bill, let's find out what you think are your weaker points as a manager. If I were to ask your colleagues this, what would they say?'

Bill: 'They would say that I tend to panic when I think there is a risk of the timing of a project getting out of control. Some of them would say that I should refrain from taking over their work when this happens. I think they're right; I do get very nervous sometimes and then I start doing their work myself.'

Denise decides to ask for exceptions: 'Bill, do you remember moments or situations when you were able to control your tendency to interfere?'

Bill: 'Yes and no. Last week I learned something. We were in the last phase of the implementation project for the new resource-planning software. It was a complicated project for the bank. It was a thrill because at two o'clock in the morning we had to go offline for thirty minutes. All data communication had to be stopped in order to load the new software and transfer the old data across. Then our servers needed re-booting. Wow, it felt like doing a heart transplant. Anyhow, around one-thirty, it hit me again. I started running around, making hectic phone calls and demanding an update every five seconds. Suddenly, Peter, who is normally the calmest person in the world, exploded: 'You %&$*!* controlling %&$*!*, stop it. You are doing it again. Get out of here and let us do our job.' Well, I can assure you that came as a shock. It felt like a slap in the face. I could understand Peter's point so I withdrew and let them get on with the proceedings. All went smoothly.'

Denise: 'Wow, what a story! Now that's interesting. So, Bill, with a little help from your friends (laughs), you can do it. What did you learn from this so that you can use it in the future?' [FQ-3/WR3]

Bill: 'I can hardly expect to have Peter around to yell at me all the time (laughs). You know what, it sounds like a crazy idea but I'm going to put a little elastic band around my wrist and every time I feel the urge to take over, I will let it snap into my arm. That sounds stupid, doesn't it?'

Denise: 'Not at all, Bill. It sure is a lot better than slapping yourself in the face (both laugh). What would you answer if I asked the miracle question?'

Bill is familiar with the miracle question technique. He smiles and says: 'If a miracle happened, I would be able to say to myself in the morning, without snap or slap (laughs), "Bill, today you will take care not to step into your little pitfall." In the coming project meeting, I would be able to refrain from asking questions all the time. Instead, I would feel confident, I would sit back and just listen to my team. I would just ask them if I could do anything to help, that's it.' [FQ-4/WR4]

Denise: 'Wonderful, Bill, now that would be a real miracle. But miracles happen every now and then. (Both laugh.) I would like to ask you to do a strange thing. For the coming weeks, I would like you to pretend in the first hour of your working day that the miracle really has happened. Then see what it is that you are doing differently. Observe how your colleagues react differently. I wonder what difference that will make for you. Are you prepared to give this a try?

Bill: 'Sure. I wonder what will happen if I try this out.'
Denise: 'Is this useful to you what we've discussed so far?' [M3-2]
Bill: 'Sure, very useful. Thank you.'

Denise: 'When do you think we should have our next meeting?'
Bill: 'Give me three weeks. I have lots of work to do plus I really want time to experiment with this assignment.'

In the next meeting, Bill takes the lead: 'You remember that you asked me to act as if that miracle really happened? Well, I didn't do that. And I didn't use that stupid elastic band either. I just kept telling myself that it was all too normal that someone in my position occasionally feels insecure, especially when the going gets tough. Nothing wrong with that, is it?'

Denise: 'Nothing at all, Bill. On the contrary, it keeps you focused. Go on.'
Bill: 'What helped me most was the fact that during the last few weeks I seem to have succeeded in just listening to my team instead of constantly being afraid that things might go wrong.'
Denise: 'How did you do that?'
Bill: 'I designed a little scale which I use a lot. It works perfectly.'
Denise: 'Now you've got me curious, Bill. Tell me about it. I think I'm going to learn something here.'
Bill: 'In the beginning of every project meeting I ask the team to choose a number between zero and ten where zero stands for 'we have no hope whatsoever that this project can possibly be done on time' and ten stands for 'we have a firm belief that this project will be on time'. [M3-2] If, during the start-up phase of a new project, their answer is zero, that means that they are convinced that they are heading for a failure and that we'd better cancel, postpone or redesign such a project. Luckily, I haven't been given a zero so far. Whatever other number they choose, e.g. a four, I accept it and ask them to explain what it is that they're already doing to get to that four. By doing this I force myself to just listen to them and they are invited to give me all the information that they've got on the project. After that, I ask them what needs to be done differently to get to a five. This helps them to work in small steps while it gives them confidence that they are in charge. I learned that is important to talk about small steps and not about giant leaps. Giant leaps got humankind to the moon, but small steps got the rocket going. (Laughs.) It's very strange, you know, but this little scaling technique helps me to keep an overview on things without urging me to ask for details. I think my team likes this method also because I noticed that they started using similar scaling techniques amongst themselves.'
Denise: 'Congratulations, Bill. I am convinced that if you keep this up, you will gradually grow more and more confident.'

Denise is very happy to see that Bill evolved into the co-expert position [WR-4], and on top of that the team took the same position by using the scaling technique themselves. That provided a good opportunity to stop supervising and limit his intervention to just encouraging the do-more-of-the-same approach. [M3-3]

Validating SoFAP-P 115

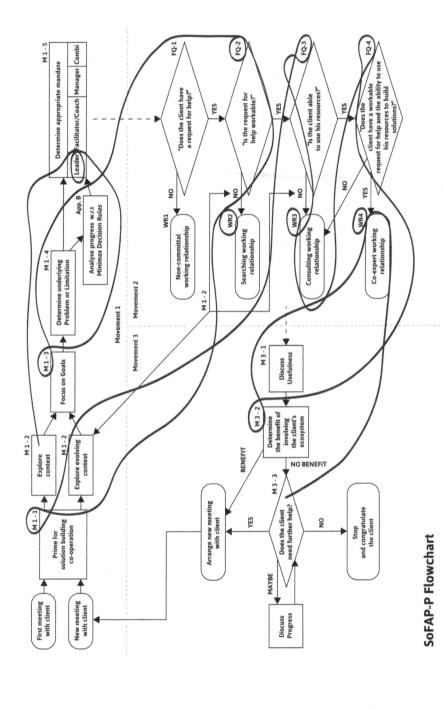

SoFAP-P Flowchart

FIGURE 5.3 Case – The devil is in the detail

5.2.4 Case – Miles & Son Inc.

(Cauffman, 2006)

Miles & Son Inc. is a family business that specializes in developing and manufacturing packaging solutions for the pharmaceutical industry. This company is one of those 'hidden champions,' extremely successful yet unknown to the general public. Mr. Miles (59) is the founder of the company and chairman of the board. Mr. Miles is half inventor and half businessman. His business acumen, combined with some inventions that he has patented, has been the basis for the corporate growth story. His only son, Stephan Miles (32), is working for the company. Stephan's job is not clearly defined. He is seen as his father's son and aide. Although Stephan's business card states that he is a marketing director, he is all over the place like a butterfly. As happens frequently in closely held family businesses, there is a great-looking organizational chart, yet the roles and mandates of top management are not clearly defined. The emphasis lies on how the business runs, not on how it should be run. The working relationship between father and son has always been good to great, even if Mr. Miles senior keeps a tight rein on things. [M1-2]

Lately, Mr. Miles senior has experienced serious health problems and consequently has been in and out of the office over the past six months. During that time, his son Stephan stepped up as CEO. He has made a few small, significant changes in the way the business is run, especially on the organizational side.

Once recovered and working again full time, a friction develops between Mr. Miles and his son. It started out small, with Mr. Miles senior expressing his amazement about things that, during his absence, had been changed within the company. On certain topics, this grew into bewilderment. Stephan was not amused by the fact that his father shared his bewilderment openly with the board of directors. Mr. Miles was happy that the business was run well during his absence, but he was less happy with the changes that Stephan had introduced, especially since Stephan had not informed him about these changes. Stephan, on the other hand, felt that as an acting CEO (and CEO in waiting) it had been his responsibility.

A serious brawl erupted between them when, unannounced and in the middle of a board meeting, his father bluntly cancelled a fact-finding trip to China that Stephan organized. Stephan reacted furiously. The board members were flabbergasted by this extreme falling out between the two, an open hostility that had never occurred before. In the following days, both sides avoided each other completely, and this avoidance then continued for weeks. Mr. Miles and Stephan went on giving instructions without consulting with each other. Soon the personnel received contradictory orders and felt like they were being used as pawns in the struggle between Mr. Miles and Stephan.

How should this problem be approached? Studying the history of the conflict and analysing the reasons behind their conflict would probably lead to more arguments and more conflicts.

Another approach might be to encourage Mr. Miles and Stephan to 'express openly' what they feel and think about each other – but then you run the risk that they hurt each other even more.

Some might even think that discussing the psychology of the father-son relationship will do the job, but there again you risk making their problem even more personal.

In contrast, the solution-focused applied psychology (SoFAP) approach is very utilitarian – our aim is to help both parties cooperate again, like they always have been cooperating, and preferably to do this in the swiftest way possible. In other words, to help them help themselves.

Mr. Miles was convinced that Stephan had seized the opportunity to take charge of the company. The son believed that it was his duty to keep the business running, and that he had earned the right to continue managing the company in the same way as he had done during his father's absence.

They had already tried to convince one another of the correctness of their own position by rational arguments. [FQ-1/WR1] This only led to a harshening of their conflict. Soon they were simply blaming each other in front of the other members of their management team. They asked staff to give their opinion, but nobody dared to take a clear stance for the simple reason that both the father and the son were very successful in running the business. The staff members were caught in their loyalty towards both men. Plus, staff members realized that whatever they said, they would run the risk of getting trapped in the conflict.

After some months of growing tensions, John, the technical director who had been working for the Miles family business for over two decades, could no longer stand it. During a meeting in which the same old disagreements paralysed the discussion yet again, John could no longer refrain himself and blurts out: 'Excuse my bold language, gentlemen, but you are messing up this company with your personal conflicts. You simply paralyze the company. If you don't stop this, this company is going to grind to a halt and we'll never get it going again. Please, shape up!' [M1-5/Leader]

Everybody in the meeting, and especially Mr. Miles senior and Stephan, are startled. Nobody expects this kind of language from the usually silent John. Mr. Miles senior feels the urge to take over as big boss yet he refrains from doing this. In a split second, he realizes that John is correct. The same goes for Stephan. John's outburst is a wake-up call for the both.

John tells everybody that it would be inappropriate to continue the meeting: 'I do apologize for my outburst. But hey, I am one of the veterans of this company and I know that both of you are very concerned with what's best for the company. I share that concern, as do all of us around this table. If you agree, I would like to have a private talk with the both of you. Let's see how you can solve this.' [M1-5/Leader]→[M1-5/Facilitator/Coach]

Before Mr. Miles senior and Stephan can answer, the other participants stand up and swiftly leave the room. Both Mr. Miles senior and Stephan agree with John that it is necessary to let things cool down a bit. They agree to meet again the next day.

118 Validating SoFAP-P

That evening, John ponders on how to tackle the next meeting. Thoughts like: 'Why did I have to stir up the hornets' nest' cross his mind. John is aware that, to avoid getting trapped in a pure rational discussion with the same old arguments, he needs a different approach. It dawns upon him that asking lots of questions might work best. [M1-1]

At the same time in their respective homes, father and son are also thinking about the next meeting. They both are aware that doing more of the same, arguing and analysing the other's behaviour, will be of no help.

Next day, at ten o'clock in the meeting room, Mr. Miles opens the meeting by thanking John for the wake-up call: 'I am so glad that you spoke your mind, John. This disagreement between me and my son has been going on for too long now.'

John:	'OK, I have been thinking about how you could tackle this problem. [M1-1] In the past twenty-two years that I have had the honor of working here, it has always been very clear to me that the Miles family is crucial for this company. The same goes for your cooperation at the top, Mr. Miles and Stephan. It has never been a problem, on the contrary, your cooperation has propelled this company towards its success. Now, if my words in the meeting yesterday were a little harsh, I apologize for this. Yet I could no longer stand to see how both of you are suffering because of the tension and how this tension threatens to spread throughout the business. I am certain that this situation is something that the both of you never had in mind but that you just got caught up in it. I am sure that you both prepared for this meeting. But, if you agree, I would like to start out with something completely different.' [M1-5/Leader]→[M1-5/Facilitator/Coach]
Both:	'Go ahead, John.'
John:	'Instead of remaining focused on the negative, I would like to invite you to look at more positive aspects. What are the things that — despite the tension that has arisen between the two of you — still function well in the company?'
Mr. Miles:	'Well, that's an open book, John. You know perfectly well what works well in our company. But I understand the reason behind your question. Actually, this would be a good question to ask every employee. It would turn their heads away from complaining about everything that goes wrong towards more positive insights. For now, I can list many things but maybe the

Validating SoFAP-P 119

	most important issue here is the cooperative style of the business.'
Stephan:	'I agree with my father, although it sounds a little silly coming from the two people in the company that lately have not been cooperating.' (All laugh)
John:	'I'm glad that you have kept your sense of humor, Stephan. Now, what is it that we should talk about so that this meeting will be useful?' [M1-3]
Stephan:	'I would like to get some clarity about what is going on between my father and me.'
Mr. Miles:	'I would like to find order and peace again between us so that we can pick up our cooperation where we left it a few months ago.'
John:	'What would be the smallest sign that your relationship has improved and that you are making little steps towards cooperating again?'
Mr. Miles's answer is quick:	'My son has to stop shutting me out.' [FQ-1/WR1]
	When John asks the same question to Stephan, he says: 'Dad has to stop interfering with my work and leave me alone.'
	These answers are not very useful. They both answer with what the other should do differently and John realizes that this isn't going to help to make some progress. Of course, John is not going to give up easily and so he continues his line of questioning. [M1-5/Leader]
John:	'Let me ask you again. What are **you** going to do differently to make things easier? And by 'you', I mean each of you. So would you please be so kind as to talk about yourself.' [M1-5/Facilitator/Coach]
Mr. Miles:	'What I could do differently to make things easier? Well, we sure can't go on this way. I will try to be friendly to Stephan but I'm not going to butter him up.'
John:	'Fine, Mr. Miles. How about you, Stephan? What would you be prepared to do differently to make things better?'
Stephan answers:	'I could invite my father to join the meetings of the steering committee that I've organised. But only if he promises not to snap at me during the meeting.'
	Nothing is solved here, but it's a start. [M1-1]
	Feeling that these answers open possibilities, John proceeds: 'When you think about the last few months, have there been any instances — however small — when there was a little less tension between you? And what did you do differently then?'

Stephan:	'Sure. I remember. The week before our falling out concerning the China trip, we were in a meeting together with some clients. The clients were complaining about our announced price raise. It was very nice to hear my father backing me up totally when I explained the reason for the raise. That support was very welcome and it made me feel good.'
Mr. Miles:	'Yes, I remember that meeting too. I was glad to be invited. It was the first time that I got to meet one of our main clients again after my sick leave. Stephan told the clients that he and the rest of the company were very glad that I was back. It was the first time that I felt welcome again in my own company.'
John:	'Great. Are there other moments that you can recall when things went OK between the two of you?' Mr. Miles and Stephan continue to talk about other examples and the tension between them slowly abides. John compliments them on the many examples of exceptions to their problem. [FQ-3/WR3]
John:	'So if I understand you correctly, what you are saying is that whenever you cooperate, you notice that this eases your tension. What do you need to be able to act more and more cooperatively again?' [M1-5, Facilitator/Coach]
Stephan replies directly to his father:	'I would need to feel more at ease and not be so on edge when you are around.'
Mr. Miles answers:	'For me, the smallest sign of betterment would be that you stop avoiding me.' As the conversation progresses, both men become more willing to change their attitude towards each other.
John:	'What are the things that you can do in the next days and weeks so that you know you will make further progress?' [FQ-3/WR3] Mr. Miles agrees to try to act positively toward his son. He translates this into being more friendly, inviting him again for the family's traditional Sunday aperitif, and agreeing with him in the presence of their employees (or remaining silent if he doesn't agree).
Mr. Miles:	'I know I am not good at this, never have been and probably never will be. But I will try to do my best to say something positive when you do something well, Stephan.'

Validating SoFAP-P **121**

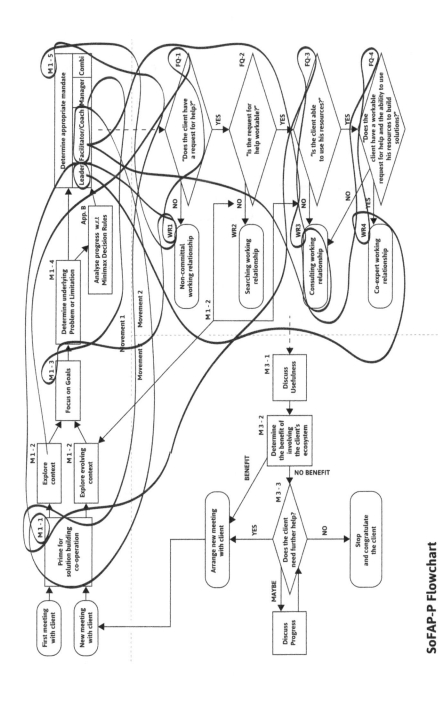

SoFAP-P Flowchart

FIGURE 5.4 Case – Miles & Son Inc.

Stephan says he will inform his father weekly about all matters concerning production and sales figures.

John ends the meeting by complimenting the two of them and wishing them good luck. In the weeks after this conversation, all parties concerned notice an improvement in the relationship between Mr. Miles and his son, much to the relief of everybody in the company. [FQ-4/WR4]

Mrs. Miles discreetly sends John a case of champagne. [M1-5/Leader] [M3-2]

5.3 Conclusions

In summary, the final version of SoFAP-P (presented in Section 4.1) passed the α- and β-test successfully. We are talking about *the final version* here because – as usual in DSR – the design was iteratively improved based on interim test results.

The indications and contraindications for SoFAP-P (given in Section 4.2) have also been completed based on interim test results.

The α-test (Section 5.1) shows that all-minus-one building blocks with which SoFAP-P is 'built' are relevant. The β-test indicates that with the help of the flowchart – in which SoFAP-P is maximally explicated – it can be reconstructed in an exhaustive way which route practitioners have taken in various real live cases. This stimulates confidence in the productivity (= effectiveness × efficiency) of SoFAP-P in ex post cases.

Notes

1 For all quantitative outcomes mentioned in this section, see also Appendix D.
2 Remember: the standard deviation (or σ) is a measure of how dispersed the data is in relation to the mean. Low standard deviation means data are clustered around the mean, and high standard deviation indicates data that are more spread out. Example: a student has taken three exams that were graded with a 5, a 6 and a 7. The average exam grade is then 6.00 and has a relatively small standard deviation: $\sigma = 0.82$. If the student had scored a 4, a 6 and an 8 for the three exams, the average exam mark would also have been 6.00, but the standard deviation would be relatively high: $\sigma = 1.63$.
3 See for further explanation, *α- and β-testing* in Section 2.3.2.
4 Ex post cases are cases that are used to test (parts of) the protocol, i.e. after the design has been made. Ex ante cases are cases from which lessons are drawn for the benefit of the design of the protocol (which is not yet available at that stage of development of the design).
5 This case was also used for the empirical grounding of the SoFAP-P design in that it is one of the 25 cases in Appendix A from which the set of 21 CIMOs used to create SoFAP-P was derived (see Section 3.3).

Here the *Keep your friends close, and your contractors closer* case is used again to β-test the protocol developed. In this way, one could say that this case acts as a kind of *linking-pin* between the cases ex ante and ex post.

6
EVALUATION OF SoFAP-P AND A GLANCE INTO THE FUTURE

In addition to suggestions for further research, this chapter highlights the contributions of the SoFAP-P design to practice and society. The chapter concludes with desired future developments in solution-focused applied psychology if this approach is to continue to expand its influence.

6.1 Suggestions for further research

6.1.1 Specifying in detail the mechanisms (the M's) in the CIMOs

As noted in Section 3.3, the CIMOs distilled from the 25 practitioner experience cases (see Appendix A) are mainly defined in terms of context, intervention and expected result (output). In most cases, less attention was paid to the wording of the mechanism by which the intervention works. This limitation is the reason for formulating a suggestion for further literature research and eventual explanatory (hypothesis testing) research to fill this gap.

6.1.2 Field testing of SoFAP-P with trained practitioners

Field testing of a design requires, among other things, transferring the design to practitioners and training them in its use. Next, the productivity of the application of the design, in this case solution-focused applied psychology protocol (SoFAP-P), is comparatively examined. Here, *productivity* is seen metaphorically as the product of the *effectiveness* of the results achieved and the *efficiency* of the intervention process (Stack, 2016). Subsequently, based on evaluation interviews and *after-action* reviews with the trained practitioners, improvements can be made to SoFAP-P. Depending on the available resources, this process of *training-application-evaluation*

DOI: 10.4324/9781003404477-6

can go through several iterations, thereby constantly increasing the validity of the design. Such a validation can take place in parallel and analogously at a lower aggregation level, namely that of the building blocks of the design, in particular the CIMOs. This can lead to a sharpening and fine-tuning of the mechanisms indicated per CIMO.

The suggestion for extended β-testing outlined here can potentially lead to the claim that SoFAP-P should be considered an evidence-based design. After all, *Evidence-Based Practice* does not require proof, but evidence.

6.2   Contribution of SoFAP-P to practice and society

Three steps back to jump further

Steve de Shazer always posited that solution-focused working should operate in stealth so that the client can unknowingly benefit from the solution-focused thinking that works as a creator of an alternative reality without having to be aware of it. Change then 'just happens' and it is the practitioner's job to help the client assume responsibility for the beneficial changes. The solution-focused way of thinking and working, its epistemology, then becomes embedded in the fabric of how the world is perceived, understood, and alternatively created.

Step 1: Same operating system, different apps

After the initial successful spread of the model, a lot was written about the future of the solution-focused approach and practice. This body of literature mainly stems from the 2010s and concerns itself with applications for different problems and in different fields of, mainly, the mental health professions.

This literature expands in two main directions. One is on the content. We saw scores of publications on 'how to apply SFT when dealing with' autism, OCD, addiction, depression, anxiety, and most of the diagnostic criteria from the DSM-V.

The other direction concentrates on different working fields and explains on 'how to apply SFT' in psychotherapy, social work, in-patient settings, nursing, physiotherapy, coaching, management, family business, and many other fields.

Although highly practical and therefore relevant to practice, this literature does not really contribute to the innovation or novelty of the solution-focused approach, as it is limited to putting into practice the solution-focused epistemology already available at the time. In summary: Same operating system, different apps.

Step 2: Same operating system, tailored apps

Outcome research dominates therapeutic fields, both in medicine and in mental health practices. The ideal here is the evidence-based model (EBM) that strives to find 'final' scientific solutions that understand, explain, and predict the outcome of interventions with the same scientific clarity as processes can be understood, explained, and predicted in physics or chemistry. The EBM research has helped solution-focused applied psychology to find its niche in the plenitude of models with proven efficacy (McDonald, 2011). This gave SFT its well-deserved place amongst the traditional treatment models.

Modern research has however put a damper on the blinding enthusiasm for EBM, for the simple reason that research dis- (or was it more un-) covered the given that EBM is about average clients with average problems that receive average therapeutic interventions. Considering the most recent developments in medical biotechnology where therapies are used that are designed to fit this individual patient with this individual problem that is treated with this individualized therapeutic intervention, EBM lost some of its luster. Even with its limitations, EBM is a far better tool to discern intervention models than the pigeon-hole approach of the old days when adherence to a model (and the accompanying reward of belonging to a club) prevailed over objectivity. To summarize: same operating system, tailored apps.

Step 3: Coat of many colours

SoFAP-P expands its scope by incorporating insights, knowledge and practical consequences from other fields. Sources of inspiration are the science of well-being (Kahneman, 2003), priming (Bargh, 2006), evolutionary psychology (Tooby & Cosmides, 2015; Trivers, 1971), cybernetics (Bateson, 1972), linguistics (Korzybski, 1995; Pinker, 1994), swarm intelligence (Kennedy, 2006).

These inspiring fields add subtle hues to the 'coat of many colors' that together constitute SoFAP-P.

6.2.1 Contributions of SoFAP-P to Practice (CP's)

CP-1: *More brevity and efficiency*

de Shazer's goal for his new approach in psychotherapy was that the time the client had to suffer from his problems would be limited. He often said: 'Therapy should be as brief as possible and not last one session more than needed'. Practitioners well versed in the approach observe that indeed fewer sessions are necessary and that they produce more sustainable results, or as one interviewee put it: 'What goes well comes faster and stays longer'.

This brevity and efficiency advantage is further enhanced by the fact that the SoFAP-P flowchart allows for the shortest path to the intended goal, without having to take intuitively chosen side paths.

CP-2: *Higher return on investment*

Time and money investment in adding the solution-focused approach to ones already existing expertise can be used across a wide variety of challenges, is not depending on diagnostic categories and transcends the division into professional categories.

CP-3: *Increased client focus*

SoFAP-P radically places the client system, its needs and goals along with its possibilities and resources at the centre of each and every intervention.

The design minimizes noise by forcing the practitioner to focus exclusively and continuously on the client's interests.

CP-4: *Augmented sustainability of outcome*

Relevant outcome research (a.o. McDonald, 2011; McKeel, 1996) shows that with a solution-focused approach, the achievement of beneficial results is reached in a much faster way (fewer sessions needed). The positive results for the client are more sustainable in two senses of the word: they last longer, and the learning effects of the outcomes generated tend to spread more easily to other life fields beyond the initial challenge.

CP-5: *Is beyond techniques*

All too often, the simple but not easy solution-focused approach was oversimplified by well-meaning novice therapists and trainers, for the (so called) sake of transferability. The quasi-protocol-like reduction of the solution-focused approach to the 4 SFT-techniques[1] is reductionistic, limiting and simplistic. This sometimes led to the erroneous statement that solution-focused work is easy. All one must do is applying the 4 SFT-techniques. It is obvious that this simplification is not what the rich epistemology of the solution-focused approach that Steve de Shazer developed is about. Therefore, SoFAP-P honours the awe for human complexity, the intricacies and difficulties of change and the needed linguistic subtleties to facilitate those changes.

CP-6: *Actively includes the ecosystem*

Although the ecosystem plays an important role in the approach, in the traditional SFT, the actual work is done primarily with individual clients.

In SoFAP-P, the ecosystem can be actively involved in the change facilitation process rather than remaining background information. The reason for this inclusion is that there are resources available in the ecosystem that can be put to use towards positive change. The participants in the relevant context of the 'identified' client are involved stakeholders. Including them in the facilitation process invites cooperation and avoids counterproductive responses. The members of the ecosystem often are the 'secret weapon' for the client in search of solutions since they represent the still well-functioning part of the client's (work) life and, finally: Why shouldn't the change facilitator make his life and work as simple as possible by using all the resources at hand?

CP-7: *Broadens the scope directly to client goals*

In the early days of the solution-focused approach, instead of asking the client directly for his goals, the practitioner inferred the client's goals from the conversation about the client's context. Some solution-focused therapists, such as the team at Brief London, a free mental health clinic led by pioneers of the solution-focused approach, simply never ask contextual questions but immediately proceed with their own special formulation of the goal-setting question: *What is your best hope for today?* If a client feels the need to talk about his problems, the immediate question is: *What would you like instead?*

From the outset, the SoFAP-P combines context-clarifying questions with goal-setting questions. Which element gets attention first and what comes next is determined by the idiosyncratic needs of the specific client or client system. After initiating the contact into a working relationship that may develop into a working alliance, the practitioner asks for background information that provides the client with space to talk about what he thinks is important, even if it is about his problems. This exchange reveals useful resources and is then followed by the most obvious question for people who come asking for help: *What should we talk about today so that this conversation will be useful for (all of) you?* The sequence of steps is not fixed in a linear protocol but follows an improvised scenario that carefully fits the situation.

CP-8: *Adds lightness*

Before SFT, psychological models tended to excel in complex theorizing, with jargon reserved for acolytes, and with more focus on internal developments of the treatment model itself than on benefits to clients. The solution-focused approach countered this, and SoFAP-P takes it a step further.

Creating a working relationship that forms the context in which the client is helped to use his own resources to find solutions for his goals adds hope. The motto 'add lightness' captures the essence of the client-practitioner interaction in SoFAP-P.

6.2.2 Contributions of SoFAP-P to Society, (CSs)

CS-1: *The concept of differentiation is able to match environmental differentiation*

Compared to the last century, the diversity of situations in today's world has increased dramatically. The term VUCA[2] is often used nowadays to make this diversity more understandable. The letters of the acronym stand for *Volatility, Uncertainty, Complexity* and *Ambiguity* as the four characteristics of the contemporary environment.

The more diverse the questions and answers in the environment, the more relevant Ashby's *Law of Requisite Variety* becomes.

> W. Ross Ashby was a British cyberneticist and psychologist who proposed a law with regard to levels of variety and regulation within biological systems. In his words:
> *When the variety or complexity of the environment exceeds the capacity of a system (natural or artificial), the environment will dominate and ultimately destroy that system* (1956).
> This law is now well known as the *First Law of Cybernetics* and applied to social systems as the *Law of Requisite Variety*.

If we apply Ashby's Law to social situations – such as a client, a client system and a practitioner – it would imply the following: When a practitioner wants to respond adequately to the strongly increased diversity of situations in the environment of the client, the practitioner should have interventions (communicative or otherwise) available that correspond to each situation that might arise in the client's ecosystem. In other words: The more divers the environment of the client-practitioner system, the more differentiated the available repertoire of interventions *within* that system must be.

With SoFAP-P, this dramatically increased diversity in society can be parried. After all, with SoFAP-P, the practitioner is not bound to a limitative number of 'diagnosis-treatment combinations' as we know them from problem-focused practice. SoFAP-P makes a continuous differentiation of actions possible, depending on the client's particular, current situation. In other words: Because of the iterative and recursive nature of SoFAP-P, the number of routes through the presented flowchart is virtually infinite, which in turn ensures that the designed approach can achieve congruence with any client situation in the VUCA world.

Two examples of how SoFAP-P can be used to differentiate according to the diversity found in the environment are as follows:

- The focus on thinking in terms of what still works well, instead of what does not work and why it doesn't work.
- Giving attention to resources as steppingstones for improvement.

Finally, two contemporary examples of this kind of differentiation are seen in other fields:

- In post-operative medical care and pain treatment, a scale from zero pain to ten (excruciatingly painful) is often used to gauge the pain level. Here more accent is given to the specific number and what it entails than to the underlying reasons for the given number. Except in the final stages of palliative care, practitioners are more interested in small changes for the better then in fully eradicating the pain experience.

- While in the past most economical magazines covering the world of business oftentimes concentrated on business failures, personal misadventures of the involved parties and the detrimental consequences of all this misery, nowadays they tend to gradually shift to more interest in success stories and what we can learn from them.

CS-2: *Shows applicability outside the challenge scope*

Thinking and acting in terms of possibilities and resources (instead of in seemingly unsurmountable difficulties and deficits) is swiftly adopted in places where people congregate and work together to a common goal: in clubs and teams, companies, families, volunteer movements, etc. As a result of the more objectified process and the guided decision-making of SoFAP-P, that protocol catches on easily and spreads rapidly to benefit members of that kind of common goal groups in our society.

CS-3: *Uses language as a change master*

Therapy and change facilitation is seen as a Wittgensteinian language game by which one can create an alternative reality. Therefore, the language and the precise words we use guide the conversations in the direction of positive change. The question *What still works?* reveals elements that are (yet) operative and on which one can build progress. The question *What would you like instead of the problem?* points the client's focus towards a constructive future. This different language, also known as *solution talk*, slowly enters the popular lingo as it becomes ever more acceptable, and even wished for, to show interest for positive elements in (personal, societal and business) life. SoFAP-P thus better matches – the dynamics of – current language use.

CS-4: *Value for (tax) money*

As a result of SoFAP-P advantages in terms of brevity and efficiency (see CP-1) and sustainability (see CP-4), a serious contribution from SoFAP-P to society is that with the same budget more clients can be helped (to help themselves). In other words: the expected outcome of the facilitation process remains as productive while being achieved in a shorter time frame and with less noise in the process. At the same time, that result contains the attributes that allow the process to update itself or adapt to developments over time.

6.3 Desirable developments in solution-focused applied psychology

Imagine that tonight you go to sleep and while you sleep, it is as if a miracle happens. And in that miracle what is it that you will notice to be different now that you have stepped into the future?

Since the future is unpredictable, we can try our best to invent it as good as possible. In furthering solution-focused thinking, its theoretical groundings and its ever expanding and deepening utilization in diverse areas of knowledge, we will hit discoveries that for the moment are unknowable or just difficult to imagine.

But what we can warn against is the following: If the solution-focused approach – containing SoFAP-P – wants to continue its development and spread, it must step away of simplistic reductionism and outdated holistic pseudo-hippy wokeness. No more solution-focused knitting and Kumbaya-singing at SF-conferences that from year to year become more and more like cult meetings.

If solution-focused applied psychology – and SoFAP-P in particular – wants to survive, several developments need to be sponsored by professional practitioners and academics that look through the new age-like fog and are willing to go to great efforts to (re)introduce this approach into the realm of science-based professional best practices.

Solution-focused applied psychology needs therefore:

- to move back to basics: it started in the clinic where professionals wanted to make a difference that makes a difference in the lives of their clients (instead of having fun in closed workshops among brethren)
- to move back to as simple as possible, but no simpler than necessary
- to move back to applying solution-focused applied psychology as a tool and not as an end in itself
- to move back to ….

The future of solution-focused applied psychology therefore needs:

- to move forward to a theoretical underpinning so that we know what we do instead of assuming *If it works, it is OK*.
- to move forward with the courage to go against novelties that are not innovations but emanations of a solution-focused sectarian dogma.
- to move forward by going beyond mere techniques, beyond the closed world of solution-focused aficionados by (re)appreciating the epistemological complexity.
- to move forward by becoming part of the academically accepted psychological methods that facilitate progress for individuals, groups and society.
- to move forward to incorporating research from crosslinked scientific endeavours so that solution-focused applied psychology truly becomes a coat of many colours.

6.3.1 Beware of trendy fog banks

On average, people in the West are healthier than they usually think themselves to be. This applies to both somatic and psychological health. Western man's self-healing capacity and resilience seems more powerful than is often thought, by insiders and outsiders alike.

However, there exists this strange tendency to be 'Vogue'-perfect. Everybody needs to be a fashion model, have fun all the time, visit exotic places and spent his time doing extraordinary things. In contrast with this 'perfection-is-hardly-good-enough' YOLO attitude, imperfections, especially mental imperfections, are often defined in fashionable terminology. Narcissism, giftedness, depression, PTSD and traumatic-whatever-things, ADHD and an autistic spectrum disorder, are 'en vogue'. With all due respect and compassion for clients diagnosed as such by true professionals, all too often these labels are used without being hindered by the required expertise to do so.

This fashionable trend leads to 'therapeutization' of language and interaction between predominantly healthy people. One is not sick or ill but one 'suffers' from trendy fog banks that invade, nebulize, and obscure the reality of our human condition. A classic from decades ago yet still alive amongst some strata of the upper class in the major cities of both coasts of the USA is that it is *bon ton* and status-enhancing to have your own 'psy' in addition to a GP for your physical condition. Brent Katz, journalist at *The New Yorker*, suggested back in 2018 that 'The New York State of Mind' should be added to the *Diagnostic and Statistical Manual of Mental Disorders*.

In contrast with this problem-inducing and energy-draining phenomenon, there exists a significantly smaller group of people who have little use for this fashionable trend. They are known for statements like 'Don't worry, be happy', 'Count your blessings' and 'Get a live!'

We opt for the latter position: a perspective that sees more solutions than problems and values the future more than the past.

Since Descartes and Heidegger, we have gradually come to believe that thinking and living, a.k.a. Being, are distinguishable but not separable. Perhaps that is why pleasant or encouraging thoughts about what is still going well or working, about what could be achieved, can indeed lead to a more pleasant life. A stronger focus on solutions than on problems fits that statement.

6.3.2 SF is no SF

Solution-focused is not *Science Fiction*, although in the (near) future we will – probably and hopefully – be able to use virtual reality in the form of augmented reality, game-like applications in exercises, training and – why not – actual consulting and coaching work, to facilitate our work as practitioners. Surely, the further development of Artificial Intelligence will play a big role in this. This will not only broaden the scope of possible SoFAP-P applications but also broaden the physical range of where we can offer services, like surgeons today operate in Boston on patients in Dubai.

Because the indescribable in science can only be approached in art, where the indescribable is guiding, William Blake shared his most intimate feelings and thoughts:

To see a World in a Grain of Sand
And a Heaven in a Wild Flower,
Hold Infinity in the palm of your hand
And Eternity in an hour.

Notes

1 See Section 2.1: Solution-focused therapy (SFT).
2 The US Army War College introduced the concept of VUCA to describe the more volatile, uncertain, complex and ambiguous multilateral world perceived as resulting from the end of the Cold War.

APPENDIX A

SoFAP-P cases ex ante

This appendix presents 25 cases from which the CIMOs of Section 3.3 are distilled. Together with the 6 points of attention (see Section 2.2), the 14 lessons learned (see Sections 2.2 and 2.3) and the 10 best and bad practices (see Section 3.2), the 21 CIMOs found are the building blocks for the envisioned SoFAP-P design.

For each case, it is indicated where within that case the antecedents for a particular CIMO are located. Most CIMOs are based on multiple clues that appear in several cases.

At the end of each case, the CIMOs to which that particular case contributed are listed again. There the phrase *among others* is used to indicate that (aspects of) other CIMOs not mentioned in the list may still transpire between the lines. After all, most of the time, different CIMOs are simultaneously at work.

The frequency of contributions from the 25 cases to the various CIMOs is shown in the table below. It may be an indication of the necessity or sheer popularity of certain CIMOs.

CIMOs based on contributions from many cases (11–22)

[cimo-1] Establish contact to build the client-practitioner alliance [based on contributions from 16 cases]
[cimo-3] Explore the context [based on contributions from 22 cases]
[cimo-4] Direct the conversation towards a goal [based on contributions from 11 cases]
[cimo-7] Ask solution-building questions [based on contributions from 16 cases]
[cimo-8] Activate resources [based on contributions from 21 cases]
[cimo-11] Offer positive feedback, give compliments [based on contributions from 13 cases]
[cimo-20] Use future-orienting questions [based on contributions from 14 cases]

CIMOs based on contributions from an average number of cases (>3 and <9)

[cimo-2] Distinguish problem versus limitation to enhance effectivity
[cimo-5] Circumvent absent intrinsic motivation
[cimo-10] Ask continuation questions to activate resources
[cimo-12] Give advice in the guise of a question
[cimo-14] Ask: What have you tried thus far?
[cimo-15] Ask for exceptions to the problem
[cimo-21] Use the miracle question

CIMOs based on contributions from just one to three cases

[cimo-6] Focus the client's attention on accepting responsibility and accountability for the client's own actions
[cimo-9] Ask the pre-session change question
[cimo-13] Ask the coping question in case of serious distress
[cimo-16] Ask the usefulness question
[cimo-17] Offer a relativistic perspective
[cimo-18] Ask differentiating questions
[cimo-19] Use scaling questions

Case-A: No time to make time

(Cauffman, 2001)

Steve is the manager-owner of a chain of real estate agencies. He built his company from scratch. Mike is a self-employed consultant and coach. They are both members of the same business club.

One day, Steve calls Mike: 'Mike, I need to talk to you in private. I know you are coaching people for a living, and I sure could use some help from a professional like you'.

They meet in Steve's office. After some preamble, [cimo-1] Steve explains why he wants to talk to Mike.

Steve: 'I really think I need some help. I have postponed this for a long time now, but I can no longer cope. It has nothing to do with my business because that is running very smoothly. It has to do with me. I finally decided to call you for help because my wife urged me to. She is right, I do need help from someone to get another perspective. I am stuck'.

Steve tells the long story of his business life. [cimo-3] He remembers the days when he worked alone and had to do everything all by himself. With regret, Steve says: 'Those were the days. I remember the pleasure and the thrill. I was lucky to start my company at a time when the real estate business was picking up, and I've been riding the waves since then. Surely, I've had bad moments but all in all, everything has gone smoothly. Although I had to do literally everything myself, I feel that I had more time in those days. Now I have several agencies and forty-five people working for me. I thought that having personnel to take care of the business would give me more freedom and time. Dead wrong! Nowadays I have no time for anything as I am always running behind'.

Mike: 'Great story. Congratulations on your success. You did a great job building this company. It's good to hear that your private life is a haven for you. [cimo-11] Now, what should we talk about today so that this meeting will be helpful to you?' [cimo-4]

Steve: 'There is a lot, of course, but two things stand out now, and they are interrelated. First, I don't have any time. I tried a time management course but that didn't work out. It was too complicated and besides, I don't have enough time to devote myself to really applying the techniques'.

Mike: 'No time to make time, that's an interesting paradox. What else?' [cimo-14]

Steve: 'I recently hired a sales manager. His job is to coach the sales team. I was hoping that this would save me some time so that I can do what I do best — making deals. I should coach him, of course, but up until now I haven't even found enough time to introduce him properly into my company. I sure tried and we set up many meetings but to no avail. It doesn't work. There is always some interference — a deal that only I can close, another meeting with a potential client that I simply can-not postpone. So instead of a solution, I have an additional problem'.

Steve realizes that both his time management method and his way of coaching his personnel are very inefficient. His sales manager isn't too happy with the way it is working either. He tries his best but without vital information from Steve, he is only scratching the surface.

Steve has talked to his wife about this. She listened to her husband and offered good advice but to no avail. Steve keeps insisting that he has tried everything and still can't change the situation due to lack of time. He is constantly solving little things but never looking at the bigger picture. 'I feel like a fireman, running around with buckets of water to kill every fire in every corner and yet the whole building is ablaze'.

Reflection

What can Steve do?

Even though resources are tools that are easy to use, it is not always easy to get clients to use the tools correctly. After all, they have made many failed attempts at solving their problem.

Usually this is because they don't have the right manual for the tools they use, or they quit before they see results. ('I tried that time management thing for about two weeks but it didn't work'.) Or they don't use them in the right way. ('In my job it isn't possible to set priorities because something else always comes up unexpectedly'.) Or they jump too quickly from one tool to the next. ('I have tried everything from written reports I didn't really have time to write, to weekly meetings that never took place. Nothing works!') The examples show that they do have resources but they don't make use of them in the correct way.

It also happens that clients have no idea about the resources they have at their disposal. Some people have never heard of time management, prioritizing, or an efficient way to share information via reports. You still (and maybe always will) meet teams that do not know how to have an efficient meeting. Then all you must do is gently teach them these resources. But these cases are rare, especially in the sophisticated business environment you are working in.

The most important strategy we use to help those clients is to help them to (again) use their tools and resources correctly. Here, questions often prove to be more effective than telling people what to do. [cimo-12]

Mike: 'OK now, Steve, let's see what you can do differently. You told me you went to that time management course, tried out some of the techniques but in the end you just gave up. What is it exactly that you tried?' [cimo-14 coupled to cimo-3]

Steve: 'One of the things they taught me was to make lists of everything I had to do. I tried this. It gave me some overview of my work. Every day I sat down and made lists, but I gave up because I was drowning in these lists. Plus, nothing came out of it because I was almost never able to do what was on my list. At the end of each day, I was even more frustrated because I was confronted with my failure. The only good thing was that I was pleased to see how much work I have'.

Mike: 'OK. So making these lists was a little bit helpful because it gave you an overview. Of course this is no instant cure. Would you be interested to learn a more useful way of making these lists?'

Steve: 'Sure. Anything is better than what I am doing now'.

Mike: 'Maybe a little adjustment can help. I assume that you agree that working too hard is not always efficient but working smart is? To-do lists are, as you noticed yourself, particularly useful to get an overview. It is a frequent mistake to think that one actually needs to do everything on the list. People tend to put too strict a timing on all the actions, and that's where frustration and failure comes from. Of course, you have so many things to do that you cannot possibly do them all. So, it is useful to adapt these to-do lists'.

Steve: 'I'm curious'.

Mike: 'Would it be a good idea to differentiate between urgent and not urgent on the one hand, and important and less important on the other? [cimo-12] That way your to-do list becomes a matrix, and you still have an overview. Would you be willing to try this in the coming weeks and see what a difference this makes?'

Steve: 'Interesting concept. So you don't want me to put timing on this list? How will this be useful then? I still have to do all these things anyhow'.

Mike: 'Correct, no timing, just the overview matrix. Then you go about your business as usual. I wonder what you will discover when you do this exercise. [cimo-7] [cimo-12] [cimo-20] By the way, this exercise works like jogging: there is no point in going out for a two-hour jog every three months — that is as dangerous as it is useless. The same applies for this exercise — it will only be useful if applied on a daily basis. You might even want to take some time every evening to reflect on what you have learned that day. Some clients tell me it helps when they take notes. Some even suggested me that, when looking at the coming day, they try to predict how the coming day will go and the observe the difference with what happens in reality'.

Steve: 'I will give it a try'. Like my father always said: 'If you don't shoot, you always miss'. Now, what should I do about my sales manager? The few meetings we did have were very useful. If only we could meet more frequently, but there are not enough hours in the day. Even a week is gone in a blink'.

Mike: 'What did you try?' [cimo-14] [cimo-15]

Steve: 'When he started working for me, we set up an ambitious plan. We agreed to meet for one hour every day. That went OK for two days but then I had to leave town for a few days, and we were never able to pick it up again. Mind you, it's not that we don't talk at all, we just don't talk enough. Lately I have been a bit worried about him. He has started complaining that I never make time for him. Last week he bluntly asked me if I am really sure that I want him as a sales manager!'

Mike: 'Do you?'

Steve: 'Sure. He is the right guy. He comes from the real estate business and has a lot of experience. I just need to give him enough inside information about my company. Plus, I want to know what he is doing all the time. He is a big investment, and I want to see results'.

Mike: 'Knowing what your personnel is doing all the time is a giant task. Maybe it's not possible or advisable'.

Steve: 'That's not what I mean. I have enough trust in my personnel to let them work in their own way. The same goes for my sales manager. But the way it's going now is wrong. We spend more time planning for meetings than actually having a meeting. We talk more about the fact that we should talk than anything else. It is frustrating'.

130 APPENDIX A

Mike: 'Good. At least this shows that you are motivated to meet with each other, no misunderstanding there. Would it be a good idea to decide first about what it exactly is that you want to tell him? And then decide what kind of information that you would like to get from him? Then think about the frequency and the method?'

Steve: 'So you propose that instead of talking content we're better off taking some time to set up a structure?'

Mike: 'Exactly. You could even ask your sales manager to draw up a proposal so that you don't have to spend time on it yourself. I am pretty sure that he will see this as a sign of trust from your side. You can always correct and fine-tune his initial proposal'.

Steve: 'OK. I will try it. This is bound to work better than what we are doing now. I just need to make a little time to make time. Let me work on this and let's meet again in a few weeks. Thanks for your advice, Mike'.

- Contributes among others to [cimo-1] [cimo-3] [cimo-4] [cimo-6] [cimo-7] [cimo-11] [cimo-12] [cimo-14] [cimo-15] [cimo-20]

Case-B: Outplacement

(Cauffman, 2001)

A corporate office that needs to cut back suggests outplacement to Luc, an administrative assistant. [cimo-3] However, Luc is not at all interested in outplacement. He feels that the company is taking his job away from him, so the company should come up with something else to get his cooperation. To build a positive relationship with Luc, the solution-focused manager shows understanding of Luc's views and respects his feelings. [cimo-1] The manager clarifies that the final decision is taken about Luc's position in the company after the reorganization. [cimo-2] By showing empathy and reformulating his rebellion as an expression of proactive and independent behaviour, the manager clarifies to Luc that he will be able to use these resources in the next phase of his career. [cimo-8] [cimo-11] Feeling understood and respected, Luc is more likely to become interested in a payout plan, or having regained his self-confidence, he might accept an outplacement programme that will help him become successful in the job market. [cimo-4]

- Contributes among others to [cimo-1] [cimo-2] [cimo-3] [cimo-4] [cimo-8] [cimo-11].

Case-C: Family perils

(Cauffman, 2006)

The owner of a very successful plastic extrusion company, Mr. Kingsley, is caught between his son-in-law and the non-family CEO. His son-in-law is a board member and shareholder, and he is demanding an increasingly central role within the company. There is a long-standing tension between him and the non-family CEO. The straw that broke the camel's back was the son-in-law's purchase of an entirely new computer system without prior consultation with the CEO. [cimo-3] The CEO threatens to quit. Mr. Kingsley is furious at his son-in-law, but his hands are tied: The son-in-law acted upon his own authority as a board member and shareholder. Plus, the deal with the computer company is already closed. [cimo-2]

Instead of venting all the negative feelings towards his son-in-law or conspiring with the CEO, Mr. Kingsley decides to take a long walk. After fuming for a while, he reflects on everything that goes well in his successful family business, on every smart move his son-in-law has made in the past, on the important role of the CEO for the further development of the company. Instead of analysing the 'whys' of his son-in-law's solo action or the history of the conflict between his son-in-law and the CEO, Mr. Kingsley visualizes all the occasions on which his son-in-law and the CEO collaborated for the best of the company. [cimo-8]

Mr. Kingsley's anger soon passes and he decides to have an open conversation with his son-in-law.

Mr. Kingsley: 'I do not appreciate nor approve of your solo action, let that be clear. Yet, what is done is done and we will not dwell on it. I would like to talk about other things with you. Let me ask you the following question instead: What, in your opinion, goes well in our company, and how did both you and our CEO contribute to that?' [cimo-10]

The son-in-law is startled. He was expecting a heavy rebuke from his father-in-law and had prepared his arguments extensively. He immediately realizes the wisdom of this question. Knowing the tenacity of his father-in-law, he drops his prepared arguments and answers in detail. After sharing the resources that make the company and their collaboration so successful [cimo-8], their conversation steers towards the future of the company. [cimo-20] The son-in-law can see the importance of a better cooperation with the CEO. At the end of the conversation, they both agree to initiate a project on corporate governance.

Mr. Kingsley then sets up a meeting with the CEO and starts off with the same question. Their conversation ends with the same conclusion.

Reflection

Talking about what goes well in spite of the problems allows all parties to voice their opinions in a constructive manner instead of remaining stuck in the classical 'who is right and who is wrong' discourse. No wonder people at Problems Inc. tend to become depressed, frustrated and hopeless. After all, the managers at Problems Inc. are trained to do just that: Go into all the possible details of the 'whys' and the 'why-nots'. As everyone attempts to reach the deepest causes of the already weighty problems, they forget to focus on what the solution might be. With every round of the discussion, another problem is unearthed, making the issues seem insurmountable. The chance that positive changes will arise from this is minimal.

At Solutions Inc. on the other hand, people discern problems from limitations. The given that the new computer system is bought is not a problem (for which an – inexpensive – solution is thinkable) but a limitation: The deed is done, and one can only make the best of it. In Solutions Inc., the focus is on what positive resources have contributed to the success and how these can be used in the future.

- Contributes among others to [cimo-2] [cimo-3] [cimo-8] [cimo-10] [cimo-20].

Case-D: Believing is seeing

(Cauffman, 2001)

For the second year in a row, a sales manager has not met his targets. The business owner is about to fire his sales manager. He doubts because he has a good relationship with this manager. Over many meetings, they worked hard together to try and solve the problem. It is clear the sales manager tries his utter best. In addition, the owner does not want the investment he made in the salesperson to go to waste. [cimo-3]

So, he decides to make one last attempt to encourage the sales manager to change his attitude and achieve better results. [cimo-2] Both agree to call in a coach who organizes a meeting that will take place in two weeks. The clients are stressed because they know that this coaching process is a one-time opportunity. When they meet, the coach first takes his time to create a trustworthy atmosphere. [cimo-1] Then he starts the process with the question: 'Has anything changed since we set this appointment?' Both clients, tot their own astonishment, respond to this 'pre-session change' question with: 'Now that you mention this, yes, some small changes happened'. [cimo-9] The sales manager says that he tried to switch his client relationship style from very cautious to a little more assertive. 'That seems to help', he reports, 'It seems that my clients prefer that I offer them choices between possible solutions instead of my previous endless double checking what it is that they need'. 'In the light of our today meeting', the owner says, 'I decided to refrain from grilling him on why he didn't sell anything yesterday and I limited myself to asking about what went well that day'. [cimo-6] [cimo-8] Happy with these small improvements, the coach then asks both parties the question: 'How would *you* notice a small improvement in the coming days and weeks? [cimo-7] [cimo-8] [cimo-20] What would you do differently?' The sales manager answers that he would no longer feel ignored and 'passed over' by the owner. The owner replies that he would notice that the sales manager would be much more assertive and stand his ground.

These are almost always the first answers: The cause is put on the other person. Then the coach must help the person look at what he himself would do differently. [cimo-6] 'How will *you* act differently when you notice that your employee keeps behaving more assertive with his clients?' [cimo-20]

The question for the sales manager might be: 'What will *you* do differently, if you got the impression of no longer being ignored?' The owner replies that he would then feel safe and secure enough to give the sales manager more space, while the sales manager states that he would have the courage to point out to the owner that he should let him do his job in peace. 'I would have continuous direct consultation meetings with all my salespeople, and I would do it on site or when on the road with my salespersons but not in the office'.

Based on these forward-looking imaginary alternatives, the coach helps both parties to further turn these statements into concrete agreements, with good results.

- Contributes among others to [cimo-1] [cimo-2] [cimo-3] [cimo-6] [cimo-7] [cimo-8] [cimo-9] [cimo-20].

Case-E: Hampered by good intentions

(Cauffman, 2006)

Jonathan, an experienced salesman, who had previously been working for a company's competitor, is hired to head the sales department. In his career to date, he has always worked exclusively as a salesman and has never had to manage other people. Jonathan did well during his training period, but once he was up-and-running in his position as sales manager, problems soon arose. Having no experience as a manager, he was uncertain what to do – so he jumped in, feet first. The first thing he did was to visit lots of customers with his salesmen. This, of course, provided a perfect introduction, but during many of these joint visits, he behaved like a salesman and took the lead in the meetings with the customers. His salesmen did not appreciate this, especially since Jonathan sometimes corrected them in front of the customer. In the car back to the office, Jonathan, in a well-intended attempt to help, always lectured his colleagues on what they should or shouldn't do or say and told endless stories about his successes as a salesman. Although well meant, these lectures showed more of his uncertainty than anything else. The ensuing conversations led to a lot of arguments between Jonathan and his team members. Jonathan felt that his colleagues did not accept him and the team accused him of putting himself too much in the forefront and not sufficiently supporting them. [cimo-3]

After a few weeks, this situation was no longer tenable and the sales team jointly asked for a meeting with George, the general manager. The team made it very clear that they understood Jonathan's well-meant efforts but that they were fed up with him treating them like beginners. 'We know he's just insecure in his new job as sales manager, but he won't listen to us'.

George sets up a meeting with Jonathan. After listening to Jonathan's version of the facts, [cimo-1] George asks him the miracle question. [cimo-21] 'Jonathan, after a long day of hard work, you will go to sleep tonight. While you are asleep, suppose a miracle happens in which all the problems you are having in the team today are sufficiently solved so that you are no longer bothered by them. Once you wake up tomorrow morning, how will you discover that this miracle has happened?' Jonathan replies, 'All my colleagues would accept all my proposals, and they would do what I tell them to do'.

In its initial form, Jonathan's answer is useless. Still, George accepts it without arguing and continues. 'Not so fast, Jonathan, you are lying in your bed, you open your eyes and wham, you notice that something special has happened but you don't know that your miracle happened. What would you be doing differently when you get up in the morning?'

Jonathan answers:	'When I wake up in the morning after this miracle, I will be in a better mood and feel a little more self-confident. I probably wouldn't go to work whistling, but still, I would be more at ease'.
George:	'Great. What difference would there be when you enter the office?' [cimo-7]
Jonathan:	'At work, instead of running around and trying to talk to as many people as possible within the first half hour, I just would say hello and start with my emails. When my emails are done, I would walk around to see if something special has come up, and then I would retreat into my office for an hour or so just to think'.
George:	'Interesting. What will be your next small step?'
Jonathan:	'Maybe I need to start out from what I know best'.
George:	'That's a good idea. [cimo-11] Would you mind explaining this to me? How will this help you?'
Jonathan:	'I realize that I might have been overstressing my new role as sales manager. If I try to walk a mile in my salespeople's shoes, maybe I can come up with things that will help them to accept me better. I could do this by writing down the things that helped me the most when I was a salesman'.
George asks:	'Good, what else would you do differently?'
Jonathan:	'Come to think of it, I realize that my former sales manager in my previous job was a great help to me'.
George:	'In what respect?'
Jonathan:	'He hardly ever told me what I should do. He was always asking questions about my work, about customers, about my planning. I might do the same'. [cimo-8]
George:	'Very good. What else?'
Jonathan:	'Instead of going along to see customers all the time, I would try to design an action plan based on the sales budget. Yes, I could think about which actions could be taken at short notice. Out of that I could distill a proposal for my colleagues'.

Just by giving these answers, Jonathan is starting to think in a different way about his job as sales manager. Now the time is right to help Jonathan expand his ideas from actions to interactions.

George: 'If I could ask your staff what changes they will notice about you after the miracle, what would they say?' [cimo-12]

Jonathan: 'They would probably tell you I am much less pushy and more easy-going. I hope they won't start taking advantage of me, though'.

George asks another solution-building question: 'Well, nobody likes being taken advantage of. If they try it on, you will know immediately. How would you react then?' [cimo-7]

Jonathan: 'Well becoming pushy again certainly wouldn't help. On the contrary. Actually, I don't expect them to do so. Why would they? They know their job better than I do'.

George: 'Do you think it would be helpful if you show them how you appreciate their professionalism? [cimo-12] How could you combine this with the next little step of the miracle? How would you act differently towards your colleagues, Jonathan?'

Jonathan: 'Yes, I could slip in some compliments about how they do their jobs instead of just proposing ready-made plans that they are not likely to accept'.

George: 'Now, how will you do that?'

Jonathan: 'When my proposal is ready, instead of just presenting it to them, I would ask one of my salesmen to go through it with me. I would ask him what has worked best for him in the past and would integrate these ideas in the final proposal. I would also ask him what should be in it so that it will be accepted more easily by his colleagues'. [cimo-20]

George: 'Very good, Jonathan. What would you need to be able to put into action what you have just told me?'

Jonathan: 'I just need to do it'.

- Contributes among others to [cimo-1] [cimo-3] [cimo-7] [cimo-8] [cimo-11] [cimo-12] [cimo-20] [cimo-21].

Case-F: Change or die

(Cauffman, 2001)

The regulations department of a high-tech multinational company came under great stress after a reorganization exercise that had swept through the whole corporation. [cimo-2] They were forced to lay off many of their highly trained technicians. Before the restructuring, the regulations department had been responsible for the regulation of services all over the company. They created, controlled and monitored the procurement of all the company's products. This ranged from the exact dimensions of pins in a socket to the density of the foam used in headphones. It's evident that they had a lot of work and a lot of power. Nobody could start production without their approval. However, this all changed radically after the reorganization when the regulation task was decentralized. Every department was required to set its own regulations and the original regulations department's task was reduced to overseeing and ensuring that these standards were streamlined and communicated throughout the consortium. The only instances in which they still executed their technical specialization were when products needed to be manufactured in different parts of the company and then needed assembling. In such cases, they still had the overall responsibility.

On top of this, every department, including regulations, was converted into an independent business unit with its own income responsibility. [cimo-3] The result was that the remaining employees of the regulations department, who once were the cream of the crop when it came to technical skill and responsibility, now had a very limited span of control. The turnover of the department was greatly reduced due to their limited tasks. The remaining staff members were living under the constant threat of not making their budgeted turnover, and the likely consequences thereof. This led them to exert their influence by using their regulations stamp whenever possible. The result was that lots of interdepartmental regulations were painstakingly slow, overly precise, and, therefore, overpriced, sometimes to the client's great dissatisfaction. The self-protective response of the regulations department, or more precisely of what was left of it, was very counterproductive as they were serving themselves instead of their clients.

Before the situation spiralled out of control and debilitated the whole company, the director of the regulations department decided to organize a two-day seminar to which she invited the complete team to consider the following topic: 'Let's go with the flow by using what we know'. [cimo-5]

Readers who have gone through a similar reorganization process will know from experience how the first hours of this seminar went – whining, complaining, telling war stories from the good old days, more whining. After a while of this, there almost always comes a moment in which the team members reach the conclusion that more whining isn't going to help them get ahead. At precisely that moment, their manager asked them to sit in small groups and to discuss their true skills and specialties and how these could be used in the future. [cimo-9] They soon found out that their know-how in technical procedures would be a perfect fit for the ongoing corporate-wide quality programme. [cimo-14] After all, developing, controlling, and securing technical procedures are what they knew best. In addition, they had in-depth knowledge of communication procedures that streamline implementation processes in a large company. [cimo-8] They decided to become service providers to the corporate-wide quality programme and offer the specialized technical support that currently had to be purchased from outside suppliers. The seminar ended with a detailed proposition for the vice president of operations. All went well and a few months later, the regulations department had a steady income from this new project on top of their specific regulations work.

- Contributes among others to [cimo-2] [cimo-3] [cimo-5] [cimo-8] [cimo-9] [cimo-14].

Case-G: It is not me! It's him

(Cauffman, 2001)

The HR manager gets an urgent phone call from one of the production managers who says: 'Look, can you do me a favor? I have this guy Eric in my team who is driving me crazy. I feel that he is constantly trying to undermine my authority within the team. We have just had a big fight and I told him to go and talk to you to get himself straightened out. I also told him that this was his last chance. If he doesn't stop his subversive behaviour right now, I will kick him out. Can you talk to the guy right now, please? He is on his way to your office'.

HR manager:	'Is this guy good at his job? Do you really want to get rid of him or, apart from regularly getting on your nerves, is he a valuable asset in your team?' [cimo-7] [cimo-16]
Production manager (taken aback a little by this question):	'Well, he is very good at his job. The best there is. The problem is that he knows it, and he feels protected by it. But this time I mean it — get him to shape up or I will ship him out'.
HR manager:	'No promises from me but I will talk to him and see what can be done'.
	Eric storms into the office of the HR manager: 'I have to come and see you because my boss told me to. He accuses me of undermining his authority within the team behind his back. But that's a lie. It's simply not true. He got so angry that he ordered me to come and see you or he would kick me out. I know, when he is under stress, he has a tendency to think digital, black-white. He is an engineer. But now, I think the guy has just lost his marbles. That's it, I have nothing more to say — it should be him who needs the shrink'. [cimo-6]
HR manager:	'Whoa! Have a seat and let's see what can be done. Tell me what happened, please'.
	Eric tells a long and winding story that can be summarized as an avalanche of mutual misunderstandings. [cimo-1] [cimo-3]

After a while, the HR manager says: 'OK, Eric, I see your point. I don't feel like getting into all kinds of rationalizations about who is right and who is wrong. You're only talking to me because you must. And it is my job to talk to you. It is obvious that your boss is upset with you. But if you look at the positive side of this: he sends you to come and talk to me, which means that he still sees a chance to get out of this mess. Otherwise, he would not make the effort of referring you to me. So, maybe it is helpful to step over the black or white position and try to look at the situation in a more relativistic way [cimo-17] Eric looks surprised and nods: Yes, you are probably correct. The HR manager continues 'Now, let me ask you a question. What do *you* need to do differently to get your boss off your back?' [cimo-5] [cimo-7]

It is clear that Eric has no request for help whatsoever on the topic that his boss rises, i.e. his presumed subversive behaviour. The HR manager decides not to delve into a fruitless search and analysis for truth: Is Eric acting subversively, yes or no? Such an intervention would lead nowhere except towards more trouble. The HR manager points out that the boss, even though he is cross with Eric, still has a positive reason for his referral. [cimo-8] This has a soothing effect. The HR manager's last question then helps Eric to think about an alternative problem – what does Eric need to do differently so that he no longer has the boss on his back? [cimo-6] Now that is a problem for which Eric might have a request for help. From that point, a useful conversation can develop. The HR manager can ask differentiating questions: 'If right now is the very worst situation of the last months, can you give me some examples of moments when it was a little bit easier to deal with each other? What did you do differently and what did your boss do differently? Follow-up questions help Eric to slowly step out of the digital position (yes/no, black/white/on/off) and start talking about what he could do differently to make his dealings with his boss easier. At the end of the conversation, the HR manager asks Eric if this conversation was useful to him. [CIMO-16]. Eric responds: 'Yes, you help me see things in a more correct perspective and that is both a relief and a good starting point for the next steps forward.

- Contributes among others to [cimo-1] [cimo-3] [cimo-5] [cimo-6] [cimo-7] [cimo-8] [cimo-16] [cimo-17].

Case-H: She doesn't know a thing about it!

(Cauffman, 2006)

A mother sends her 15-year-old son for a consultation with the request to talk him out of using cannabis. [cimo-3] However, the young man has no request for help and does not want to change his behaviour, let alone the use of the controversial substances. An attempt to make him aware of the dangers of soft drug use through information on the so-called steppingstone theory – it starts with a joint and ends in the gutter – is unlikely to yield much. What will work better is to ask him what he could do differently at home so that his mother would be less concerned, and he would be saved from having to come to the consultation. [cimo-7] Using this elegant method, his practitioner helps him to adopt a more open attitude. If he is willing to develop an alternative request for help, he is at least giving you a mandate to work on issues other than the one he was initially sent for. [cimo-5]

Practitioner: How do you feel about your mother being worried?
Client: She always is. She doesn't understand a thing about it.
Practitioner: About what?
Client: Well, the way me and my friends interact and have fun.
Practitioner: But that isn't the problem, is it?
Client: No, I mean we sometimes drink too much and so.
Practitioner: What do you mean, 'and so'?
Client: Well, you know, we take a smoke.
Practitioner: weed?
Client: Yeah, crazy, she was young herself.
Practitioner: I don't know if soft drugs were so commonly available in her day.
Client: I think so, but of course she was afraid …
Practitioner: Afraid of what?
Client: Well, that things will get out of hand. She obviously thinks I'll move to the needle in no time.
Practitioner: Does she really think that?
Client: Yeah, she's always talking about addiction and stuff.
Practitioner: Any idea how you could convince her that you won't become an addict?
Client: But she doesn't know anything about it.
Practitioner: And you, do you know everything about it?
Client: Well, everything. I know what I'm doing and what I won't do. For example,
  I *would* never swallow pills, snort, or use a needle.
Practitioner: Good for you! What makes you so sure of that? [cimo-11]
Client: You don't believe I'm crazy, do you? Later I want to join the police; if that gets out, I can shake it. Besides, it scares me of. You then no longer have control over yourself.
Practitioner: Never tried?
Client: No. Sometimes its offered, but I always just shrug. No, I don't do that stuff.
Practitioner: Where does that happen?
Client: Where not, you better ask. In clubs, but also at school. I'd rather not talk about that.
Practitioner: And you're able to say no whenever you are offered that stuff? [cimo-11]
Client: Yes, I mean it's no problem for me to say no.
Practitioner: Good on you. They'll try very hard to get you around.
Client: Hm.
Practitioner: Do you think your mother would be proud if she knew?

148 APPENDIX A

Client:	She does know that. I'm not crazy.
Practitioner:	Is that really the case? I mean, it's very likely that you're not crazy. But does she really know that you can turn down all the junk that is offered to you?
Client:	Maybe not.
Practitioner:	Do you think you could tell her?
Client:	Maybe when my dad is home.
Practitioner:	What do you mean your dad has to be there?
Client:	Well, if I say something like that when he's there, she'll believe it.
Practitioner:	And when will he be home?
Client:	He's sailing, so it won't be until Friday afternoon.
Practitioner:	And you go out that night?
Client:	No, when my dad comes home, I always stay in.
Practitioner:	The whole weekend?
Client:	No, the day he comes home, I stay home too.
Practitioner:	Does he know about the drugs and stuff?
Client:	I don't think so. He'd be furious.
Practitioner:	But you are able and willing to tell them what's happening to you? And especially how you manage to resist those temptations?
Client:	I think so.
Practitioner:	Then he will be proud of you.
Client:	(chuckling) And rightly so. My mother too, by the way.
Practitioner:	Well, what are you waiting for?

It is agreed that, at an appropriate time, the youngster will tell his parents about the temptations he manages to resist. Then he will report back. In the second conversation, we talk about his school performance. After all, he wants to join the police force and will therefore have to have a diploma. He has come to realize that smoking a lot of cannabis and good grades do not go well together. He realizes that his drug use limits his future possibilities. He has agreed with his mother that he will limit his drug use and that, if things go well at school, she will not nag him. In his own words, 'I just make sure my grades are good. Easy enough'.

- Contributes among others to [cimo-3] [cimo-5] [cimo-7] [cimo-11].

Case-J: Redirecting your focus

(Cauffman, 2010)

Client:	Whenever I catch myself not feeling anxious for a moment, I immediately start to panic, and then I'm completely lost. I can't help it, it's stronger than myself.
Practitioner:	Are there moments when you notice that you are not anxious, and still find a way to keep the panic at a distance for a while? [cimo-15]

APPENDIX A **149**

Client: I can do it when I'm busy at work. In those moments I'm so focused on my work and my colleagues that the panic can't get hold of me.
Practitioner: How do you do this? [cimo-13]
Client: No idea, that's just how it is.
Practitioner: So, if you manage to focus your attention on something else, you also gain control over your panic. Brilliant!
Client: Thanks. Do you think it could work in my spare time as well?
Practitioner: Of course, but it will require some effort.
Client: Doesn't matter. Now the panic also costs a lot of energy. It's better to put all that energy into something else, if only I knew how.
Practitioner: Do you want to look together for a way that you could do that? [cimo-8]
Client: Sure. If that would be possible.
Practitioner: Do I understand you correctly when you say that you can keep the panic at bay by intensely focusing your attention on something else? [cimo-12]
Client: Correct.
Practitioner: Would you be so kind as to close your eyes for a minute. Try not to think of an elephant. What are you thinking about?
Client: An elephant.
Practitioner: Obviously. Now let's proceed. While you try not to think of an elephant, you can feel how you sit on your chair, how you breath, how your hands are in your lap, how your feet feel on the ground. Now where is the elephant?
Client: Gone until you mentioned him.
Practitioner: Excellent. It shows that you can focus your attention and that you can do this in a 'distributed' manner. [cimo-11] You just need to practice this method a few times per day. Take some time for yourself in a spot where you can be alone for a while. Relax and concentrate on your breathing. When you feel you are relaxing, allow thoughts of your panic and when those difficult feeling grow, then deliberately focus you attention on the way you sit, where you are, the colors of your clothing, the sounds you can hear ... slowly add all these impressions to your panicky feelings and see what happens next. Don't you think this will 'water down' your panic?
Client: I will try this. But will my panic be gone forever then?
Practitioner: Probably not. But you can learn to be in control of your panicky feelings instead of being controlled by them.
Client: Well, better than nothing.
Practitioner: Is this useful when we talk like this? [cimo-16]
Client: I think so. I will give it a try. Still, I realize that I will need to work hard and take my time.

150 APPENDIX A

- Contributes among others to [cimo-8] [cimo-11] [cimo-12] [cimo-13] [cimo-15] [cimo-16].

Case-K: A detour through China

(Cauffman, 2010)

Practitioner:	Before you continue, I would like to know a bit more about you. What do you like to do in your spare time?
Client:	I do a lot of sports.
Practitioner:	Like what?
Client:	I'm into football, but mostly I run. [cimo-1] [cimo-3]
Practitioner:	Great. I do a bit jogging myself, but I always find that the first few meters from the couch to the front door are the most difficult. What about you?
Client:	I was the same, but I got through it. I motivate myself thinking about the shower afterwards and the positive feeling I get after a big effort.
Practitioner:	I wish I was as determined as you. Are you like that in all your endeavors? [cimo-7] [cimo-8] [cimo-12]
Client:	A few months ago, I started a course in Chinese. It's extremely difficult and I often need to give myself little pep talks to keep going.
Practitioner:	I'm sure you do, it's a difficult language. Things like that require intelligence and perseverance. Is it going alright?
Client:	It's going ok. This summer I'm going to China. I want to be able to read the street names and ask directions. And I want to order food in a restaurant without the help of my book.
Practitioner:	Wow!
Client:	I'm a bit nervous because it'll be my first time flying and travelling alone.
Practitioner:	WOW!
Client:	About time I become more independent.
Practitioner:	That's really exciting. Everything you just told me says a lot about you, don't you think?

- Contributes among others to [cimo-1] [cimo-3] [cimo-7] [cimo-8] [cimo-12].

Case-L: Coping at minus 27

(Cauffman & Van Dijk, 2014)

Practitioner:	On a scale from 0 to 10, where 0 stands for 'the situation just before we started our sessions' and 10 for 'this is good enough for me', where would you say you are now? [cimo-19]

APPENDIX A **151**

Client:	It's completely hopeless. My partner threatens to leave me, I'm about to lose my job, and I get more and more depressed each day. [cimo-3] I'm at minus 27.
Practitioner:	How do you cope? [cimo-13]
Client:	I really can't do this any longer. It's unbearable and it gets harder and harder.
Practitioner:	*looks client in the eye with compassion and stays silent.*
Client:	I need to. I can't let my kids starve, can I? They must go to school in the morning.
Practitioner:	*remains silent and nods.*
Client:	I must go to my work, or else they'll kick me out. And if I let myself go, my partner turns even more distant, and I don't want that. So, I scrape together all my energy in order to keep functioning. I don't want to lose my marriage, I want to take care for my family, and I need the money from my job.
Practitioner (has heard enough to break the silence):	So, if I understand correctly, even though you are at minus 27 and experience extreme difficulties, you manage to pull yourself together and keep going. Even through your despair, you've found the strength to look after your children, to drag yourself to work and do your best so you won't get fired. You even manage to let the responsibility that you feel for you family prevail over your own miserable state. And the relationship you have with your partner is important enough to try hard to make it work. [cimo-8] [cimo-11]
Client:	If you say so, well, yes.
Practitioner:	What should be different so that you could give yourself a number that is slightly higher? [cimo-18]
Client:	If only I could see for myself that there is some truth in what you just told me.
Practitioner:	What do you need to be able to do this? [cimo-20]
Client:	I must use what self-confidence that remains and not allow myself to let go completely. I realize that I am using all my strength to do what is necessary for my family.

- Contributes among others to [cimo-3] [cimo-8] [cimo-11] [cimo-13] [cimo-18] [cimo-19] [cimo-20].

Case-M: The crying client

(Cauffman, 2010)

As a very young therapist, with a lot of ambition and full of theories, but unbiased by any practical experience, I once talked to a young woman. After she had given me her address, she started sobbing. It was clear that this woman was carrying a heavy burden and during the first session I used all my skills to support her: '… it's okay to cry. … I understand you are facing hard times. [cimo-1] Take a deep breath, try to tell me what the problem is'. [cimo-3] Result: zero. The woman sobbed her heart out and I had no idea what was going on. She couldn't put it into words. At the end of the session, I still didn't understand what the problem was. I kindly asked her if she wanted to come back. She could only nod 'yes' and we made a new appointment. For the second session, I had prepared a series of questions. I had to find out what was going on with her. But it went the same: tears, sobbing and sighing, but no words. I didn't know what else to do and I was starting to get very worried about her, so I tried a more direct approach: 'Try to say something …. Take a deep breath and tell me …. Is there something wrong with your relationship or with your child … or with your work? What is going on? Calm down'. No improvement, the woman kept crying and I seriously started to doubt my professional skills. The client wanted a new appointment, at least that was what I could tell from her nod. Once again, I was well prepared: It will work this time. However, I was very surprised when I started the third session. She looked different, she was excited and told me: 'I'm cured. I want to thank you for your help'. I was speechless. A bit thrown off, I asked her what she meant, she said: 'I've never felt so understood. You were so patient with me. I could finally be myself during our sessions'. To this day, I still don't know what was wrong with this woman ….

- Contributes among others to [cimo-1] [cimo-3].

Case-N: Burnt out with St. Bernard

(Cauffman, 2022)

Sid (talking to his external coach Dick):	Things aren't much better yet, Dick. Since I've been at home with my burnout, I've been slouching from one chair to another couch. When I get up in the morning, I'm still tired. Or should I say already tired? Because by then I've usually been lying around wide awake in my bed for several hours. This has been going on for more than two months now. I feel ashamed when I think that my colleagues have so much extra work because of this, while I am just hanging around at home.
Dick:	Burnout is a serious issue, Sid. It's grossly underestimated. It's to your credit that you're so concerned about your colleagues. Can I ask you some questions?
Sid:	Please because I'm not getting anywhere on my own.
Dick:	You just said that things are not much better yet. Do I understand correctly that this means that things are going a little better anyway? [cimo-7]
Sid:	One day it is, the next day I have the feeling I'm back to square one.

Dick:	OK. I'm sorry to say but those fluctuations are normal. Slowly crawling out of the pit of burnout and then slowly beginning to feel firmer ground under your feet again is how the recovery process works. And – especially in the beginning – there are days when one has the feeling of sliding backwards.
Sid:	That's exactly how it is.
Dick:	Sid, imagine that, on a scale of minus ten to zero, where the minus ten represents when you had to stop work and yet found the courage to seek help because you didn't want to stick with it alone and the zero represents 'now it's sufficiently good to be able to slowly take up my schoolwork again, where do you stand now? [cimo-19]
Sid:	At a minus six.
Dick:	Fine. What is already different so that you can already give yourself a minus six?
Sid:	I don't think a minus six is great yet. But anyway, I'm starting to get up the nerve to do something fun again. In the beginning I felt guilty when I sat at home and read a book, not that I enjoyed it.
Dick:	What else? [cimo-8]
Sid:	When I get up, I'm usually still tired but I get up with my family. We have breakfast together. I think that's important. When my wife and son are out of the house, at work and at school, I clean up the breakfast table. Then I dare to crawl on the couch. I don't sleep then but I still have the feeling of resting a bit.
Dick:	Excellent, you scrape together your energy to be busy with your family and then allow yourself some rest. [cimo-11] What else is in that minus six?
Sid:	Now that you ask me, it comes to mind. Last week I started walking the dog in the afternoon. That is, the dog walks me. It's a Saint Bernard, a colossus (both laugh). Before that, I didn't dare show myself in the street for fear that the neighbors would say 'what is Sid doing now, shouldn't he be working?'. I got over that. I just told my neighbors what was going on.
Dick:	And?
Sid:	All understanding. That was kind of nice.
Dick:	Anything else?
Sid:	No, that's it.
Dick:	What could be the smallest next step forward? What would you do, think, feel differently? [cimo-20]

- Contributes among others to [cimo-7] [cimo-8] [cimo-11] [cimo-19] [cimo-20].

Case-O: High potential

(Cauffman, 2006)

William (29) has been promoted twice during the last couple of years. He has a PhD in economics and is labelled as a 'high potential' within his company. He is the assistant to Tom, the Vice President of a soft drinks production plant. William's job is to control production planning. A minor heart problem forced Tom to stay home for some weeks, and William was asked to temporarily take over Tom's position. [cimo-3] Top management said to William: 'If you manage this well, you are on your way up the corporate ladder'. William tackled his new task like the proverbial bull in the china shop and his over-enthusiasm showed in his behaviour: 'eyes-wide-shut and full speed ahead'. He jumped into the task feet first. With a lot of theoretical knowledge but little work floor experience, he started ordering others around. Feeling justified by the top manager's remark, he started to overstretch himself by introducing all kinds of changes in the production planning. He started acting like a newly appointed crisis manager and was talking about wonderful new goals for the production department. 'If we really set our mind to this, this production plant can become the world's top. We can double production, lower personnel cost, we can even give a lot of advice to marketing and sales since they hardly know anything of the production possibilities we have'. In short, William got carried away by aspiring to unrealistic and unachievable goals. Along the way, he also forgot to connect to the reality of life 'in the trenches' and he lost the connection with his team. William was quickly overwhelmed. The unions were on his back, and his co-workers didn't like having an 'upstart' as a boss. Within a few weeks, William's position became untenable. Top management considered removing him from the position. Fortunately, from his sickbed, Tom showed more wisdom than anyone else. He wrote an email to the management, to William and to the workers on the production floor: 'Give William a fair chance. [cimo-1] Let him take on tasks that he can fulfill and use your years of experience to get us through the peak season. I will coach William from behind the scenes as much as I can, given my health situation. Please continue to do what all of you have been doing for years now: take care of the company'. [cimo-10] The gist of this email was practical. It said to management: 'Don't overestimate William by expecting things from him that he can't handle'. [cimo-2] The message for the people on the shop floor was as follows: 'Don't underestimate him and write him off, either'. In the following weeks, Tom invited William to his house twice a week to coach him on his management methods and to soften him up. Tom asked a lot of detailed questions on how William proceeded daily. He took every chance to compliment William on the things that he did well. [cimo-11] The questions gave their working relationship enough leverage to deliver the necessary criticism and feedback to coach William towards a more useful and less bossy style. [cimo-12] William accepted the fact that he needed more guidance. The co-workers became much less critical and more understanding. Positive changes were soon underway.

- Contributes among others to [cimo-1] [cimo-2] [cimo-3] [cimo-10] [cimo-11] [cimo-12].

CASE-P: Samia

(Ratner & Yusuf, 2015)

Samia was a 16-year-old girl who was referred by her social worker. She was living away from home and had experienced many difficulties and challenges in her life.

Samia told me that she usually tried to wrap up her thoughts in a bag and ignore them – but that it was difficult to do this. [cimo-3] The thoughts were often very self-critical, and she wanted to be less harsh towards herself, believe in herself more and not give up on herself all the time – to have a different bag of thoughts perhaps. [cimo-4] The difference this would make for her was that she would feel more confident and perhaps do some things in other ways, and this became our contract of work. I asked her what sort of things she might notice the next morning when she woke up if she were more confident and doing things differently. [cimo-7] [cimo-8] [cimo-20] Some of her ideas included the following:

- Looking into the mirror first thing and smiling
- Holding her head up in the bus
- Going to the front or at least to the middle of the rehearsal room, and not straight to the back
- Sitting closer to other people at lunchtimes
- Taking her headphones off sometimes when with other people

We talked about this day, about how other people would respond to her and about how she would react to this. During this conversation, there were some very small things she recognized that she had already been doing, such as sitting a bit closer to other students and not storming out of the studio so often. [cimo-14] We explored these instances, how she had done them, and how others had reacted; for example, one or two students included her in conversations when she was sitting nearer and other people had offered to help her when she stayed in the studio.

- Contributes among others to [cimo-3] [cimo-4] [cimo-7] [cimo-8] [cimo-14] [cimo-20].

CASE-Q: Keni: Walking in a different way

(Ratner & Yusuf, 2015)

Keni was a 12-year-old boy referred for coaching because of the number of fights he was getting into. He experienced other students as picking on him and making his life unhappy and would become very angry and lash out. [cimo-3] Keni had many ambitions: He wanted to be famous and run a hotel. He wanted to get some good exam passes, earn money, and buy smart clothes. [cimo-4] The school wanted him to manage his anger. Keni's best hopes from the coaching were to get on better at school so that he could achieve his ambitions. We looked at what sort of life he wanted for himself in school which would help him on his way to the sort of life he wanted outside school. [cimo-7] [cimo-8] [cimo-20] I encouraged him to describe this in detail. [cimo-1] It included taking part more in lessons, ignoring other students' negative comments, walking in a different way around the school, smiling and starting conversations, and playing basketball more with others. [cimo-3] I asked Keni to show me what he meant by some of these descriptions. He was good at drama and so he role-played talking, smiling, focusing, answering questions, and especially walking in a different way around my room. [cimo-8]

- Contributes among others to [cimo-1] [cimo-3] [cimo-4] [cimo-7] [cimo-8] [cimo-20].

CASE-R: James and the oxygen bottle

(Ratner, Georges & Iveson, 2012)

James is 25, well educated but stuck in what he considers to be a dead-end job. He has recently been discharged from hospital after taking an overdose. He lives with his parents who do not get on. His mother is severely disabled by multiple sclerosis and his father works long hours 'to avoid being at home' (according to James, who 'hates' his father). [cimo-3] James provides most of his mother's support [cimo-8] and this, he says, prevents him from having a life of his own. He would like to have more confidence. [cimo-4] This extract is from half-way through the first meeting. James has described getting up, chatting with his mother, being more polite to his father and more conscientious at work. [cimo-8]

Therapist[1]: And after work, how would your confidence show then? [cimo-10] [cimo-20]
James: I'd like to go for a drink, but I can't really leave my mother that long.
Therapist: Would she be upset if you stayed out?
James: Probably not because she always says I should get a life before she dies otherwise, I'll be really stuck.
Therapist: So, your mum might even be pleased to see you going out more? [cimo-12]

James:	She would if she didn't need me so much or if my dad did more, but he won't because they don't even speak to each other most of the time.
Therapist:	So if they got on better you think your dad might help more?
James:	Yes, but he won't.
Therapist:	If they did, what would be the first sign?
James:	They wouldn't. It's too far gone.
Therapist:	If a miracle happened and they did start to get on, what would be the first sign? [cimo-21]
James:	They'd communicate.
Therapist:	About?
James:	Anything and everything.
Therapist:	And what would be the first sign of them just beginning to talk? [cimo-7] [cimo-20]
James:	He'd help mum more.
Therapist:	What would be the first sign of him helping your mum more?
James:	He'd help her with her oxygen; she needs oxygen now and she can't change the bottle herself, so if I saw dad helping her with the oxygen, I'd know they were getting on better. [cimo-15]
Therapist:	What difference would that make – seeing your dad change the bottle? [cimo-20]
James:	A huge difference.
Therapist:	Like?
James:	Like I'd think I could have a life of my own at long last.

- Contributes among others to [cimo-3] [cimo-4] [cimo-7] [cimo-8] [cimo-10] [cimo-12] [cimo-15] [cimo-20] [cimo-21].

CASE-S: A healing speech

(Ratner, Georges & Iveson, 2012)

Paul is in his early 20s. His life has been dominated by ill health and by the failure of the medical world to take his condition seriously. [cimo-3] After the first part of the interview, [cimo-1] the therapist took a break and spoke as follows, after the thinking pause:

> *Paul. It would be clear to anyone listening to you just how tough things have been for you, not just your struggles with your health, the time that you have spent in hospital, the pain that you have experienced but also the failure of the medical world to get to grips with your situation and to take you seriously. As you said, at times it has felt like living within a never-ending nightmare. And alongside that what has been just as clear had been your extraordinary capacity to keep yourself going, to keep hope alive in your live, to keep struggling and fighting for people to take you situation seriously to get the medical treatment that you have needed.*

[cimo-8] *And beyond that you have fought determinedly to hold on to your hopes for your life and for your future, you have held on to your wish to be useful to others and even after the recent setback you have been determined to improve your mobility, to be independent again, to live. You have been going out more, you have been connecting with people again, you have, as you said, been 'living again'.* [cimo10] [cimo-11] *As to the future you are more than clear about your goals for yourself and your best hopes from our talking and you have a very clear picture of the small signs that will tell you that you are moving on from this point that you have already reached.* [cimo-20] *Above all you have '10' confidence that you will progress* [cimo-19]*, and that confidence is based on firm evidence.*

- Contributes among others to [cimo-1] [cimo-3] [cimo-8] [cimo-10] [cimo-11] [cimo-19] [cimo-20].

Case-T: The glass company

(Polgár & Hankovszky, 2015)

This is the story of how the solution-focused approach was introduced to a small business – a company making and selling glass giftware. The questions we asked during the preliminary interview clarified the following situation. Starting with just 2 people, the company had grown steadily and at the time of the coaching work together it employed about 30 people. They were engaged in the whole range of activities: making the giftware in a factory and selling it through its own retail outlets (three shops) as well as through major department stores throughout the country. [cimo-1] [cimo-3]

The prospect of two days in a training room is not very enticing, even when the invitation comes from the top! The event was to end with the company's Christmas party, but to many, this seemed a minor consolation. Most of the people working in the company had left school as soon as they could; the prospect of coming into a training room filled some of them with dread and others with resentment that their busy lives were being interrupted. This had to be handled carefully! The project of engaging the participants started long before they came into the meeting room. [cimo-1] [cimo-3] Everyone received a personal invitation from us, telling them what to expect and whom to contact if they wanted to talk about the event beforehand. [cimo-5] We also asked them to think about achievements that they were particularly proud of, times when they had felt really good at work ('sparkling moments') and challenges that they were facing at work. [cimo-8] [cimo-9] [cimo-14]

Twenty-eight people crowded into the company's meeting room and we knew it was very important to get them actively involved right from the start – this was not a group used to sitting quietly and listening to long expositions of theory. After a few introductory remarks from Bob and us, we got everybody's voice into the room by asking them to introduce themselves by name, role in the company [cimo-3] and by briefly describing a sparkling moment at work. [cimo-8]

Then they all produced a poster showing two achievements or skills and two challenges that they were facing at work. Displaying all these colourful posters on the walls was a great way of displaying the wealth of talent in the room, as well as letting everyone – not least Bob – become aware of the range of challenges that people could see. [cimo-4]

Not surprisingly, several people identified many of the issues and so the group decided to tackle the most common issues first. [cimo-4] These included:

- stock control, which had been identified as an issue from many perspectives: the production line workers who didn't always have the raw materials they needed, the retail shops who didn't always have the finished goods they wanted and the dispatch department dealing with department store orders who saw themselves as last on every list when it came to getting the finished goods they needed;
- 'housekeeping' – keeping premises tidy;
- making time for developing new products;
- getting new people up to speed.

Rather than dividing people up in to groups ourselves, we asked everyone to work with the issue they felt most strongly about and then to form themselves into groups of about four or five to work together.

The afternoon was spent in the review phase, with participants working together in their workplace groups (raw material handling, production, retail, administration) to pool their learning and decide on one or two small steps for each individual to take in the general direction of the ideal. We made sure to offer positive comments [cimo-8] [cimo-11] on all issues, themes and topics that pointed the group towards their goals [cimo-4]. We asked question about the progress that they wanted to achieve [cimo-20] on the foundation of what already went well in their collaboration [cimo-10].

- Contributes among others to [cimo-1] [cimo-3] [cimo-4] [cimo-5] [cimo-8] [cimo-9] [cimo-10] [cimo-11] [cimo-14] [cimo-20].

Case-U: High-flying Tony

(Iveson, 2014)

In this ultra-short case study, many solution-focused elements are concealed between the lines and it is the task of the facilitator to hear them, unearth them and hand them back to the client.

He was the father of a boy I had helped overcome 'school phobia'. [cimo-1] A high-flying executive in a US-based multinational Tony's sparkling career had led him and his family through several capital city postings. [cimo-3] Though financially well rewarded, this was a tough life for a family whose hope was that a home posting would eventually be offered so they could return to the States. [cimo-4] Tony had been invited to apply for such a job much earlier than expected. If he succeeded, he would be the youngest vice president in the company. [cimo-8] In the run-up to the interview, his high hopes for a yes became a big stress factor. He had lost his nerve and even become afraid of flying. [cimo-3]

We met once. Tony said he could overcome his fear sufficiently to board a plane [cimo-15] but as to facing the interview he could not see a way. [cimo-2] The interview was to be in his hometown, and he would be staying on familiar territory at his parents' house. [cimo-8]

Facilitator: Let's imagine it's the morning of your interview and during the night a miracle has happened and sorted out your fear! [cimo-21] So you're ready for it – absolutely at your best. [cimo-7] [cimo-8] What's the first thing you'd notice when you woke up? [cimo-20]
Tony: I wouldn't be dreading the interview! [cimo-15]
Facilitator: What would you be doing instead? [cimo-7] [cimo-8]
Tony: I'd be thinking it's going to be a tough day but I'm lucky to have the chance. [cimo-8]
Facilitator: Great! And if you woke up with those thoughts and feelings what difference will[2] that make? [cimo-8] [cimo-11] [cimo-20]
Tony: I'd want to get straight up!

- Contributes among others to [cimo-1] [cimo-2] [cimo-3] [cimo-4] [cimo-7] [cimo-8] [cimo-15] [cimo-20] [cimo-21].

Case-V: Two is a crowd

(Iveson in: Hoyt & Bobele, 2019)

Joseph was described as a 'revolving door schizophrenic' a characterization that carried little hope for his future well-being. He was referred by Donna, a community psychiatrist.

Joseph was a very jolly man and member of a 'celebrity' family. From his late teens to his early 40s, he had been in and out of psychiatric hospitals and had made numerous suicide attempts, some very serious. [cimo-3] Sitting at ease in our clinic, he was happy to tell me all his history. [cimo-1] Listening to his – sometimes – harrowing tale, I began to see a man of great personal strength and resourcefulness hidden behind the man most professionals had written off. Through Joseph's account of a seemingly failed life, there began to appear a 'shadow story' of survival, struggle, determination, perseverance and hope. [cimo-8] To hear this story, to read between the lines of what was being said, required of me a very intense form of listening verified by the occasional question. [cimo-7]

Chris: What are your best hopes from our talking together? [cimo-4]
Joseph: I don't know, my social worker told me to come. [cimo-5]

Chris:	And if coming here proves to be a good idea what difference do you hope it will make? [cimo-7] [cimo-8]
Joseph:	To be honest, I don't really expect it to make a difference – nothing has.
Chris:	If it did?
Joseph:	If it did! Then I'd be able to get on and lead a normal life get a job, get married.
	At this point Joseph took a long look at the empty space to his right then turned back to me with a hopeless shrug saying,
Joseph:	She's angry. She didn't want me to come here.
	Not wanting to step into this strange territory without more familiarity with its contours, I sought to confirm with Joseph his desired outcome:
Chris:	So, if our talking together led in some way to you leading a normal life, getting a job and possibly even getting married would that mean it had been worthwhile? [cimo-4]
Joseph:	Yes. (*turning again to the empty space on his right*) What do you think, Jenny?
Chris:	If a miracle happened tonight while you were asleep, and it set your life on track towards a normal life with a job and a wife what might be the first thing you'd notice? [cimo-21]
Joseph:	(*Turning to his right*) She wouldn't tell me to kill myself. [cimo-6]
Chris:	What would she do instead? [cimo-7]
Joseph:	She'd agree to marry me! (*a laugh and turning to his right, saying to the empty space*) You don't have to marry me if you don't want to.
	This 'three-way' conversation continued for a few minutes with Joseph, more often than not, putting my questions to the silent and invisible 'Jenny' whose answers, if she gave any, I was unable to hear.
Chris:	Joseph, would you mind if I asked Jenny some questions?
Joseph:	(*looking to his right and then rather suspiciously at the therapist*) Okay.
Chris:	Obviously I can't see her so; will you be her for a few minutes?
Joseph:	(*looking a bit confused*) Okay.
Chris:	Jenny, what are your best hopes from this conversation? [cimo-4]
Jenny (Joseph):	I'd like Joseph to ignore me when I get angry and tell him to kill himself. [cimo-8]
Chris:	So, you don't really want him to kill himself?
Jenny (Joseph):	Definitely not!
Chris:	How come?

Jenny (Joseph):   Because I love him.
Chris: What do you love about him?
Jenny (Joseph):   He's very kind. [cimo-8]
Chris: What else?

    Jenny went on to list Joseph's numerous positive qualities and when prompted was able to give concrete examples of these qualities enacted. [cimo-7] [cimo-8] Then I asked,

Chris: What might be the very first small sign that Joseph is beginning to ignore your instructions? [cimo-15]
Jenny (Joseph):   He won't shut himself away. He tries to hide in his room when I'm angry. [cimo-15]
Chris: What might he do instead?
Jenny (Joseph):   He'll carry on with his routine. [cimo-8]
Chris: What else will tell you that he is ignoring your instructions?
Jenny (Joseph):   He'll keep taking his medication because his body needs them. [cimo-2]
Chris: What difference do you think that will make?
Jenny (Joseph):   He goes crazy when he stops his medication and that makes me even more angry.
Chris: What difference might it make to you if Joseph carries on with his routine and keeps taking his medication?
Jenny (Joseph):   I won't have to worry about him so much.
Chris: What do you think will replace the worry?
Jenny (Joseph):   Worry makes me angry, so I won't get so angry.
Chris: What will replace the anger?
Jenny (Joseph):   I'd be more calm [cimo-15]
Chris: What difference will that make?
Jenny (Joseph):   We'd get along better. [cimo-8]
Chris: Is this useful, Jenny, when we talk like this? [cimo-16]
Jenny: Not for me, but for Joseph, certainly.

    I drew out a little more description of what 'getting along better' might look like, then thanked Jenny and went back to a direct conversation with Joseph.

Chris: So, Joseph, what would be the first sign of this miracle happening? What would tell you that your life was beginning to move forward normally towards a job and possibly even marriage? [cimo-21]
Joseph: I wouldn't lie in bed half the day.
Chris: What would you do instead? [cimo-20]

The session now continued routinely without further asides to 'Jenny'. Joseph was able to describe many features of what, for him, would be a 'normal' life.

- Contributes among others to [cimo-1] [cimo-2] [cimo-3] [cimo-4] [cimo-5] [cimo-7] [cimo-8] [cimo-15] [cimo-16] [cimo-20] [cimo-21].

APPENDIX A **163**

Case-W: Death defeated

(Iveson in: Hoyt & Bobele, 2019)

Rosa, a suicidal young woman, had been admitted over the weekend and was being detained against her will so she could be force-fed. Though only 19, she was well known to the hospital. From the age of 12, she had been struggling against a compulsion to starve herself to death and was now close to losing the struggle. Being familiar with the system, she had come prepared, this time, with a lethal overdose sewn into her clothing. Only the vigilance of a nursing assistant had saved her. But pumping out her stomach had left her very weak. The staff's choice was to risk killing her by force-feeding or let her die from starvation. [cimo-3] This was not the first time that I had encountered desperate patients being protected from self-harm on locked wards nor was it the first time I had offered to meet with the client.

Chris: What are your best hopes from our talking together? [cimo-1] [cimo-4]
Rosa: I don't do hope.
Chris: If you did? If you did do hope?
Rosa: (*With the same flat tone*) I ... don't ... do ... hope.
Chris: How come you agreed to see me?
Rosa: It's something to do.
Chris: Is it? Seeing a counselor? Most people in here would run a mile before seeing someone like me! [cimo-1] [cimo-5]
Rosa: That's true!
Chris: So how come you agreed? [cimo-1]
Rosa: You don't know how bad it is in here!
Chris: Don't you like it?
Rosa: What do you think?
Chris: I don't know, but I bet there are people here that like it so much they can't be persuaded to leave.
Rosa: (*With the first sign of animation*) Well, I'm not one of them!
Chris: So, you want to leave? [cimo-4]
Rosa: (*Forcefully*) Yes, I do!
Chris: So, if our meeting, in some way helps you leave here, that means it will have been useful? [cimo-20]
Rosa: Maybe
Chris: I mean leave here in a way that is right for you?
Rosa: (*With renewed animation*) Yes!
Chris: So, let's imagine that tonight, while you are asleep, a miracle happens; it doesn't get you out of here, but what it does do is set off the process which will enable you to leave this hospital .... leave this hospital in a way that is absolutely right for you ...... absolutely right for you – and right for the hospital. What will be the first thing that you notice that tells you that a miracle has happened? [cimo-21]
Rosa: I suppose I wouldn't feel so bad when I woke up.

Chris: How would you feel instead?
Rosa: I wouldn't be happy.
Chris: So how do you think you would feel after this miracle even though you weren't actually feeling happy.
Rosa: I don't know, maybe a sense of just getting on with it.
Chris: What time would that be?
Rosa: Too early! When they start clanking around and changing shifts.
Chris: Who might be the first to notice at that early time that you had woken up ready to 'get on with it'? [cimo-7]
Rosa: Probably, Angela, she's one of the ward sisters and she's on this week.
Chris: What do you think Angela might notice that gives her the first hint that this miracle has happened, and you have decided to 'get on with it'?
Rosa: (*Laughing*) I'll say 'Good morning' to her.
Chris: Will she be surprised or does that happen anyway? [cimo-8]
Rosa: She'll definitely be surprised – I don't talk to anyone at that time! [cimo-15]
Chris: How do you think she'll respond?
Rosa: She'll probably want to hug me!
Chris: Would you like that?
Rosa: (*Looking at her body*) as long as she didn't snap me in half!
Chris: What would Angela notice about your response to her hug that fitted with you deciding to 'get on with it'? [cimo-8] [cimo-11]
Rosa: I'd probably tell her she didn't have to worry, not this time anyway.
Chris: How might she respond to that?
Rosa: Knowing Angela, she'd probably cry – we'd both probably cry!
Chris: What might be the next small sign that this miracle had happened? [cimo-20]

- Contributes among others to [cimo-1] [cimo-3] [cimo-4] [cimo-5] [cimo-7] [cimo-8] [cimo-11] [cimo-15] [cimo-20] [cimo-21].

Case-X: A damn good boss

(Iveson & Coach in: Burgstaller, 2015)

The client wanted to deal better with her middle management position. [cimo-4] It starts two minutes into the session after the coach had expressed his admiration for the delicate work of managers in a middle management position. [cimo-1]

Coach: I guess the most important question is, what are your best hopes for the result of this session. [cimo-4]
Client: My best hope would be I find some – not strategy, but some way to support people in their strive to get better and what they do, and to support them ... to be there. I am not going to say cheerleader, but I can't find

	another word. And try to plant a seed ... for them to see that the new management isn't all bad.
Coach:	OK.
Client:	And they'd feel good about their job and what they do. Yeah. Many things.
Coach:	Many things, yeah, I've noticed at least three so far. [cimo-11]
Client:	Oh, yeah. But I guess mostly to make them feel good about what they do. [cimo-8]
Coach:	OK.
Client:	So they can be proud.
Coach:	OK. Now that was the first thing you said actually, yes, support them in becoming ... being good and be proud. OK. And you said it is not a strategy you are looking for as a result of this session but more of a way ...? [cimo-12]
Client:	Yeah. How can I, ... with my ... can I say behaviour plant the seed ... or what kind of signals can I send out for them to pick up, and well ....
Coach:	Signals, behaviour, and maybe your contribution. Yeah, OK? – Hm. – I am trying to locate where you are on your way. How long have you been doing this kind of work? [cimo-3]
Client:	A year.
Coach:	A year? OK. And so on a scale from one to ten, and ten meaning you have found your way of planting the seed, reinforce, make them, you know, do whatever they can do, so they feel reinforced. So that would be ten. And one would be, when you first started this kind of work in this position in-between. What would you say where you are right now? [cimo-20]
Client:	I would say at 5.
Coach:	At five. OK. More 4.9 or more? [cimo-18]
Client:	5.1.
Coach:	5.1? And there came this beautiful smile. [cimo-1] So there seems to be a difference between a 5 and a 5.1.
Client:	It is.
Coach:	It is a difference. Yes, I can see. Can you reveal a little bit about the difference when you are able to say, hey, I am at 5.1, and not at 5 or lower anymore?
Client:	Well because I know in my heart that I am on the right way, but I really want to see faster results.
Coach:	OK.
Client:	I want to see if I can push them hard in a positive way.
Coach:	Yeah, OK, good. With this in mind, how might you know this at the end of our session, that your best hopes are well on the way to become realized? ... how would you know by the end of this session? [cimo-20]
Client:	I would probably feel more secure in my own – what's it called – in my ability to do such a thing.

166 APPENDIX A

Coach: More secure in your ability. I suppose more secured at the end of the session. What might be some of the effects then? So I get a clear idea of "more secured". What does that mean for tomorrow – probably you are going back (to work), right? OK. So if you are going back more secured, what might be some of the effects? [cimo-20]

Client: I guess people would notice that, maybe I change my posture, right? And more positive ... maybe I say even more positive things, cheer on them more, like they are doing a real great job ... yeah.

Coach: OK. So, being more secured about this might be one of the results of the session, what else?

Client: Like what they would notice?

Coach: Like that, for example, yes.

Client: Well I guess, my management, my boss would notice. That I am doing a great job too.

Coach: Is that a new boss or the old one?

Client: The old one, the new one hasn't arrived yet.

OK. And you are already preparing the field?

Client: Yes.

Coach: Wow! [cimo-11]

Client: Because we need to, we need to have staff that is confidence in what they do, or happy and proud of what they do.

Coach: Before the new management arrives.

Client: Yes.

Coach: Well I am really impressed ... that means that somehow in this middle position apparently you manage to think much further then the next day ... you know, putting out the fires that burn. You seem to have a long-term perspective, long term goals that you ... wow! OK. I am even more impressed. OK. [cimo8] [cimo-11]

Client: Thank you.

Coach: So you said, your old boss might notice.

Client: Uhm.

Coach: OK, what else might be the signs of the result of this session that tell you, yeah, I am well on the way towards my best hopes for the session? [cimo-20]

Client: Well I think probably my friends, and my family would notice as well. Maybe I am more like – I don't know – positive perhaps?

Coach: It is interesting when you said that, you made this kind of (forward) movement and I started to wonder ... now we are going to make it challenging it for the people at the camera ... you say, being on the way includes a movement, right? I don't know whether it's going to be possible for them (*pointing towards camera*), but, would it be possible that you make a couple of steps and we could see how you would be on the way now and how you would like to be on the way after your best hopes. Would it be interesting to try out? [cimo-18] [cimo-20]

Client: OK. Sure. Here I am right now.
Coach: OK. Yeah.
Client: And when I am on my way, I hold my head up.
Coach: You hold your head up. OK. Yes. How would that make a difference for you?
Client: It would boost my confidence in myself, I guess.
Coach: OK. How else? – I suppose boost the confidence in yourself – what might be the effects, … some of the effects, … how might that change some of the things in your life … or how would that show?
Client: You know, I think it would make a very big change actually.
Coach: OK.
Client: So, I think yeah, it would.
Coach: Could you share a little bit about that very big change, share some of the effects – or I don't know maybe it's beyond words – I don't know, would it be possible to …? [cimo-8] [cimo-10]
Client: I don't know, I am striving to be … I wanted to do something else in my work life, and I think that this positive change could … maybe I send out different signals when I am like applying for management roles.
Coach: So in that sense, hm. And again, it pops up, your ability to see a big span not only for others and for the company and for your people but also for yourself.
Client: Yes.
Coach: OK. I start to get an idea about our common project. … There is one more curiosity left. If we take the big span of your life … your professional life. What's around the ten in that big span, do you have an idea where you are heading towards? [cimo-7] [cimo-20]
Client: Well, if I am at ten, I would probably use all my capabilities in my …. I am looking for a word. Let's rephrase. I think that if I am at number ten … well, I would make a damn good boss.
Coach: OK, … sounds like a good common project. [cimo-11]

- Contributes among others to [cimo-1] [cimo-3] [cimo-4] [cimo-7] [cimo-8] [cimo-10] [cimo-11] [cimo-12] [cimo-15] [cimo-18] [cimo-20] [cimo-21]

Case-Y: Keep your friends close, and your contractors closer[3]

(Cauffman, 2007)

Bill, a facilities manager responsible for the coordination of technical building projects in an oil refinery, is constantly frustrated. He complains to his employees that the contractors, and particularly their respective subcontractors, are not keeping their promises. Consequently, the building projects are chronically behind schedule. From fear of losing face, he doesn't talk to his boss about these problems. The problem comes to a head when the work on a special production unit doesn't finish in time, causing the whole production line to be stopped with big financial losses consequently. At that point, Bill is put on the spot by the management. The production manager and the financial manager are furious. They order Bill into their office: 'What the %&$*!* is happening, Bill? You never tell us anything. We just have to guess how things are going in your part of the organisation. And now you shut down production without warning us. This can't go on any longer'. When Bill tries to defend himself by blaming the contractors, the management reminds him that he is the one who is paid to get things done on time. The management agrees to give him another chance. They appoint Bruce, an experienced project manager, as Bill's supervisor. 'You seem not to be able to get things straightened out on your own, Bill. You have been working hard in the past, that's why we aren't firing you on the spot. But our patience is wearing thin. We no longer accept that you keep us uninformed about progress. You accept help now or you are out'. It should be no surprise that Bill doesn't welcome this move from the management, but he has no choice but to accept.

In their first meeting, Bill tells Bruce: 'I don't see why my management is after me like that. I have been working extremely hard and have done everything possible. To me, the fact that they're forcing you upon me seems more like a punishment than support. Mind you, I have nothing against you – you are just following orders. I don't see what you can do for me unless you have a magic trick to make sure that the contractors get their work done on time'.

Bruce is immediately aware that Bill is not asking for help on how he can proceed differently to appease the management and accepts that Bill is stuck in his focus on the unwilling contractors. This is clearly a non-committal relationship. Bruce realizes that entering a discussion is useless so instead, he decides to give Bill the chance to vent some of his frustrations.

Bruce: 'OK, Bill, you and I are not going to change the world, let alone the contractor's behaviour. Why don't you first explain your viewpoint to me, then we can investigate how you can use your skills to improve your management of the situation'.

Bill relaxes a bit and, insisting that it wasn't his fault that the projects were behind schedule, he offers a litany of explanations and excuses. 'I have done everything in my power to make the contractors do their work on time. You surely agree that I can't go after them with an Uzi. Constantly yelling at them doesn't work either. That just invites them to make up even more lame excuses that would cause even more problems for our company. The contracts I give them are already as clear and as strict as legally possible. In this business, you have to understand, Bruce, that you need to give people some leeway, or you find nobody who is willing to accept the job. Whenever I finally contract a certain party that will do the job, I just don't have the time to sit down with them and talk it through with them. Once they take a job, the contractors are on their own — it is their responsibility to do a good job, not mine'.

Bruce:	'How do you communicate with your management during these processes?'
Bill:	'Are you kidding? I don't even have time to talk to the contractors, let alone time to talk to the management about how I proceed. I leave them alone and they leave me alone — everyone to their own work'.
Bruce:	'So, if I understand correctly, what you are telling me is that, once the contracts are drawn up, you have blind faith in the outcome'.
Bill:	'Well, basically that's it, yes. Isn't that normal? I mean, when I say that I will do something, I just do it. I don't see why my contractors shouldn't behave in the same way. And I totally do not see why my management wouldn't trust me on this. But apparently, they don't trust me or we wouldn't be talking now'.

Bruce now goes for the second (appreciative) part of the intervention: 'There is a lot that is still going well, Bill, despite the problems. You have earned a good reputation within this company. Most of your projects are on time, even if it's often a close shave. The fact that your management is worried and sent me over to work with you intrinsically means that they don't want to lose you. Plus, amid storms, you have been able to maintain a positive attitude toward your contractors. However difficult your job is, you keep going at it.

Feeling supported, Bill relaxes some more and becomes a little less defensive. Then Bruce goes for the third part of the intervention: 'What is it that you could do differently so that your management no longer feels that you and I need to talk about this?'

Bill:	'If I could get all my contractors to do as they promise, I wouldn't have to talk to anybody at all. But I guess that that's a fairy tale'.
Bruce:	'Correct, and fairy tales sometimes happen but it is best not to count on them happening. What about your management? What could you do differently, so that they would no longer be breathing down your neck?'
Bill:	'Well, maybe I should cover my back a little bit more. As it goes now, I only do my best to get the contractors aligned, but there will never be a full guarantee there. Up to now, I have only taken care of putting the entire project into the planning software so that the contractors have an overview. I will of course keep doing that but maybe it would be good if I gave more feedback to my management about what's going on in the process. If things spin out of control, then they at least know this straight away. What do you think, Bruce?'
Bruce:	'Seems like a good idea. Any thoughts on how you could combine that with giving/getting more feedback to and from your contractors? It would be nice to kill two birds with one stone, don't you think?'
Bill:	'That would be perfect but how on earth could that be done?'
Bruce:	'It is obvious that you haven't much time, yet you will probably need to make some time to get more time. I know that your department is using

	planning software. Do you see any possibility of putting together reports from this software?'
Bill:	'Sure, whatever you put in can be shuffled into almost any report one can think of. Ah, it's dawning! Since I put every assignment into this planning software, I can easily create two different reports from it. One could serve as an implementation guide for the contractors and another could go to management so that they can follow what is happening'.
Bruce:	'Excellent idea, Bill, excellent. Would it be feasible to take your idea one little step further? When you assign a contract, might it be a good idea to fix a meeting with the contractor and go through your implementation plan step by step? That way you can involve the contractor from the very beginning. The report of this meeting then can be sent to your management and at the same time it can be used as a continuation protocol'.
Bill:	'That's it. I can use that continuation protocol — must find a better name though — to satisfy my management, it keeps them in the loop. At the same time, it obliges me to talk more to the contractors. Although I have little time, this will save me a lot of time in the long run. You know, Bruce, this brainstorm is really useful to me. And to the company.
Bruce:	'Congrats. Go for it'.

The result of this intervention is that Bill finds a different way to deal with his own management and that he develops an alternative method for dealing with the contractors.

- Contributes among others to [cimo-1] [cimo-2] [cimo-3] [cimo-4] [cimo-5] [cimo-7] [cimo-8] [cimo-11] [cimo-12].

Case-Z: A wonderful surprise

(Cauffman, 2007)

John is a successful software engineer who, over the years, has not only been given responsibility for technical matters but also was invited to become a team leader. However, he does not succeed in his role as a team leader: He fails to manage his team in an efficient manner. The company believes that the problem lies with John, because he does not use good communication techniques and does not have a good understanding of leadership.

John is convinced that the problem lies with his colleagues: They don't want to follow him, even though he is a technical genius. He also thinks of himself as a good explainer. He believes that the company does not support him enough in his position as manager, because the management does not want to convey the same message to his employees as he does.

It is easy to understand that this kind of situation quickly leads to deadlocks and stalemates.

We were able to solve the problem by asking John what, besides this 'problem', was going well with the employees. That same question to the team members yielded a host of exceptions: John turns out to be someone who is highly regarded for his technical expertise and his social behaviour outside of actual working together. As the goalkeeper of the company soccer team, he is highly regarded. As chairman of the team meetings, he is reviled.

When asked the miracle question, John answers, among other things, that the day after the miracle everyone will understand him better. When asked what he should do differently in order to be better understood, he – unexpectedly – makes the following proposal: 'Apart from all this nonsense about miracles, I think it would be better if I spent my time on a course in internal communication rather than on the umpteenth technical course. Let someone else get skilled in those technical matters. I'm going to focus on how to do my actual job better. The time has come for me to focus more on dealing with people'.

We are pleasantly surprised by this flood of words. Until now, we have only heard John speak so smoothly about technical matters, or when he was lamenting about others.

- Contributes among others to [cimo-7] [cimo-8] [cimo-10] [cimo-21].

Notes

1 The term *(psycho)therapist* is used in the original source. It equals the term *practitioner* in this book.
2 Please notice the difference if one uses the word *will* instead of *would*.
3 This case was also used in the β-testing section as case ex post to test the validity of the SoFAP-C design. See Section 5.2.1.

APPENDIX B

The four minimax decision rules in detail

Our thinking, acting, feeling and interacting is modified by the thinking, acting, feeling and interacting with our context, of which our fellowmen are a dominant factor.

Change facilitation is a process of interaction in which involved parties continuously must make decisions. The client must decide what he says or does not say. The practitioner must decide what he asks or does not ask. In addition to that, there is an inevitable mutual influence that also decides what the client and practitioner decide. To handle this complexity and obtain optimal efficiency, the following decision rules are helpful.

Rule 1: *If something still works (a.k.a is not broken), do not repair it but show respect and appreciation for what still works.*

Even in dire situations, there are always things that go well. Contrary to traditional types of therapy that focus on the (*why* of the) problems, a solution-focused approach should not be blind to the problems but must have a keen eye for those things that still function well, despite those problems. This means that when the time is right, the practitioner should ask for those things: *Despite of all the suffering and misery that you just described, can I ask you a slightly different question? What are the things in your life that still go well enough, so that you want to keep them?*

It happens that the client is so despondent that he is unable to answer this question. Then the practitioner should search for things that he assumes are important and still work well enough in the life of the client. The practitioner offers these issues in the form of a question: *Would you agree that X and Y in your life still work well?*

This should be done in a gentle, subtle and yet incisive manner, in order to help the client to detect his resources. The professional thereby must show respect and appreciation for the client's efforts and for the resources that surface.

Rule 2: *If something does not work, or no longer works, or does not work well enough after trying it for a while, stop, learn from it, and do something else.*

If something does not work

One can offer an intervention once, twice but if the client does not respond, then it is better to let that intervention go. One of the most common mistakes is to drone on when an intervention, however well intended, does not work.

Some things the practitioner and/or the client does just don't work and it is wise to acknowledge this. Practitioners and/or clients sometimes seem to be 'in love' with the things they keep on repeating without getting the desired effect. Bad habits are also included in this category.

or no longer works

Man is a creature of habit, and basically this is a good thing. Imagine returning from work, but instead of going home you walk into any random house…. Routines, habits, fixed patterns may be useful in most situations, but there are exceptions. Some habits are rather counterproductive. What was helpful yesterday may not work in today's changing circumstances. Certain psychological symptoms may once have had a function, but due to its repetitive and chronic character, this function has been lost. The alcohol that may have helped a patient through a stressful situation can just as well turn into alcohol abuse, stress or no stress. Benzodiazepines may be useful in certain situations, but frequent use of this medication may lead to long-term dependency. In short, a client can continue doing something that no longer works. Even worse: He now has an additional problem.

or does not work well enough

Some things the practitioner and/or client do are not sufficiently effective. It is important that the practitioner recognizes this on time to avoid counterproductive persistence.

after trying it for a while

Sometimes the practitioner and/or client must show some persistence. A message, insight, suggestion does not always come across from the start. If you give up immediately after a first attempt, you won't get very far in life. When offering an intervention, show some persistence, if need be, offer the same message in different forms or words. Be aware of the word 'offer': persistence is different from stubbornness.

stop

Letting things go in due time is better than doggedly pushing on. Continuing to push without the desired response can be counterproductive. Then the practitioner may develop the idea that the client is exhibiting resistance. From a solution-focused perspective, one can define this so-called resistant behaviour as a stage direction, read: additional information that shows the practitioner that, instead of pushing on, a different path should be taken which means doing something else.

learn from it

A good question now is: *What have you tried before that hasn't worked?* By asking this question, you are showing respect and consideration for the time and energy the client has already put into it, even if that effort has not helped. An additional benefit is that the practitioner gets direct information about which things not to try again. Sometimes this question shows you that the client has good intentions but has handled the issue in a suboptimal way.

and try something else

What that 'something else' is depends entirely on the context. To paraphrase Gregory Bateson: *We are going to look for a difference that makes a difference.* There are two categories of this difference: One is caused by the practitioner, the other by the client.

- Category 1: Practitioner acts differently

The practitioner can do something different. For example, instead of allowing the client to constantly talk about complaints, you can suggest other topics in a polite and respectful manner. The following questions can be helpful here: *I understand how serious your problems are and how frustrated you are because you seemingly can't do anything about them, but can I ask you a question: Are there things that, in spite of this big issue that you're facing, are still going well in your life?*, or *What are things in your life you would definitely like to keep?* Here, the 'continuation question' is recognized which is based on the resource orientation that assumes that there are always things that are still going well. By asking this question, you help the client to focus on those things. Over time, this could help the client to let go problem-focused mindset.

- Category 2: Client acts differently

You can ask the client if he wants to try something different instead of staying in a rut. In case the client agrees, he will give you permission to try something else. By phrasing your suggestion as a question, the client becomes the owner of the answer.

To clarify this, we give an example: Some people have problems with their energy levels. The practitioner then hears things like: I can't go on like this, I don't feel good, I'm always tired, I get nothing done and other vague complaints. They tell how they manage to get a lot of work done one day, only to collapse completely the next. Their approach is harmful: One day, they work too much and too hard, the next day, their energy is wasted and they stay on the couch all day, wallowing in guilt.

This behavioural pattern can become repetitive because, after a day on the couch, the client forces himself to work at full throttle. This way of using their energy is like running a marathon at sprinting speed. The practitioner can help the client to deal with his energy in an alternative manner: *Would you be interested to see if there is a way to handle your energy in a slightly different way?*

You then can suggest alternative working methods in the form of questions regarding: *Would it make a difference if you divided tomorrow's chores in small parts with regular breaks in between?* In short: by using suggestive questions, you can help the client to do something that does work.

Rule 3: *If something works well, well enough, or better, keep doing it and/or do more of it.*

If something works well or well enough

Rule 1 teaches us to acknowledge and respect what still works and therefore does not need mending. Rule 3 goes one step further and teaches us to actively look out for what is working well enough so that these things can be used as a launching platform for further enhancements. This can be things that in daily life are often overlooked because they seem evident. Healthy people have the tendency to take their health for granted. It is only when something goes wrong that they become aware of the preciousness of their health. 'Count your blessings' became a cliché because it is the truth. It is a skill to be happy with what you've got and striving for perfection will usually leave you empty-handed.

or works better

When we try to make small changes in life, sometimes coincidence intervenes. We do things without intention, but they seem to work better than what we tried before. It is good to pay attention to those moments, seize them and use what is beneficial in them.

The husband who's working from home is waiting in full anticipation of his wife returning from work. When she gets home, he immediately overwhelms her with all kinds of questions and news. His wife, however, has had a hard day at work and would rather have a break. They often have discussions because the husband thinks that his wife isn't interested in talking to him, whereas she thinks her husband doesn't give her any space. If he made her a cup of tea and kept working for another half an hour, this cycle would be broken quickly.

keep doing it

Some things that are useful are so mundane that we overlook them or underestimate their importance and therefore do not continue to practice them.

> A general practitioner is confronted with a hard-working patient who never gives himself a moment off and who complains of stress symptoms. The doctor cautiously advises him to have a 15-minute walk with his dog every evening. The patient follows this advice, but in a following session, the doctor begins to wonder whether this is sufficient. Should the exercise be extended to 30 minutes or perhaps even an hour? Or is it wise to simply congratulate the client on his daily exercise and encourage him to keep it up?

and/or do more of it

Physical exercise is beneficial for mind and body. If a client tells you he went to the gym for 10 minutes in the past week, he should be encouraged to go more often. Ten minutes won't make a huge difference but may lay the groundwork for lots of 10-minute workouts in the future. If you see actions that work, your automatic reaction should be to fully support and stimulate the client to do more of it. In this way, chances are big that small improvements will slowly grow into substantial and sustainable progress.

Rule 4: *If something works well, well enough, or better, then offer it to, or learn it from someone else.*

When something works well, well enough, or better

We have already discussed this in Rule 2 and Rule 3.

learn it from someone else

You can be open to information and expertise from colleagues, literature and refresher courses. When you've found out from your colleagues which interventions are efficient in certain circumstances, why wouldn't you make it easier for yourself and try similar methods? Of course, you shouldn't mindlessly copy these interventions, but you needn't start from scratch. The client for that matter is your main source of information because he constantly gives you stage directions that you help him in a better way.

or offer it to someone else

The same applies to useful interventions you have used yourself: Is there a greater professional pleasure than sharing the things that work with your clients and colleagues? If you're working in a group practice or in a team, this axiom is even more practical. You could think of the word *team* as the acronym 'together each achieves more'. Change facilitation is teamwork at its best because you always form a team with your client.

'In the relationship between patient and clinician, you have one goal in common. The patient wants some type of care and you are prepared to give the desired care. There are two people joined together, working for a common goal – the welfare of the patient' (Erickson, 1966).

Taking a step back to jump further

To avoid that the simplicity of the Minimax decision rules is reduced to simplism, there need to be awareness of the rules that regulate the use of those decision rules:

- The rules have nothing to do with you-should-do this or that.
- The rules aren't about the intervention by one single party, but about the interaction between parties.
- The result of each rule may prompt parties to use another rule.
- All rules are valid in all circumstances.
- The rules do not depict the truth.
- The rules are epistemological instruments that can help (re)shape reality.
- The rules don't help to understand, but to change.
- The rules are simple, but it is difficult to follow them consistently.
- The rules are contentless and only serve the interactional process.

The rules direct the cooperation between parties towards co-evolutionary processes.

APPENDIX C

Use of building blocks in the SoFAP-P design

In the methodology section (Section 2.3.2), the following was reported:

For the sake of clarity, we would like to point out that the methodology of Design Science Research does not require that the building blocks found in literature and empirical research (such as CIMOs and best and bad practices) are explicitly addressed in the design. They are implicitly recognizable in the design, but it is not required to indicate which building block underlies which rule or part of the design. Nevertheless, for those interested: the SoFAP-P design is 'deconstructed' into building blocks in this appendix.

That commitment is honoured in the matrix presented here:

M1	Points attention	Lessons learned	Best practices	Bad practices	CIMOs
M1-1		10,12a,12b,14	1	1,5	1,11
M1-2					
M1-2.1	1	2,5,6,10,12a	4	-	1,3
M1-2.2	1	5,12a	4	1,2,3	9
M1-2.3	3,4	1,2,5,6,10,12a	4	–	1,3
M1-3					
M1-3.1	1,2	1,2,4,5,9,10	2	1,2,3,4	4
M1-3.2	1,2,3	1,2,3,4,5,6,9,10,12a	2,3	1,2,3,4	3,4
M1-3.3	6	2,4,7,10,14	1,2,3,5	1,5	4,17
M1-4					
M1-4.1	6	3,5	4	–	2,4,12
M1-4.2	1,2	3,5,7,9,10	4	2	2,4,8

(*Continued*)

Appendix C

M1	Points attention	Lessons learned	Best practices	Bad practices	CIMOs
M1-5	–	12b,14	1	5	1
M2					
FQ-1	–	2,10,11	–	1,5	–
FQ-2	3,4,6	2,3,5,7	4	1,2	4,17
FQ-3	1,2,6	1,2,5,7,10,12a	4	1,2	8,17
FQ-4	1,2,3,4,6	1,2,3,5,7,10,12a	4	1,2	4,8,17
WR1	5	2,5,6,10,11,12b	1,4	1,5	1,5,6,11,21
WR2	1,2,3,4	1,2,3,4,5,7,8,9,10, 12b,14	1,2,3,4	1,3,4,5	1,2,10,11, 12,15,
WR2-1	–	5,10,14	1	1,5	1,11
WR2-2	1,2	1,2,3,4,8,10	2,3	1,3,4	2,4,7,19
WR2-3	1,2	1,2,4,5,7,8,9,10	2,3	1,2,3,4	2,4
WR2-4	–	2,5,7,9,11,14	1,4	2,5	2,4,5,6
WR2-5	1	5,12a	1,4	1,2,3,5	9
WR2-6	1,2	2,5,6,12a,14	1,4,5	1,2,3,5	3,4,8,10
WR2-7	1,2	2,5,6,12a	4,5	1,2,3	3,4,8,10
WR2-8	2	7,12a,14	1,4,5	1,2,5	8,15
WR2-9	2,3,4	5	4	2	4,12,19
WR2-10	–	13	–	–	18,20
WR2-11	1,2	1,2,7,9,10,14	1	1,2,3,4,5	4,22
WR3	1,2	1,2,4,5,7,9,12a,12b,14	1,4	1,5	1,7,8,10,11, 12,14
WR3-1	2	2,10,12a,14	1,4,5	1,5	8,14,15
WR3-2	2	2,3,7,10,12a,14	1,4,5	1,5	8,14,15
WR3-3	1,2	2,5,10,13	4	1	8,20
WR3-4	2	2,10,12a,14	1,4,5	1,5	3,8,14,15
WR3-5	1,5	1,2,5,6,12a	4	1	3,8
WR3-6	5	2,6,12a	4	1,5	3,8
WR3-7	n.a.	n.a.	n.a.	n.a.	n.a.
WR3-8	1,2	2,5,10,14	1,4	1,2,5	8,13
WR3-9	2	2,10,12a,14	1,4,5	1,2,5	8
WR4	4	1,2,4,5,7,8,9,10,12a, 12b,14	1,2,3,4,5	1,2,3,4,5	11,12,21
M3					
M3-1	2,3,4,6	1,2,4,10,14	1,5	1,5	17
M3-2	1,5	6,12a	4	1	3
Instance-1	1,2,6	2,5,8,10,14	1,5	1,2,5	8,20
Instance-2	1,2	2,5,10,13	4	1	8,20

APPENDIX D

Opinion survey among solution-focused applied psychology practitioners; questions and results

PA-1a:
Most approaches show an unbalanced methodological focus. They pay more attention (= time and energy) to past experiences and to the historical context of the client, than to his present situation and his wishes for change.

$\bar{X} = 3.67$ $\sigma = 0.89$ n = 76

PA-1b:
This unbalanced methodological focus goes at the expense of exploring possible future options to bring the desired changes closer.

$\bar{X} = 3.80$ $\sigma = 0.92$ n = 76

PA-2a:
The emphasis in problem-oriented approaches is on the detailed description of problems.

$\bar{X} = 3.55$ $\sigma = 1.09$ n = 67

PA-2b:
This emphasis easily results in a situation where there is (too) little attention paid to finding a solution to solve the client's problem.

$\bar{X} = 3.90$ $\sigma = 0.87$ n = 67

PA-3:
Client's problem descriptions typically result in classifications of diagnoses and typologies of mental problems and disorders. Such classifications, like DSM V, have the advantage of being convenient, although they can also easily lead to confusion and simplifications that leave little or no room for the complexity of human life.

$\bar{X} = 4.23$ $\sigma = 0.84$ n = 77

The causal linearity from *anamnesis* and *diagnosis* to *therapy* and *prognosis*:

- **PA-4a**: obscures the complexity of each client's life;

  $\bar{X} = 3.62$ $\sigma = 0.99$ $n = 77$

- **PA-4b**: oversimplifies the situation that causes the problem;

  $\bar{X} = 3.43$ $\sigma = 1.05$ $n = 76$

- **PA-4c**: reduces the opportunity for robust and sustainable solutions.

  $\bar{X} = 3.66$ $\sigma = 0.93$ $n = 76$

PA-5:
The linear problem-oriented theories (from *anamnesis* to *prognosis*) show an unbalanced stakeholder focus.

The emphasis of attention mainly goes to the client as an individual, even if the treatment format is the couple, the family or a group.

$\bar{X} = 3.68$ $\sigma = 0.94$ $n = 77$

PA-6:
In general, problem-oriented approaches suffer to a greater or lesser extent from a lack of efficiency in the use of time, money and other resources.

$\bar{X} = 3.76$ $\sigma = 0.91$ $n = 76$

LL-1:
Abandon analytic classifications of mental problems; focus instead on integrated holistic solutions.

$\bar{X} = 3.77$ $\sigma = 1.02$ $n = 77$

LL-2a:
The client's goals and resources should be the center of attention.

$\bar{X} = 4.60$ $\sigma = 0.65$ $n = 77$

LL-2b:
The paradigm the practitioner uses to guide his interventions is no more than a tool in the client's facilitation process.

$\bar{X} = 3.99$ $\sigma = 0.95$ $n = 77$

Useful client goals:

- **LL-3a**: are practical;

  $\bar{X} = 4.29$ $\sigma = 0.79$ $n = 77$

- **LL-3b**: are realistic;

  $\bar{X} = 4.29 \quad \sigma = 0.82 \quad n = 77$

- **LL-3c**: are achievable;

  $\bar{X} = 4.27 \quad \sigma = 0.82 \quad n = 77$

- **LL-3d**: can be phrased in behavioural terms (*What will you do different if ...*);

  $\bar{X} = 4.16 \quad \sigma = 0.84 \quad n = 77$

- **LL-3e**: preferably go from small to large.

  $\bar{X} = 3.91 \quad \sigma = 1.15 \quad n = 77$

LL-4:
Refrain from the linearity of *anamnesis, diagnosis, therapy* and *prognosis*; work iteratively, recursively and circularly instead.

$\bar{X} = 4.26 \quad \sigma = 0.85 \quad n = 77$

LL-5:
Start from the client's present situation as it relates to his momentary goals and then develop a future orientation.

$\bar{X} = 4.32 \quad \sigma = 0.77 \quad n = 77$

LL-6:
Incorporate the client's actual context directly and explicitly in the approach.

This means involving all relevant stakeholders in the client's actual ecosystemic context in such a way that they can contribute additional resources for the client or that they can benefit from the progress of the client or both.

$\bar{X} = 4.26 \quad \sigma = 0.85 \quad n = 77$

LL-7:
First focus on potential solutions and then iterate intermediate steps to create a robust, self-learning, client-specific solution methodology.

$\bar{X} = 4.19 \quad \sigma = 0.76 \quad n = 77$

Solutions can be:

- **LL-8a**: outcomes, results;

  $\bar{X} = 3.77 \quad \sigma = 0.84 \quad n = 77$

- **LL-8b**: process effects (since thoughts change actions and vice versa);

  $\bar{X} = 4.01 \quad \sigma = 0.79 \quad n = 76$

- **LL-8c**: combinations from the first two.

    $\bar{X} = 4.09 \quad \sigma = 0.80 \quad n = 77$

LL-9:
Instead of concentrating on the (*why* of the) problems in the past, the focus of the practitioner should be on constructing possible solutions and desired outcomes.

$\bar{X} = 4.40 \quad \sigma = 0.82 \quad n = 77$

LL-10:
Stimulate a client-driven or steered approach, instead of a client oriented or focused one.

$\bar{X} = 3.95 \quad \sigma = 0.98 \quad n = 76$

There are three major tendencies that prevent clients from being open to a solution-focused applied psychology approach:

- **LL-11a**: no intrinsic motivation to change;

    $\bar{X} = 3.14 \quad \sigma = 1.14 \quad n = 76$

- **LL-11b**: 'resistance' to change;

    $\bar{X} = 3.08 \quad \sigma = 1.13 \quad n = 76$

- **LL-11c**: translating mental issues into physical problems.

    $\bar{X} = 3.07 \quad \sigma = 0.91 \quad n = 76$

LL-12a:
Integrate the exploitation of non-specific therapeutic factors seen from the client's point of view, into the facilitation approach (instead of regarding them as a welcome by-product).

$\bar{X} = 4.22 \quad \sigma = 0.80 \quad n = 77$

Non-specific factors that are common to all successful interventions are as follows:

- **LL-12a1**: *I feel understood*

    $\bar{X} = 4.65 \quad \sigma = 0.58 \quad n = 77$

- **LL-12a2**: *I get the appropriate authentic attention*

    $\bar{X} = 4.61 \quad \sigma = 0.65 \quad n = 77$

- **LL-12a3**: *I feel respected as a person*

    $\bar{X} = 4.77 \quad \sigma = 0.54 \quad n = 77$

- **LL-12a4**: *I get the perspective that change for the better is possible*

    $\bar{X} = 4.58$ $\sigma = 0.64$ n = 77

Facilitation interventions that activate the non-specific factors in an effective way, mentioned in the previous question:

- **LL-12b1**: contain an emotional and confidential relationship with a person who is trying to help,

    $\bar{X} = 3.97$ $\sigma = 1.04$ n = 77

- **LL-12b2**: take place in a setting in which the client believes that the help offered, is professional,

    $\bar{X} = 4.08$ $\sigma = 0.91$ n = 77

- **LL-12b3**: give a credible explanation for the client's symptoms, and

    $\bar{X} = 3.32$ $\sigma = 1.20$ n = 77

- **LL-12b4**: offer reliable procedures to cope with these symptoms.

    $\bar{X} = 3.84$ $\sigma = 0.96$ n = 77

LL-13:
Put the effect of psychological and inter-relational facilitation techniques into a more differentiated perspective by asking differentiation questions (including scaling questions).

$\bar{X} = 3.82$ $\sigma = 0.97$ n = 77

LL-14:
Allow the therapeutic relationship to develop into a therapeutic alliance.

$\bar{X} = 4.08$ $\sigma = 0.94$ n = 77

BP-1:
A relationship reflects a connection while an alliance is a relationship between parties that share a common goal. Therefore, transform the working relationship with the client into an alliance.

$\bar{X} = 3.97$ $\sigma = 0.94$ n = 67

BP-2:
Set goals in an active manner by actively asking questions to help the client set his targets and to translate them into a list of useful objectives.

$\bar{X} = 4.18$ $\sigma = 0.80$ n = 67

BP-3:
Once a partial goal is achieved, this change becomes the context for a follow-up challenge until the *mother of all goals* is reached: The client is helped to help himself reach his own goals by using his own resources. So set goals in a continuous manner.

$\overline{X} = 4.06 \quad \sigma = 0.83 \quad n = 67$

BP-4:
Concentrate on the client's resources and possibilities to take steps forward towards a desired future.

$\overline{X} = 3.36 \quad \sigma = 0.73 \quad n = 67$

Use the minimax decision rules:

- **BP-5a:** *Rule 1*: If something still works, do not repair it but show respect and appreciation for what still works.

  $\overline{X} = 4.69 \quad \sigma = 0.53 \quad n = 67$

- **BP-5b:** *Rule 2*: If something does not work, or no longer works, or does not work well enough after trying it for a while, stop, learn from it, and do something else.

  $\overline{X} = 4.52 \quad \sigma = 0.80 \quad n = 67$

- **BP-5c:** *Rule 3*: If something works well, well enough, or better, keep doing it and/or do more of it.

  $\overline{X} = 4.70 \quad \sigma = 0.58 \quad n = 67$

- **BP-5d:** *Rule 4*: If something works well, well enough, or better, then offer it to, or learn it from someone else.

  $\overline{X} = 4.18 \quad \sigma = 0.98 \quad n = 67$

BaP-1 (inverted – *don't*):
Don't give primacy to a theory, model or method over the idiosyncratic needs and possibilities of the client.

$\overline{X} = 4.40 \quad \sigma = 0.80 \quad n = 67$

BaP-2 (inverted – *do not*):
Do not delve into speculations about the *why* of what goes wrong.

$\overline{X} = 3.54 \quad \sigma = 1.08 \quad n = 67$

BaP-3 (inverted – *refrain from*):
Refrain from an obsessive focus on the past.

$\overline{X} = 3.97 \quad \sigma = 0.97 \quad n = 67$

BaP-4 (inverted – *do not*):
Do not limit the desired goals to the mere absence of problems.

$\bar{X} = 4.15 \quad \sigma = 0.91 \quad n = 67$

BaP-5 (inverted – *don't*):
Don't treat the working relationship as an asymmetric one in which the client is the source of all difficulties and the practitioner is the all-knowing expert.

$\bar{X} = 3.75 \quad \sigma = 1.60 \quad n = 67$

CIMO-1:
From the first contact, establish, ensure, maintain, and constantly update the best possible contact with the client. That way you create a constructive relational foundation for accomplishing the joint effort in psychological facilitation.

$\bar{X} = 4.30 \quad \sigma = 0.72 \quad n = 67$

CIMO-2:
To avoid disappointment or disillusionment, the practitioner must determine at the start of the working relationship, whether the client's complaints are the result of a problem or a limitation.

A limitation – such as difficulties caused by age, background, disability or past events – cannot be solved by any conceivable action. Problems are defined by their possible solutions.

$\bar{X} = 4.18 \quad \sigma = 0.92 \quad n = 67$

CIMO-3:
Explore the context. No problem occurs in a vacuum. This implies that the context in which the client lives is always of significance.

$\bar{X} = 4.48 \quad \sigma = 0.70 \quad n = 67$

CIMO-4:
Since the psychological facilitation process is a professional encounter with a purpose, you must steer this process in a direction where the practitioner employs his expertise to help the client verbalize what he wants to accomplish, and what his goals are (instead of his problems).

$\bar{X} = 4.24 \quad \sigma = 0.82 \quad n = 67$

CIMO-5:
Whenever a referred client does not feel intrinsically motivated to engage in a facilitating conversation and shows no immediate goals for himself. Then, the practitioner can help the client to circumvent this obstacle by asking a triangular question as follows: *What do you need to talk about so that you don't have to come here anymore?* With this question, the practitioner shifts the attention from the absent motivation of the client to the wishes of the referring party.

$\bar{X} = 3.99 \quad \sigma = 1.09 \quad n = 67$

CIMO-6:
If a client blames a third party for his problems and shows that he is not (yet) willing or able to assume accountability, the task of the practitioner is to help the client to adopt a more responsible and constructive attitude.

$\bar{X} = 3.90$ $\sigma = 0.96$ $n = 67$

CIMO-7:
Ask solution-building questions if the client is able and/or willing to answer these questions, pathways to possible solutions emerge immediately.

$\bar{X} = 3.94$ $\sigma = 0.87$ $n = 67$

CIMO-8:
The resource orientation that is so characteristic of the solution-focused approach is founded on the axiom that every human system, be it an individual, a family or a group of whatever constellation, always has resources at its disposal, even in times of trouble.

$\bar{X} = 4.46$ $\sigma = 0.68$ $n = 67$

CIMO-9:
Ask the pre-session change question to explore if there are some things which have already changed for the better since the appointment was made.

$\bar{X} = 4.21$ $\sigma = 0.85$ $n = 66$

CIMO-10:
Ask continuation questions to activate resources. These questions invite the client to look beyond his problem-focused perspective and prime the idea that there is always something positive in a person's life (large or small) and makes the client aware of resources he has at his disposal.

$\bar{X} = 4.33$ $\sigma = 0.84$ $n = 67$

CIMO-11:
Offer positive feedback, give compliments. This strengthens the alliance and stimulates the client to do more of what works well.

$\bar{X} = 4.36$ $\sigma = 0.86$ $n = 77$

CIMO-12:
Advice is best given in the form of a question. This works because it gives the client ownership of the solution, even if this solution is suggested by the practitioner.

$\bar{X} = 4.22$ $\sigma = 0.94$ $n = 77$

CIMO-13:
Ask the coping question if the client is in dire straits: *If the situation is as bad as you say it is, how do you cope?* This question not only shows recognition for the

client's difficult situation but most importantly implies that the client has resources that keep him going.

$\bar{X} = 4.29 \quad \sigma = 0.79 \quad n = 77$

CIMO-14:
The question, *What have you tried thus far?*, hones the alliance between client and practitioner and helps the client to get access to his resources.

$\bar{X} = 4.11 \quad \sigma = 0.95 \quad n = 76$

CIMO-15:
Ask for exceptions to the problem, because answers reveal details about the partial solutions that emerge during the exceptional moments.

$\bar{X} = 4.22 \quad \sigma = 0.85 \quad n = 77$

CIMO-16:
When there is the impression that the facilitation is not resulting in sufficient progress or that feedback is indicated, ask about the usefulness of the relationship.

$\bar{X} = 4.13 \quad \sigma = 0.82 \quad n = 76$

CIMO-17:
When clients have the impression that they are in deep trouble, they often tend to think in black-and-white terms which petrifies their vision. Then the client must be helped to find nuances to counteract this dismal viewpoint. The desired differentiation can be elicited by asking questions that suggest a relativistic perspective.

$\bar{X} = 4.38 \quad \sigma = 0.71 \quad n = 76$

CIMO-18:
When the client is stuck, the practitioner can ask differentiating questions, as follows: *Are there moments when you are less burdened with the problem?* or *Have there been moments when it was even worse than it is now?* These questions will help the client to direct his attention towards the things in life that are going well or better.

$\bar{X} = 4.36 \quad \sigma = 0.78 \quad n = 77$

CIMO-19:
To facilitate differentiation in all kinds of different contexts, use scaling questions. The generic scaling question goes like this: *Imagine if I asked you to give a number on a scale where the starting point, the zero, stands for X (to be filled in according to the specific situation to be assessed) and the 10 stands for Y (ditto), then where are you now?*

$\bar{X} = 3.95 \quad \sigma = 0.94 \quad n = 77$

CIMO-20:
To help the client disengage from staying stuck in the past, ask questions that allow them to 'retroject' possible solutions from the future into the reality of today.

$\bar{X} = 4.23$ $\sigma = 0.83$ n = 77

CIMO-21:
If a client is stuck in his problem-oriented worldview, a positive, imagined perspective might be suggested by asking the so-called miracle question. *Suppose that, while you are sleeping, a miracle happens which solves all your problems (just enough so that they no longer bother you so much). How would you notice that it is as if a miracle happened for you?*

$\bar{X} = 4.09$ $\sigma = 0.93$ n = 77

E-1:
I am familiar with problem-oriented applied psychology approaches

$\bar{X} = 3.83$ $\sigma = 0.92$ n = 105

E-2:
I am familiar with solution-focused applied psychology approaches

$\bar{X} = 4.25$ $\sigma = 0.75$ n = 77

If you scored 4 or 5 on question E1 and question E2, then go to the 4 E3 questions.

If you scored 1, 2 or 3 on E1 or E2, then you are now done with this survey.

In view of the intended interpretation of the two key concepts in question E3, first, operational definitions were provided of the terms *efficient* and *effective*:

- *Efficient*: in the most economical way, a way that costs relatively little time and little money;
- *Effective*: achieving the intended goal, meeting the targets set.

E-3a:
With the same case and comparable practitioner expertise, problem-oriented applied psychology is generally more *efficient* than solution-focused applied psychology.

$\bar{X} = 1.89$ $\sigma = 0.81$ n = 70

E3-b:
With the same case and comparable practitioner expertise, solution-focused applied psychology is generally more *efficient* than problem-oriented applied psychology.

$\bar{X} = 4.13$ $\sigma = 0.72$ n = 70

Consensus and convention

Most approaches in the field of applied psychology show an unbalanced methodological focus. They pay more attention (i.e. time and energy) to past experiences and to the historical context of the client, than to his present situation and his wishes for change.

                1   2   3   4   5

Strongly disagree ○ ○ ○ ○ ○ Strongly agree

This unbalanced methodological focus goes at the expense of exploring possible future options to bring the desired changes closer.

                1   2   3   4   5

Strongly disagree ○ ○ ○ ○ ○ Strongly agree

Descriptions of the client's problem typically result in classifications of diagnoses and typologies of mental problems and disorders. Such classifications, like DSM V, have the advantage of being convenient, but they can easily lead to confusion and simplifications that leave little or no room for the complexity of human life.

                1   2   3   4   5

Strongly disagree ○ ○ ○ ○ ○ Strongly agree

The linear problem-oriented theories (from anamesis and diagnosis to therapy and prognosis), show an unbalanced stakeholder focus. The emphasis of attention mainly goes to the client as an individual, even if the treatment format is the couple, the family, or a group.

                1   2   3   4   5

Strongly disagree ○ ○ ○ ○ ○ Strongly agree

In general, problem-oriented approaches suffer to a greater or lesser extent from a lack of efficiency in the use of time, money and other resources.

                1   2   3   4   5

Strongly disagree ○ ○ ○ ○ ○ Strongly agree

FIGURE APPENDIX D   Part of the opinion survey with five questions

E-3c:
With the same case and comparable practitioner expertise, problem-oriented applied psychology is generally more *effective* than solution-focused applied psychology.

$\bar{X} = 2.13$ $\sigma = 0.83$ $n = 70$

E3-d:
With the same case and comparable practitioner expertise, solution-focused applied psychology is generally more *effective* than problem-oriented applied psychology.

$\bar{X} = 4.01$ $\sigma = 0.81$ $n = 70$

LITERATURE

Ackoff, R. L. (1979): The Future of Operational Research Is Past. *Journal of the Operational Research Society*, 30(2).
Argyris, C. (1996): Unrecognized Defenses of Scholars: Impact on Theory and Research. *Organization Science*, 7.
Ashby, R. W. (1956): *An Introduction to Cybernetics*. Methuen.
Bachelor, A. (1995): Client's Perception of the Therapeutic Alliance: A Qualitative Analysis. *Journal of Counseling Psychology*, 42(3).
Bandler, R. and Grinder, J. (1975): *The Structure of Magic: A Book about Language and Therapy*. Science and Behaviour Books.
Bannink, F. and Jackson, P. Z. (2011): Positive Psychology and Solution Focus – Looking at Similarities and Differences. *Interaction*, 3(1).
Bargh, J. A. (2006): What Have We Been Priming All These Years? On the Development, Mechanisms, and Ecology of Nonconscious Social Behavior. *European Journal of Social Psychology*, 36(2).
Bateson, G. (1972): *Steps to an Ecology of Mind*. University of Chicago Press.
Bateson, G. (1972): *Mind and Nature*. Dutton.
Blake, W. (1988): Erdman, David V. (ed.). *The Complete Poetry and Prose* (Newly revised ed.). Anchor Books. p. 490.
Boring, E. G. (1950): *A History of Experimental Psychology*. Appleton-Century-Crofts.
Boulding, K. (1956): General Systems Theory – The Skeleton of Science. *Management Science*, 2(3).
Bowen, M. (1978): *Family Therapy in Clinical Practice*. Jason Aronson.
Britannica, The Editors of Encyclopaedia. *Applied Psychology*. Encyclopedia Britannica, 31 Oct. 2021, https://www.britannica.com/science/applied-psychology.
Burgstaller, S. (ed.) (2015): *Lösungsfokus in Organisationen. Zukunftsorientiert beraten und führen*. Carl Auer.
Bushe, G. R. (2013): The Appreciative Inquiry Model. In: Kessler, E. (ed.): *Encyclopedia of Management Theory*. Sage.
Cauffman, L. (2001): *Oplossingsgericht Management en coaching*. Boom.

Cauffman, L. (2006): *The Solution Tango: Seven Simple Steps to Solutions in Management and Coaching.* Cyan Books.
Cauffman, L. (2007): *Oplossingsgericht Management & Coaching.* Boom. (in Dutch)
Cauffman, L. (2010): *Simpel. Oplossingsgerichte positieve psychologie in actie.* Boom. (in Dutch)
Cauffman, L. (2022): *Developing and Sustaining a Successful Family Business: A Solution-Focused Guide.* Routledge.
Cauffman, L. (2023): *Creating Sustainable Results with Solution-Focused Applied Psychology: A Practical Guide for Coaches and Change Facilitators.* Routledge.
Cauffman, L. (2022a): *Oplossingsgericht werken voor de klas.* PICA.
Cauffman, L., en Van Dijk D. (2014): *Handboek oplossingsgericht werken in het onderwijs.* Boom.
Cooperrider, D. L. and Srivastva, S. (1987): Appreciative Inquiry in Organizational Life. In: Woodman, R. W. and Pasmore, W. A. (eds.): *Research in Organizational Change and Development.* JAI Press.
De Jong, P., and Berg, I. K. (1998): *Interviewing for Solutions.* Thomson Brooks/Cole.
De Shazer, S. (1980): *Putting Difference to Work.* Norton.
De Shazer, S. (1982): *Patterns of Brief Family Therapy: A Ecosystemic Approach.* Guilford Press.
De Shazer, S. (1984): The Death of Resistance. *Family Process.* 23.
De Shazer, S. (1985): *The Keys to Solution in Brief Therapy.* Norton.
De Shazer, S. (1989): Resistance Revisited. *Contemporary Family Therapy*, 11(4).
De Shazer, S. (1994): *Words Were Originally Magic.* Norton.
De Shazer, S. and Dolan, Y (2007): *More Than Miracles, The State of the Art of Solution-Focused Brief Therapy.* Routledge.
Denyer, D., Tranfield, D. and Van Aken, J. E. (2008): Developing Design Propositions Through Research Synthesis. *Organization Studies*, 29(3).
Diodorus Siculus, (60 – 30 BC): Βιβλιοθήκη ιστορική. Historical library.
Dolan, R. J. and Matthews, J. M. (1993): Maximizing the Utility of Customer Product Testing: Beta Test Design and Management. *Journal of Product Innovation Management*, 10.
Duncan, B. L., Miller, S. D., Wampold, B. E. and Hubble, M. A. (2010): *The Heart and Soul of Change: Delivering What Works in Therapy.* American Psychology Association.
Eisenhardt, K. M. (1989): Building Theories from Case Study Research. *Academy of Management Review*, 14.
Erickson, M. H. (1966): Experiential Knowledge of Hypnotic Phenomena Employed for Hypnotherapy. *The American Journal of Clinical Hypnosis*, April, 8.
Erickson, M. H. and Rossi, E. (1979): *Hypnotherapy: An Exploratory Casebook.* Irvington.
Frank, J. D. and Frank, J. B. (1991): *Persuasion and Healing. A Comparative Study of Psychotherapy.* John Hopkins University Press.
Freud, S. (1899): *Die Traumdeutung.* Wien.
Freud, S. and Breuer, J. (1885): *Studien über Hysterie.* Leipzig und Wien.
Galbraith, J. R. (1973): *Designing Complex Organizations.* Addison-Wesley.
Gioia, D. A., Corley, K. G. and Hamilton, A. L. (2013): Seeking Qualitative Rigor in Inductive Research. *Organizational Research Methods*, 16(1).
Guba, Y. and Lincoln, E. (1989): *Fourth Generation Evaluation.* Sage.
Guyatt, G. H. (1991): Evidence-Based Medicine (Editorial). *ACP Journal Club, Annals of Internal Medicine*, 114(2).
Haley, J. (1973): *Uncommon Therapy. The Psychiatric Techniques of Milton H. Erickson.* Norton.

Hoyt, M. and Bobele, M. (eds.) (2019): *Creative Therapy in Challenging Situations*. Routledge.
Hubbard, R., Vetter, D. E. and Little, E. L. (1998): Replication in Strategic Management: Scientific Testing for Validity, Generalizability and Usefulness. *Strategic Management Journal*, 19.
Hubble, M. A., Duncan, B. L. and Miller, S. D. (2008): *The Heart and Soul of Change: Delivering What Works in Therapy*. American Psychology Association.
Iveson, C. (2014): *At Your Best, Single Session Coaching*. www.brief.org.uk.
Iveson, C. (2019): However Great the Question, It's the Answer That Makes a Difference. In: Hoyt, M. and Bobele, M. (eds.): *Creative Therapy in Challenging Situations*. Routledge.
Iveson, C. and Szabo, P. (2015): The Cuddle Case/A Damn Good Boss: Two Coaching Cases With Chris Iveson and Peter Szabó. *InterAction – The Journal of Solution Focus in Organisations*, 7(2).
Jackson, P. Z., and McKergow, M. (2007): *The Solutions Focus: Making Coaching and Change SIMPLE*. Nicholas Brealey.
Kahneman, D. (2003): *Well-Being: Foudations of Hedonic Psychology*. Russel Sage.
Kennedy, J. (2006): *Swarm Intelligence*. In: Zomaya, A. Y. (eds.): *Handbook of Nature-Inspired and Innovative Computing*. Springer.
Keskin, D. and Romme, G. (2020): Mixing Oil with Water: How to Effectively Teach Design Science in Management Education? *BAR – Brazilian Administration Review*, 17(1).
Korzybski, A. (1995): *Science and Sanity: An Introduction to Non-Aristotelian Systems and General Semantics*. Institute of General Semantics.
Kottler, J. A. and Carlson, J. (2003): *Bad Therapy: Master Therapists Share Their Worst Failures*. Routledge.
Lambert, M. J. (1992): *Psychotherapy Outcome Research: Implications for Integrative and Eclectical Therapists*. In: Norcross, J. C. and Goldfried, M. R. (eds.): *Handbook of Psychotherapy Integration*. Basic Books.
Likert, R. (1932): A Technique for the Measurement of Attitudes. *Archives of Psychology*, 140.
Maslow, A. H. (1954): *Motivation and Personality*. Harper & Row.
Maslow, A. H. (1962): *Toward a Psychology of Being*. Van Nostrand.
Maslow, A. H. (1964): *Religions, Values, and Peak Experiences*. Ohio State University Press.
McDonald, A. (2011): *Solution-Focused Therapy: Theory, Research and Practice*. Sage.
McKeel, A. J. (1996): A clinician's Guide to Research on Solution-Focused Therapy. In: Miller, S. D., Hubble, M. A. and Duncan, B. L. (eds.): *Handbook of Solution-Focused Brief Therapy*. Jossey-Bass.
McKenney, S. and Reeves, T. C. (2012): *Conducting Educational Design Research*. Routledge.
Merriam-Webster Dictionary, (2016).
Miller, G. and McKergow, M. (2012): From Wittgenstein, Complexity, and Narrative Emergence: Discourse and Solution-Focused Brief Therapy. In: Lock, A. and Strong, T. (eds.): *Discursive Perspectives in Therapeutic Practice*. Oxford University Press.
Mischel, W. (2020): *Encyclopedia Britannica*: Psychology. https://www.britannica.com/science/psychology.
Norcross, J. C., Koocher, G. P., Garofalo, A. (2006): Discredited Psychological Treatments and Tests: A Delphi Poll. *Professional Psychology: Research and Practice*, 37(5).
Pawson, R., and Tilly, N. (1997): *Realistic Evaluation*. Sage.
Peterson, C. (2006): *A Primer in Positive Psychology*. Oxford University Press.
Pinker, S. (1994): *The Language Instinct*. William Morrow.

Polanyi, M. (1966): *The Tacit Dimension*. University of Chicago Press.
Polgár, N. and Hankovszky, K. (eds.) (2015): *Brief and Simple: Solution Focus in Organizations*. Books on Demand.
Prior, M. (2021): *MiniMax-Interventionen: 15 minimale Interventionen mit maximaler Wirkung*. Carl Auer Verlag.
Ratner, H., Georges, E. and Iveson, C. (2012): *Solution-Focused Brief Therapy: 100 Key Points & Techniques*. Routledge.
Ratner, H. and Yusuf, D. (2015): *Brief Coaching with Children and Young People: A Solution-Focused Approach*. Routledge.
Rogers, C. (1951): *Client-Centered Therapy: Its Current Practice, Implications and Theory*. Houghton Mifflin.
Romme, A. G. L. (2003): Making a Difference: Organization as Design. *Organization Science*, 14(5).
Romme, A. G. L., and Dimov, D. (2021): Mixing Oil with Water: Framing and Theorizing in Management Research Informed by Design Science. *Designs*, 5(13).
Romme, A. G. L., and Reymen, I. M. M. J. (2018): Entrepreneurship at the Interface of Design and Science: Toward an Inclusive Framework. *Journal of Business Venturing Insights*, 10.
Rosenzweig, S. (1936): Some Implicit Common Factors in Diverse Methods of Psychotherapy. *American Journal of Orthopsychiatry*, 6(3).
Sackett, D. L., Rosenberg, W., Muir Gray, J. A. (1996): Evidence-Based Medicine: What It Is and What It Isn't. *BMJ*, 312.
Sarasvathy, D. S. and Venkataraman, S. (2011): Entrepreneurship as Method: Open Questions for an Entrepreneurial Future. *Entrepreneurship: Theory and Practice*, 35(1).
Schön, D. A. (1983): *The Reflective Practitioner*. Ashgate Publishing.
Simon, H. (1969): *The Sciences of the Artificial*. MIT Press.
Simon, H, (1996): *The Sciences of the Artificial, Third Edition*. MIT Press.
Snowden, D. (2005): Strategy in the Context of Uncertainty. *Handbook of Business Strategy*. Emerald.
Stack, L. (2016): *Doing the Right Things Right: How the Effective Executive Spends Time*. Berrett-Koehler.
Stam, C. (2007): *Knowledge productivity. Designing and testing a method to diagnose knowledge productivity and plan for enhancement*. PhD-thesis. Universiteit Twente.
Tooby, J. and Cosmides, L. (2015): The Theoretical Foundations of Evolutionary Psychology. In: Buss, D. M. (ed.), *The Handbook of Evolutionary Psychology*, Second Edition. Volume 1: Foundations. John Wiley.
Trivers, R. L. (1971): The Evolution of Reciprocal Altruism. *The Quarterly Review of Biology*, 46(1).
Tsang, E. W. K. and Kwan, K. M. (1999): Replication and Theory Development in Organizational Science: A Critical Realist Perspective. *Academy of Management Review*, 24.
van Aken, J. E. (2004): Management Research Based on the Paradigm of the Design Sciences: The Quest for Field-Tested and Grounded Technological Rules. *Journal of Management Studies*, 41(2).
van Aken, J. E. (2005): Management Research as a Design Science: Articulating the Research Products of Mode 2 Knowledge Production in Management. *British Journal of Management*, 16.
van Aken, J. E. (2019): Design Science Research to Produce Instrumental Knowledge for Evidence Based Practice in OCD. In: Hamlin, R. G., Ellinger, A. D. and Jones, J. (eds.): *Evidence-Based Initiatives for Organizational Change and Development*. IGI Global.

van Aken, J. E. (2013): Design Science: Valid Knowledge for Socio-Technical System Design. In Helfert, M. and Donnellan, B. (eds.): *Proceedings of the European Design Science Symposium, Dublin, 2012.* Springer.

van Aken J. E. and Andriessen, D. (eds.) (2011): *Handboek ontwerp gericht wetenschappelijk onderzoek. Wetenschap met effect.* Boom Lemma.

van Aken, J. and Berends, H. (2018): *Problem Solving in Organizations: A Methodological Handbook for Business and Management Students.* Cambridge University Press.

Wampold, B. E. (2001): *The Great Psychotherapy Debate. Models, Methods and Findings.* Erlbaum.

Weiner-Davis, M., De Shazer, S. and Gingerich, W. (1987): Building on Pre-treatment Change to Construct the Therapeutic Solution: An Exploratory Study. *Journal of Marital and Family Therapy,* 13.

Wiener, N. (1948): *Cybernetics: On Control and Communication in the Animal and the Machine.* MIT Press.

Wittgenstein, L. (1953): *Philosophical Investigations.* Basil Blackwell.

Zeig, J. K., and Geary, B. (2000): *The Letters of Milton Erickson.* Zeig Tucker & Theisen.

ACKNOWLEDGEMENTS

A book that bridges the gap between applied psychology in the field of change facilitation and the innovative methodology of design science research could not come about without the help of many colleagues:

Ben Furman
Bert and Lillian Erickson
Chris Iveson
Fedor Schafranski for his artwork
Haiko Jessurun
Joan van Aken
Karel Geeraedts
Matthias Varga von Kibed
Peter de Jong
Zoe Adams

The anonymous professionals and academics, who peer reviewed the manuscript, made recommendations and were enthusiastic about its publication and the 77 practitioners who completed the survey.

Posthumously, our thanks go to Steve de Shazer, Insoo Kim Berg, Betty Alice Erickson and Milton H. Erickson.

With gratitude,
Louis Cauffman and Mathieu Weggeman

CURRICULUM VITAE

Louis Cauffman is a clinical psychologist and business economist. One of the first to introduce the solution-focused approach in Europe, Louis remains passionate in his further development of the solution-focused approach as an epistemological tool.

His book, *The Solution Tango: Seven Simple Steps to Solutions in Management and Coaching*, introduced the solution-focused approach in China and became a bestseller. He published the famous Canoe Diary of Dr. Milton H. Erickson, *Developing and Sustaining a Successful Family Business: A Solution-Focused Guide* (Routledge 2022) and *Creating Sustainable Results with Solution-Focused Applied Psychology: A Practical Guide for Coaches and Change Facilitators* (Routledge 2023).

Mathieu Weggeman is full Professor of *Organizational Science and Innovation Management* at Eindhoven University of Technology (TU/e). At that university, he also obtained his MSc in *Industrial Engineering* and he holds a PhD in *Strategic Management* from Tilburg University.

Weggeman served on the editorial board of *Organization Studies* and has published in *R&D Management, Journal of Product Innovation Management, Human Relations, Journal of Organizational Change Management* and many other journals.

In recent years, Weggeman has been particularly committed to further developing and applying the design science research methodology within the *Sciences of the Artificial*.

AUTHOR INDEX

Ackhof, R. L. 37
Adler, A. 10
Andriessen, D. 36–37, 39, 42, 45
Argyris, C. 41
Ashby, R. W. 127–128

Bachelor, A. 49
Bandler, R. 17
Bargh, J. A. 125
Bateson, G. 14, 15, 17, 125, 174
Beck, A.T. 11
Berg, I. K. 68
Blake, W. 132
Bobele, M. 160, 163
Boring, E. G. 19
Boulding, K. 38
Bowen, M. 14
Breuer, J. 10
Britannica 65
Burgstaller, S. 97n10, 164
Bushe, G. R. 20

Cade, B. 20
Carlson, J. 74
Carroll, L. 5, 8n3
Cauffman, L. 6, 17, 24, 46n6, 52, 98, 100, 104, 108, 112, 116, 134, 138, 140, 141, 143, 145, 146, 148, 150, 151, 152, 154, 167, 170
Chomsky, N. 14
Cooperrider, D. L. 20
Corley, K. G. 38

Cosmides, L. 125
Csiksentmihalyi, M. 19

Davanloo, H. 10
De Jong, P. 20, 68
Denyer, D. 37
Descartes, R. 131
De Shazer, S. 4, 5, 15, 20–24, 32, 49, 57, 99, 124–126
Dimov, D. 39, 195
Diodorus 2
Dolan, R. J. 41
Dolan, Y. 20, 23
Duncan, B. L. 50

Ebbinghouse, H. 19
Eisenhardt, K. M. 41
Ellis, A. 11
Erickson, M. H. 3, 16–19, 21, 24, 62, 177

Frank, J. B. 50
Frank, J. D. 50
Freud, A. 10
Freud, S. 10–11

Galbraith, J. R. 90, 91
Garofalo, A. 46n3
Geary, B. 3
Georges, E. 156, 157
Gergen, K. xiii
Gingerich, W. 20, 57
Gioia, D. A. 38

Gray, E. 12
Grinder, J. 17
Guba, Y. 41
Guyatt, G. H. 5

Haley, J. 14, 15, 17
Hamilton, A. L. 38
Hankovszky, K. 158
Heidegger, M. 131
Heraclitus Ephesus 95
Hoyt, M. 160, 163
Hubbard, R. 41
Hubble, M. A. 50

Iveson, C. 93, 156, 157, 159, 160, 163, 164

Jackson, D. D. 15
Jung, C. G. 10

Kahneman, D. 19, 125
Katz, B. 131
Kennedy, J. 125
Keskin, D. 37
Klein, M. 10
Koocher, G. P. 46n3
Korzybski, A. 125
Kottler, J. A. 74
Kwan, K. M. 41

Lacan, J. 4
Lambert, M. J. 50
Likert, R. 99, 100
Lincoln, E. 41
Lipchik, E. 20
Little, E. L. 41

Malan, D. 10
Marshall, B. 66
Maslow, A. H. 13
Matthews, J. M. 41
McDonald, A. 71, 125–126
McKeel, A. J. 71, 126
McKenney, S. 40
McKergow, M. 68
Mead, M. 14–15, 17
Merriam-Webster 7, 46n7, 97n7
Miller, G. 68
Miller, S. D. 50
Mischel, W. 1
Muir Gray, J. A. 5

Norcross, J. C. 46n3

O'Hanlon, B. 20

Pavlov, I. 11
Pawson, R. 38, 41

Peirce, C. S. 47
Peterson, C. 19
Pinker, S. 125
Polanyi, M. 90
Polgár, N. 158
Prior, M. 68

Ratner, H. 155, 156, 157
Reeves, T. C. 40
Reymen, I. M. M. J. 39
Richardson, H. 14
Rogers, C. 13
Romme, A. G. L. 37, 39
Rosenberg, W. 5
Rosenzweig, S. 49–50
Ross Ashby, W. 128
Rossi, E. 62

Sackett, D. L. 5
Sarasvathy, D. S. 39
Schön, D. A. 37, xv
Seligman, M. 19
Sifneos, P. 10
Simon, H. 36–38, 45, xv
Skinner, B. F. 11
Snowden, D. 91
Srivastva, S. 20
Stack, L. 35, 68, 123
Stam, C. 40
Szabo, P. 164

Taubes, G. 97n8
Tilly, N. 38, 41
Tooby, J. 125
Tranfield, D. 37
Trivers, R. L. 125
Tsang, E. W. K. 41

Van Aken, J. E. 36–43, 45
Van Dijk, D. 150
Venkataraman, S. 39
Vetter, D. E. 41
Von Bertalanffy, L. 14

Wampold, B. E. 50, 51
Warren, R. 66
Watzlawick, P. 14
Weakland, J. D. 14–15
Weggeman, Mathieu 46n4, 100, xii–xiii, xiv, xvi
Weiner-Davis, M. 20, 57
Wiener, N. 14, 15
Wittgenstein, L. 4, 23, 55, 129

Yusuf, D. 155, 156

Zeig, J. K. 3

SUBJECT INDEX

Note: Page number in *italics* refer to the figures and page numbers with "**n**" for notes.

4-D model 20; *see also* discover, dream, design and deploy
α-testing 40–41, 45, 98–103, 122
β-testing 40–41, 45, 98, 104–122

abduction 45, 46–47n10
accountability 56–57, 73, 134, 187
action-based research 40
action research 46
activate resources 57
advice 85, 135, 154; in guise of question 58, 73, 134, 187; study and career 65
agency 39; in human beings 12; ideas of 12, 32
alliance: client-practitioner 55, 79; collaborative 49; therapeutic 73, 184; working relationship with client into 52
ambition 4, 6, 33, 41, 151, 156
anamnesis-diagnosis-therapy-prognosis 28
applied interventions xv–xvi
applied psychology theories: behaviourism 11–13; cognitive behavioural therapy (CBT) 11–13; Ericksonian practices 16–19; extended solution-focused therapy (extended SFT) 24–27; family systems therapy 14–16; humanistic psychology 13–14; lessons learned from 31–33; limitations of 28–29; methodological flaws in 9–29; psychoanalysis and psychodynamic approaches 10–11; solution-focused therapy (SFT) 20–24
appreciative inquiry (AI) 19–20
appropriateness 42, 94, 95–96
arrangement of interventions 75–90; conclude 78–79; movements 79–90; reading guide 76–78; valid for movements 78
Artificial Intelligence 131
augmented sustainability of outcome 126

bad practices *see* best practices
behaviourism 11–13, 28, 32; *see also* cognitive behavioural therapy (CBT)
best practices 73; client's resources and possibilities 53; goals 52–53; minimax decision rules 53–54; by solution-focused practitioners 52–54; working relationship 52
brevity 125
Brief Family Therapy Center (BFTC) 20
building blocks 39, 45; CIMOs 54, 62; extended-SFT approach 46n6; in SoFAP-P design 71–74, 98–99, 100, 178–179; standard deviation 100; types of 102–103; validating SoFAP-P 98–103
buzzwords 22–23, 24

CAMO-variant 39
The Canoe Diary (Erickson) 24
cases *see* ex ante cases; ex post cases

cause-effect chain 91
caveat 66
challenges 3, 9, 26, 34, 66, 92, 95, 129, 158–159; of client 33, 41; client's ecosystem 36; clients' problems as 94; real-life field 38; solution-oriented guidelines for 39
change facilitation 7, 25, 95, 96, 126, 129, 172, 177; creativity and flexibility 95; ecosystem 126; process of interaction 172; psychological 25; therapy and 129
change model: in behaviourism and cognitive behavioural therapy 11; in family system therapy 14–16; in humanistic psychology 13–14; in psychoanalysis and psychodynamic approaches 10
CIMOs: building blocks 54, 62; -construct 38–39; -logic 39–40; mechanisms in 123; *see also* design propositions
circumvent absent intrinsic motivation 56
client 96n2, xii; centred instead of theory/model centred 25; driven 48, 73, 183; ecosystem 26; focus 126; goals 127
Client-Centered Therapy: Its Current Practice, Implications and Theory (Rogers) 13
client-practitioner alliance 55, 79
Clues: Investigating Solutions in Brief Therapy (de Shazer) 5
coach/coaching 6, 25, 31, 43, 112, 131, 158, 164–167; mandate of 27, 67; organizational 27; sports 17
co-expert working relationship 82, 86–87
cognitive behavioural therapy (CBT) 11–13, 28, 32; *see also* behaviourism
coherent validation xvi
collaborative alliance 49
common factors 50; *see also under* non-specific
complementing 27, 42, 48
complexity 42, 127; adequate 24; epistemological 130; of human life 29, 72, 126, 180; of mental problems 28; theories and models and 2
compliments 21–22, 58, 83, 187
comprehensive theory, quest for 1–3
confidence 89; in productivity 122; scaling question 61, 86; therapist 51
confirmation bias 2
consulting 97n7
consulting working relationship 82, 85–86
contentment 3, 57

context 5, 14–15, 39, 55–56, 78, 123; actual 35–36, 182; of business ventures 6; exploring 55–56, 80; historical 28–29, 71, 180; of mental problems 9; professional 26; sensitive interventions 43; situational 19; social work 45; working 45
continuation questions 21, 83
continuation-task 84
contra indications for using SoFAP-P 93
contributions of SoFAP-P: to practice 125–127; to society 127–129
coping 150–151; mechanisms 12; question 58, 73, 86, 89, 187; social work movement 14; working relationship 55
Creating Sustainable Results with Solution-Focused Applied Psychology (Cauffman) 6
creative leap 45
cross-case analyses 45, xvi
cybernetics, defined 15

data collection 43–44
depth of SoFAP-P 66–71
design: methodology 36; objective 34–35, 36, 37, 41, 44, 54, 62; principle 35, 38–39, 44, 70; process 44–45, xv
design propositions 35–39, 54–60, 70, 73–74; activate resources 57; advice in guise of question 58; based on contributions 133–134; circumvent absent intrinsic motivation 56; client-practitioner alliance 55; context-exploring 55–56; continuation questions to activate resources 57; conversation towards goal 56; coping question in case of serious distress 58; derived from client cases 54–62; differentiating questions 59; equally relevant 100–101; exceptions to problem 58–59; future-orienting questions 61–62; mechanisms in 123; miracle question 62; positive feedback 58; predicting future task 101; pre-session change question 57; problems *versus* limitations to enhance effectivity 55; question 58; relativistic perspective 59; responsibility and accountability for client's actions 56–57; scale of confidence 61; scale of difference 60; scale of hope for change 61; scale of motivation 61; scale of progress 60; scale of usefulness 61; scale of well-being 61; scaling questions 59–60; solution-building questions 57; usefulness question 59; *see also* CIMOs

design science 38; characterization 38; methodology 38
design science research (DSR) 41–42, xii, xii, xiv–xv; action research and 46; characteristic of 41; methodology 27, 41, 98, xv; in philosophy of science xvi; randomized controlled trials (RCTs) vs. 43; research approach 36–38
design specification 94–96; appropriateness 95–96; non-obviousness 95; operational relevance 95; practical relevance 95
desirable developments in solution-focused applied psychology 129–132
Developing and Sustaining a Successful Family Business: A Solution-Focused Guide (Cauffman) 6
developments: desirable 129–132; envisaged SoFAP-P design 11, 12–13, 14, 16, 19, 23–24; innovative 3–4; of solution-focused brief therapy (SFBT) xiii; in solution-focused method 4
diagnosis 2, 8n1, 12, 28; concept of 46n7; of problematic cognitive-behavioural 12; of problem-oriented model 15
diagnosis-root cause-action chain 12, 27
diagnosis-treatment combinations 128
Die Traumdeutung (Freud) 10
differentiation 4, 22, 26, 59, 73, 127–128, 188
differentiation questions 84
discover, dream, design and deploy 20
DODO-effect 5
dysfunction 12, 15, 16, 28

early family systems 15
ecosystem 126
effectiveness 13, 18–19, 37, 52, 68, 95, 100, 122, 123; problem-focused vs. solution-focused approach 69–70; productivity 35; professionalism and 81; therapeutic 32
efficiency 13, 29–30, 35, 42, 68, 69–70, 123, 125; brevity and 125, 129; maximal 78; of solution-focused working 99
empirical grounding 48–74; best and bad practices 52–54; building blocks 71–74; design propositions 54–62; lessons learned from professional and scientific literature 48–52; support questions 62–71
epistemological keystones 4
epistemology 6, 23, 31, 52, 124, 126
Ericksonian practices 16–19

evaluation of SoFAP-P 123–132; contribution of SoFAP-P 124–129; desirable developments 129–132; field testing 123–124; specifying in detail mechanisms 123
evidence 5; within EBM 43; objective 41; supporting 41
evidence-based: methodology 6; practice 43
evidence-based medicine (EBM) 5, 43
Evidence-Based Medicine (Sackett) 5
evidence-based model (EBM) 124–125
ex ante cases 122n4, 133–171; change/die 143–145; coping 150–151; crying client 151–152; death, defeated 163–164; detour through China 150; family perils 138–140; friends and contractors 167–170; glass company 158–159; good boss 164–167; hampered by good intentions 141–143; healing speech 157–158; high potential 154–155; outplacement 138; seeing 140–141; surprise 170–171; time 134–138
exception questions 84
exception-to-the-problem concept 22
experiential learning xiv
explanatory psychological theory xvi
ex post cases 104–122, 122n4
extended solution-focused therapy (extended SFT) 3, 24–27
extremes 101–102

face validity 42, 99, 100
facilitation 3, 7, 25, 30, 31, 126; change 7, 25, 95, 96, 126, 129, 172; interpersonal 43; inter-relational 51, 73; interventions 50, 87, 102; psychological 50–53, 55, 56, 73; solution-focused 57, 70
facilitor 7, 67
family-business 25, 27, 116, 124
family systems approach 15–16
family systems therapy 14–16, 28
feasibility 40
field problem: to design objective 33–35; DSR methodology 41; exploration of 9–29
field testing of SoFAP-P 123–124; *see also* α-testing; β-testing
flowchart 76, *77*, 89–90, *107*, *111*, *115*
formula first session task 21
fundamental questions (FQ) 78
further research 123–124
future 22, 87, 180, 182, 185; adequate 24; adjustment of patient 18; client's life 24;

evaluation of SoFAP-P and 123–132; orientation 26, 29, 30, 64; oriented technique 79; orienting questions 61–62; solutions 31–32
future orientation 64
future-oriented thinking 18
future-orienting questions 61–62, 84–85
future task 101

generic scientific method (GSM) xv; validation in xvi
goal orientation 64
goal-setting 26, 61, 78, 80, 83, 127
group think 2

habits 18, 173
happiness 8n2
Helicobacter Pylori 66
history diagnosis-therapy-prognosis 31
homeostasis 15
humanistic psychological approach 32
humanistic psychology 13–14, 28

image of Humankind 3, 63
incremental 21, 31, 81, 86, 95
indications for using SoFAP-P 90–96; contra-indications 93; design specification 94–96; indications 91–92; pseudo-contra-indications 93–94
individualized design 6
innovative development 3–4
innovative techniques 22, 24
interactional constructivism 23
intermezzo 19–20
interpersonal facilitation 43
inter-relational: facilitation 51, 73, 184; influence 12, 32; interventions 66; nature 66; problems 66
inter-relational facilitation 51, 73
intervention process 25–27, 67, 75–76, 78–79, 81, 87, 95, 123
intrapsychic 10–15, 28, 96n2
investment 125–126

Keys to Solution in Brief Therapy (de Shazer) 5

language 11, 23, 35, 65, 71, 83, 94, 117, 129, 131
last longer 70–71
Law of Requisite Variety 127–128
leadership mandate 67
lessons learned 72–73; from applied psychology theories 31–33;
behaviourism 11–13, 28, 32; behaviourism and CBT 12–13; client-driven/steered approach 48–49; cognitive behavioural therapy (CBT) 11–13, 28, 32; Ericksonian practices 16–19; facilitation approach 49–50; family systems therapy 16; humanistic psychology 14; non-specific factors 49–51; from professional and scientific literature 48–52; psychoanalysis and psychodynamic approaches 11; psychological and inter-relational facilitation techniques 51; for SoFAP-P 30–31; solution-focused applied psychology approach 49; solution-focused therapy (SFT) 23–24; therapeutic relationship 51–52
lightness 127
Likert scale 99, 100
limitations: of applied psychology theories 28–29; behaviourism and CBT 12; CIMO-logic 39–40; ericksonian practices 18; family systems therapy 15–16; humanistic psychology 13–14; of psychoanalysis and psychodynamic approaches 10–11; solution-focused therapy (SFT) 22–23
limitations *versus* problems 79

management mandate 67
mandate 26; appropriate 81; client 49, 56; as coach and facilitator 67; of coach/coaching 27, 67; of leadership 26–27, 67; management 67; therapeutic 26
mechanisms 39–40; in CIMOs 123; coping 12; in design propositions 123; in evaluation of SoFAP-P 123; in future-oriented question 61; intrapsychic 96n2
meeting point 45
methodological flaws: in applied psychology theories 9–29; behaviourism 11–13; cognitive behavioural therapy (CBT) 11–13; Ericksonian practices 16–19; extended solution-focused therapy (extended SFT) 24–27; family systems therapy 14–16; humanistic psychology 13–14; limitations of reviewed applied psychology theories 28–29; psychoanalysis and psychodynamic approaches 10–11; solution-focused therapy (SFT) 20–24
methodology: design 36; design science 38; design science research (DSR) 27, 41, 98, xv, xv

Miles & Son Inc. 116–122
minimax decision rules 53–54, 64–65, 103, 172–177
miracle question 4, 22, 62, 85
modern psychology 1
modus operandi 3
More Than Miracles, The State of the Art of Solution-Focused Brief Therapy (de Shazer) 23
motivation 10; circumvent absent intrinsic 56; no intrinsic 49; scale of 61
Motivation and Personality (Maslow) 13
movements 75, 96n1; continuation and evaluation 87–89; movement 1 seven-step dance 25–26; movement 2 types of working relationships 75, 78, 81–82, 87; movement 3 next session or ending of cooperation 75, 78, 87–89; SoFAP-P intervention process 79–81; working relationship (WR) 81–87

Neuro Linguistic Programming (NLP) 17, 46n3
The New Yorker 131
no intrinsic motivation 49
non-committal working relationship 81–82, 108
non-obviousness 42, 94, 95
non-specific: factors 24–25, 32, 49–50, 68, 103, 183–184; therapeutic variables 3
noteworthy extremes 101–102

on-line opinion survey 98–99
operational relevance 42, 94, 95
opinion survey 44, 68, 98–99, 180–191; on-line 99; purpose of 98–99; questions and results 180–191; simulation-based conversations and 98
organizational science 35
orientation: of DSR 37; future 64; goal 64; resource 57, 63
outcomes: of interventions xvi; quantitative 122n1; research 4–5, 6, 42, 124; results 14; sustainability of 126; therapeutic 51
outliers 103

patient and clinician relationship 17
patient's behaviour 17
Patterns of Brief Family Therapy: An Ecosystemic Approach (de Shazer) 3, 21
perfection 61, 131, 175
physical exercise 176
points of attention (PAs) 29–30, 71–72
positive feedback 58

positive psychology (PP) 19
possibilities 24, 28, 32, 53, 63
post-operative medical care and pain treatment 128
practical relevance 42, 95
practices *see* bad practices; best practices
practitioner and client relationship 75
pragmatic validity 37–39, 42
pre-session change question 57, 60, 83
problem-focused *versus* solution-focused approach 69–70
problem-phobic 3
problems *versus* limitations to enhance effectivity 55
problem talk *versus* solution talk 65
productivity 34–35, 39, 68, 70, 100, 122
protocol, defined 7
pseudo-contra-indications 93–94
psychoanalysis 10–11
psychodynamic approaches 10–11
psychological and inter-relational facilitation techniques 51
psychological change facilitation 25
psychological facilitation 50–53, 55, 56, 73
psychological theories 2
psychological treatments xvi
psychotherapy 25; behavioural models of 11; research 4–6; sine qua non of 18; systemic 15
Putting Difference to Work (de Shazer) 3, 20

QR code 76, 90
quest for comprehensive theory 1–3
questionnaire 99–100
questions: advice in guise of 58, 73, 134, 187; continuation 21, 83; coping 58, 73, 86, 89, 187; differentiation 84; exception 84; exceptions to the problem 4; future-orienting 61–62, 84–85; miracle 4, 22, 62, 85; pre-session change 57, 60, 83; relativizing-questions 84; scaling 4–5, 22, 61, 86; solution-building 57; usefulness 59, 87; *see also* support questions (SQs)

randomized controlled trials (RCTs) 43, 71
reading guide 7–8, 76–78
recursive: application 22; interventions 81; methodology 31, 33; path 7, 75; process 53, 68
relapse 14, 31, 33, 70–71
relativizing-questions 84
research: activities 44–45

resistance 2, 10, 49, 173
resource-focused working 63
resources: activation 73; defined 3; orientation 57, 63, 174, 187
responsibility 42, 56–57, 58, 83, 105, 110, 116, 124, 134, 144, 151, 168, 170
root causes 3–4, 34, 56, 64, 68

scale of motivation 61
scaling questions 4–5, 22, 59–60, 84; types of 60–61
schizophrenogenic mother 15
science fiction 131–132
The Sciences of the Artificial (Simon) 37, xv
scientific: design approaches 36; experiment, treatment or procedure 7; foundation 7; grounding 34; methodologies 6, 37
searching working relationship 82, 83–85
self-actualization 13, 32
self-awareness 32
self-efficacy 59, 71
self-healing 3, 51, 131
self-improvement 32
self-worth 13
seven-step dance 25, 78, 81
SF-methods 5
SFT-techniques 126
simulation-based conversations 40, 44–45, 46, 98
sine qua non of psychotherapy 18
single case design 18
solution-based conversations 28
solution-building: cooperation 79–80; questions 57
solution-focused: approach 5–6, 15, 91; facilitation 57, 70; method 3–6; practitioners 68, 98, 103; validating building blocks of SoFAP-P 98–103; thinking and working 1, 3, 5–6, 96, 124, 130
solution-focused applied psychology protocol (SoFAP-P) 1–8, 75–96, xii, xiv; ambition with 6; appropriate mandate 81; appropriateness 95–96; arrangement of interventions 75–90; client focused xii; context exploring 80; continuation and evaluation 87–89; contra-indications 93; contribution of, to practice 125–127; contribution of, to society 127–129; depth of 66–71; design specifications 94–96; desirable developments in 129–132; empirical grounding of 48–74; evaluation of 123–132; field testing of 123–124; flowchart 76, 77, 89–90, *107*, *111*, *115*; goals 80–81; indications 91–92; intervention process of 79–81; lessons learned for 30; non-obviousness 95; operational relevance 95; points of attention (PAs) 29–30; practical relevance 42, 95; problem and limitation 81; pseudo-contra-indications 93–94; QR code 76, 90; quest for comprehensive theory 1–3; to SoFAP-P 27; width of 65–66; working relationship (WR) 81–87; β-testing 104–122
solution-focused brief therapy (SFBT) xii
solution-focused therapy (SFT) 20–24, 49
solution talk 24
The Solution Tango (Cauffman) 6, 24
soundness 40
stakeholders 5, 7, 20, 30–32, 35, 44, 72, 126, 181–182
standard deviation (σ) 100, 122n2
strange attractors 3, 92, 97n8
Studien über Hysterie (Freud) 10
suggestions for further research 123–124
sunken cost fallacy 2
support questions (SQs) 35, 62–71; caveat 66; characteristics of SoFAP-P 62; depth 66–71; future orientation 64; goal orientation 64; image of Humankind 63; minimax decision rules 64–65; precedence over explanations 64; problems 63; resource orientation 63; solution talk 65; width of protocol 65–66
survey: questions 99–100, 103, 180–191; results 99–103; *see also* on-line opinion survey
sustainability 70, 126, 129
sustainable 68, 72, 92, 102, 125–126, 176, 181
synthesis-evaluation iterations 45

tailor-made guidelines 31
test: α-testing 40–41, 45, 98–103, 122; β-testing 40–41, 45, 98, 104–122
theories: defined 1–2; psychological 2
therapeutic: alliance 73, 184; interventions 12, 125; relationship 51–52
therapeutization 131
therapy 3, 17
Toward a Psychology of Being (Maslow) 13
training-application-evaluation process 123–124
trendy fog banks 130–131

Uncommon Therapy (Haley) 17
uninvolved observer 36
usability 40
usefulness question 59, 87

validating SoFAP-P 98–122; application 104–122; building blocks 98–103; Italian way 108–110
validity/validation: coherent xvi; face 42, 99, 100; pragmatic 37–39, 42
value for (tax) money 129

Volatility, Uncertainty, Complexity and Ambiguity (VUCA) 127, 132n2

well-being 2–3, 8n2, 61, 92, 160
width of SoFAP-P 65–66
wish for change 3, 26, 65
Words were originally magic (de Shazer) 22
working relationship (WR) 25, 81–87; co-expert 82, 86–87; consulting 82, 85–86; non-committal 81–82, 108; searching 82, 83–85
works better 70–71